Britar

Encyclopædia Britannica, Inc., is a leader in reference and education publishing whose products can be found in many media, from the Internet to mobile phones to books. A pioneer in electronic publishing since the early 1980s, Britannica launched the first encyclopedia on the Internet in 1994. It also continues to publish and revise its famed print set, first released in Edinburgh, Scotland, in 1768. Encyclopædia Britannica's contributors include many of the greatest writers and scholars in the world, and more than 110 Nobel Prize winners have written for Britannica. A professional editorial staff ensures that Britannica's content is clear, current, and correct. This book is principally based on content from the encyclopedia and its contributors.

Introducer

Mary Dejevsky is chief editorial writer and columnist at the *Independent*. A Russia specialist by training, she witnessed the collapse of the Soviet Union as Moscow bureau chief for *The Times*. A regular visitor to Russia, as special correspondent for the *Independent*, she is a member of the Royal Institute of International Affairs (Chatham House) in London and of Russia's Valdai Club for international specialists in the region.

Also available

The Britannica Guide to the 100 Most Influential Americans
The Britannica Guide to the 100 Most Influential Scientists
The Britannica Guide to the Brain
The Britannica Guide to Climate Change
The Britannica Guide to the Ideas
that Made the Modern World
The Britannica Guide to India
The Britannica Guide to the Islamic World
The Britannica Guide to Modern China

ENCYCLOPÆDIA
THE **Britannica**® GUIDE TO

RUSSIA

The essential guide to the nation, its people, and culture

Introduction by Mary Dejevsky

RUNNING PRESS
PHILADELPHIA · LONDON

Constable & Robinson Ltd
3 The Lanchesters
162 Fulham Palace Road
London W6 9ER
www.constablerobinson.com

Encyclopædia Britannica, Inc.
www.britannica.com

First published in the UK by Robinson,
an imprint of Constable & Robinson, 2009

A copy of the British Library Cataloguing in Publication
Data is available from the British Library

UK ISBN 978-1-84529-921-7

1 3 5 7 9 10 8 6 4 2

First published in the United States in 2009 by Running Press Book Publishers

9 8 7 6 5 4 3 2 1
Digit on the right indicates the number of this printing

US Library of Congress Control number: 2008931536
US ISBN 978-0-7624-3621-7

Running Press Book Publishers
2300 Chestnut Street
Philadelphia, PA 19103-4371

Visit us on the web!

www.runningpress.com

Printed and bound in the EU

CONTENTS

ILLUSTRATIONS AND MAPS

Illustrations

Cathedral of St Basil the Blessed, Moscow © *Corbis, courtesy of Encyclopædia Britannica Inc.*

Red Square, Moscow © D. *Staquet/DeA Picture Library, courtesy of Encyclopædia Britannica Inc.*

Portrait of Catherine the Great (1729–96) by Fyodor Rokotov (1735–1808). The Moscow State Tretyakov Gallery © *RIA Novosti/Topfoto.co.uk.*

Gallery in the Hermitage Museum, St Petersburg *Richard Nowitz–National Geographic/Getty Images, courtesy of Encyclopædia Britannica Inc.*

Demonstrators gathering in front of the Winter Palace in Petrograd in January 1917, shortly before the Russian Revolution *Hulton Archive/Getty Images, courtesy of Encyclopædia Britannica Inc.*

Monument to the Third International; model designed by Vladimir Tatlin, 1920. Reconstruction by U. Linde and P. O. Ultvedt in the Modern Museum, Stockholm © *Tatlin; photograph Moderna Museet, courtesy of Encyclopædia Britannica Inc.*

Soviet leader Vladimir Ilyich Lenin (1870–1924) addressing a crowd in 1920 © *Photo.com/Jupiterimages, courtesy of Encyclopædia Britannica Inc.*

Joseph Stalin (1879–1953) © *Photo.com/Jupiterimages, courtesy of Encyclopædia Britannica Inc.*

Aleksandr Sergeyevich Pushkin (1799–1837): portrait copied by Fyodor Igin from original by Orest Kiprensky © *RIA Novosti/Topfoto.co.uk.*

Leo Tolstoy (1828–1910) *The Bettman Archive, courtesy of Encyclopædia Britannica Inc.*

Boris Leonidovich Pasternak (1890–1960) with companion Olga Iwinskaja and their daughter Irina in the late 1950s © *ullstein-bild/Topfoto.co.uk.*

Aleksandr Isayevich Solzhenitsyn (1918–2008), August 30, 1970 © *Topfoto.co.uk.*

Yury Alekseyevich Gagarin (1934–68) in 1961 *Keystone/Hulton Archive/Getty Images, courtesy of Encyclopædia Britannica Inc.*

Mikhail Gorbachev (b. 1931) on a state visit to Poland © *Bernard Bisson & Thierry Orban/Sygma/Corbis.*

Military parade in Moscow's Red Square in 1985 *Tass/Sovfoto, courtesy of Encyclopædia Britannica Inc.*

Vladimir Putin (b. 1952) *President of Russia, The Kremlin, Courtesy of Encyclopædia Britannica Inc.*

Maps

INTRODUCTION

MARY DEJEVSKY

Russia can claim to be one of the most grievously misunderstood countries of the early twenty-first century. A vast land mass, with a harsh climate and declining population, the country boasts as rich a history and as glorious a culture as any in the world. Yet the upheavals it experienced in the twentieth century – from the Bolshevik Revolution of 1917 to the largely peaceful reversal of that revolution before the century was out – left the country and its people exhausted, while striving to catch up with a European and global mainstream that had largely passed them by.

In between came a brutal civil war, mass emigration of the aristocracy and professional classes, enforced collectivization of agriculture, Stalin's purges, the battle for national survival that was Russia's experience of the Second World War, and ultimate defeat in the Cold War that pitted East against West. By the late 1980s, Russians could do little more than watch as the Soviet empire dissolved around them and the thought-system that had anchored so much of their lives was discredited. Few would have emerged unscathed from such a catalogue of adversity, whether self-inflicted or not.

It is a sign of Russian resilience that after a century of such turmoil, and less than 20 years after the collapse of the Union of Soviet Socialist Republics, Russia is settling as smoothly as it is into a new age and a new political system inside new state borders. With three-quarters of the territory and only half the population of the Soviet Union, it is more ethnically and culturally homogeneous (though ethnic minorities still constitute roughly one-fifth of the population) in its reconstituted statehood. But it is also – as it appears from Moscow – more vulnerable.

When the predominantly non-Slav republics became independent in 1991–2, Russia lost what had been a substantial buffer zone to its west, east, and south. The former Soviet bloc countries of east and central Europe and the Baltic states that had formed a reluctant western flank of the Soviet Union then allied themselves with the West, by joining the North Atlantic Treaty Organization and the European Union, and Russia's age-old fears of hostile encirclement returned. Security and domestic stability became the twin preoccupations of Russia's post-Soviet leadership.

For all the disappointment regularly expressed outside Russia about the country's slow pace of political and economic development in the post-Soviet years, it is rarely recalled that the consequences of the Soviet Union's demise could have been much, much worse. As the communist system breathed its last and in the often chaotic years that followed, Russia remained intact and – for the most part – free of conflict. Yet at the time this could not have been taken for granted.

When the last Soviet leader, Mikhail Gorbachev, resigned on December 25, 1991, and the Soviet flag was lowered over the Kremlin for the last time, the West feared a catastrophe of epic proportions. Contingency plans were in place to prevent already severe food shortages escalating into famine and to cope with perhaps hundreds of thousands of refugees fleeing west in the depths of winter. There were fears, too, of a replay of the 1918–20 civil war, if local Communist Party officials and their opponents tried to make a grab for power, even as the national leadership conceded that the game was up.

In the event, the break-up of the Soviet Union was mostly peaceful. The republics that had made up the USSR either seized their independence ahead of time, through leaders who successfully challenged ebbing Soviet power, or – as in much of Central Asia – reluctantly accepted the independence that was thrust upon them. What violence there was erupted at long-tense ethnic fault-lines inside the newly independent states – Georgia, for one – but the main frontiers held.

That the Soviet Union ended less with a bang than a whimper was not due to good fortune alone. It also owed much to measured leadership. As Soviet president, Mikhail Gorbachev understood that neither the Eastern European Warsaw Pact nor the Soviet Union could be held together by force; he did not fight the inevitable. The president of the post-Soviet Russian Federation, Boris Yeltsin, chose for the most part a constitutional route to power, seeking a mandate for his popular appeal through the ballot box. Outside Russia, the then US president, George H. W. Bush, and the German chancellor, Helmut Kohl, grappled with the largely unforeseen and fast-moving collapse of communism across Europe with flexibility and without panic.

The formal transfer of power in Russia, when it came, was also conducted for the most part with a due sense of dignity and responsibility. Those who had witnessed Yeltsin's public taunting of Gorbachev only four months before, following the aborted coup against the latter, might have anticipated an outburst of unseemly triumphalism. As president of the restored independent state of Russia, however, Yeltsin behaved with the modesty and generosity appropriate to a national leader in victory. There was no vicious settling of old scores.

So it was that Russia, with Yeltsin at its head, was internationally recognized as the Soviet Union's successor state, inheriting – on the positive side – its permanent seat on the UN Security Council, and its considerable nuclear arsenal. Russia also gained a place at the top table of the world's economies when it formally joined the Group of Seven (making it the Group of Eight) in 1997. But on the negative side it fell heir to the USSR's international debts and heavily subsidized export obligations to its former allies and constituent republics in Europe and Central Asia.

The reasons for the Soviet Union's decline and eventual fall will long be debated, but they surely include the extensive central planning system, the suspicions harboured by the state towards its citizens, and the inability of the political system to renew itself. Greater exposure to the outside world, as modern communications forced open borders, and the cost of trying to match the US military challenge are also part of the equation.

But an equally significant factor, often underestimated, was the aspiration of Russians to reclaim their national sovereignty. As the countries of east and central Europe, the Baltic states, and the Caucasus sought to retrieve their independent national identities through the 1980s, so Russians, too, started to question the balance sheet left by 70 years of communism. To the rest of the world, the Soviet Union and Russia might have seemed synonymous, but many Russians saw themselves as powerless within their own country, overburdened by imperial power.

Unlike other constituent republics of the Soviet Union, Russia – or the Russian Soviet Federated Socialist Republic as it was then – had no parliament or Communist Party organization to call its own. (In this respect, its position was somewhat analogous to that of England in the devolved United Kingdom.) Of course, ethnic Russians held the lion's share of leadership posts in the Soviet Union's central party and government apparatus. But there were no institutional mechanisms through which Russians could express their Russianness. In this respect, Boris Yeltsin's epic struggle against Mikhail Gorbachev in the last years and months of the Soviet Union was not just political and personal, although undoubtedly it was both of these: it was a duel between a declining Soviet Union and a resurgent Russia. The dissolution of the Soviet Union was Russia's victory and marked its rebirth as a nation.

The rise of Russia and the return of a specifically Russian national consciousness from the late 1980s on was accompanied, and fostered, by an at first hesitant rediscovery of the tsarist past. Gorbachev's policies of *perestroika* ("restructuring") and *glasnost* ("openness") had facilitated an examination of many hitherto closed chapters of Soviet, but also pre-Soviet, Russian history. In intellectual and political circles the search was on to recover what many felt had been lost, to pick up where Russia's modernization, they felt, had been artificially arrested in 1917.

Old, and sometimes embarrassing, groupings crawled out of the rotten Soviet woodwork around this time, including monarchists, anarchists, and the openly anti-Semitic nationalist group *Pamyat* ("Memory"), whose adherents paraded on the margins of the pro-democracy demonstrations of 1989–91. A self-styled Liberal Democratic Party, created and led by the rabble-rousing Vladimir Zhirinovsky, capitalized on Russia's national sense of grievance and a growing mood of xenophobia to become, for a time, the third-largest political grouping – in terms of votes received – after the centrist Russian party of power (now called United Russia) and the rump of the once all-powerful Communist Party.

One of the greatest beneficiaries of the new embrace of Russian national sentiment was the Russian Orthodox Church, whose dignitaries became a fixture at national events, starting from Gorbachev's inauguration in 1989. Soviet-era restrictions on church-building and church services were progressively lifted. Congregations across Russia raised funds and rebuilt churches despoiled and desecrated in successive waves of Soviet-era persecution. The reappearance on the rural horizon of freshly gilded domes was an early sign of Russia's national renaissance.

At state level, Russia's spiritual rebirth was symbolized by the rebuilding of the vast Cathedral of Christ the Saviour in central Moscow, which had been notoriously dynamited by Stalin in 1931. The project was initiated by Yeltsin, as Russian president, and the popular mayor of Moscow, Yury Luzhkov, and completed – thanks to almost superhuman effort – within the decade. It was paid for by voluntary contributions, raised in part from Russia's new rich – the "oligarchs" and smaller entrepreneurs who had profited from the disorderly privatizations of state industry in the early 1990s. But there were gifts from Russia's "old rich", too – the descendants of noble families who had fled abroad from Soviet power. Their names, as benefactors – linking old Russia and new across a century – are inscribed in the cathedral entrance.

But the visibility of the Orthodox Church in Russia today is not only, or even primarily, an expression of Russians' religious faith. Only a minority claim to be believers or attend church regularly. It is at least as much an expression of

Russianness. In Soviet times, church weddings or christenings tended to be confined to rural areas and were, even then, acts of personal defiance. Today, the number of church weddings, christenings, and funerals has soared. As president, Yeltsin was a regular at services on Russian holidays, and he reinstated Christmas and Easter as national holidays. Vladimir Putin and now Dmitry Medvedev have followed suit, the former having apparently disclosed early in his presidency that he had been christened and still wore the pectoral cross given to him by his grandmother.

But the revival of interest in pre-revolutionary Russia extends far beyond the reintegration of the Orthodox Church into the life of the post-Soviet Russian state. And it goes far beyond simple nostalgia. With the communist system demonstrably bankrupt in every sense and the accelerated free-market reforms of the 1990s summarily ended by the crash of the ruble in 1998, there has been a quest to find other, Russian, ways of doing things. Pyotr Stolypin, the great reforming prime minister under the last tsar, Nicholas II, has been a particular object of study. He and other political and judicial luminaries of the early twentieth century are frequently cited as reference points by, among others, Russia's current president, Dmitry Medvedev.

Class and money are also back as strands of national life, if not in the mass return of aristocratic families and those who sought intellectual freedom in the emigration, then in a revival of some of their ways. Etiquette and formal manners are in the ascendant. Winter balls, modelled on those described so graphically by Leo Tolstoy, are a feature of the social scene. Even the language is changing, as Soviet concepts and formulations are dropped, to be replaced by more elegant, often older, turns of phrase.

The appearance of a new moneyed class, initially in Moscow, but extended now to St Petersburg and increasingly other major cities, was accompanied in its first wave by ostentatious consumption. Moscow's western car showrooms and luxury boutiques could not restock fast enough for their Russian clientele. Many of those early excesses, though, have been attenuated.

The 1998 economic collapse swept away some fortunes. But among the surviving billionaires, spending habits have been changing. As well as funding property purchases abroad and children's education at British public schools, Russian money has fuelled the international art and antiques market, as wealthy Russians see themselves honour-bound to repatriate masterpieces lost to their homeland as a result of revolution and war.

Townscapes are changing fast. Many cities, not only Moscow and St Petersburg, are now ringed with new housing, both high-rise and in executive estates, much of it for private sale. Out-of-town shopping malls have mushroomed, catering to a new generation of urban blue- and white-collar workers with disposable income, and homes to equip. Standards of dress and nutrition are now mostly indistinguishable from those across the western world.

Even so, the discrepancies between rich and poor, and between Russia's private and public domains, remain glaring. In Moscow and St Petersburg some of the most expensive shops and restaurants in the world coexist with stalls where street-sweepers snack on pancakes and pies bought for pennies. Glitzy casinos and clubs tout for custom, even as the destitute elderly or disabled beg from passers-by.

Although many town centres are in the course of impressive renovation, with Moscow and St Petersburg leading the way, much public housing remains sub-standard. In rural areas, more remote villages are dying, their mostly elderly populations marooned by changed social priorities. Even in the many newly prosperous villages, where every house seems to have new window frames and a new roof, serviceable footpaths, let alone roads or even mains water and electricity, remain a distant dream. What changes the individual can make are mostly complete; where state effort is needed, however, work has barely begun.

The bonus from surging oil and gas prices in the first years of the new century may have boosted the Russian state's image at home and influence abroad, but it has not – yet – been translated into urgently needed modernization in any generalized way. A recent master plan outlines projects to bring the dilapidated infrastructure up to international standards by 2020. But neglected transport networks, school buildings, and medical facilities all represent large bills accumulating for the future.

Image, though, counts for much. At grass-roots level, resurgent Russian patriotism is tangible, matched by a revival of regional and civic pride. The contemporary art and literary scene has a dynamism and fearlessness reminiscent of Berlin in the decade after the Wall fell. Theatre, ballet, and cinema, which languished when Soviet state subsidies fell away, are starting to flourish once again.

Yet it is not just in material things that the Soviet era still casts its shadow. Although a whole generation of young adults has now grown up without communism, their parents and grandparents bear the scars of those years, in terms of poor health, damaged family life, and an unspoken fear of arbitrary state power. To all this, during the 1990s, was added sudden exposure to a capricious free market, an increase in violent crime, and the risk that the still-fragile state might fracture further.

It was these old and new fears that Vladimir Putin set out to allay when he became president. But the hand he applied was at times heavy. The degree of force used against the Caucasus region of Chechnya when separatists there renewed their fight for independence was condemned outside Russia, and by brave souls within. Putin set limits on the freedom of state broadcasting, although the Internet and satellite stations are increasingly available and uncensored. What were conceived of as ambitious reforms of the judiciary and state bureaucracy were compromised by corruption. At the same time, the fast-growing middle class, a rediscovery of family life, and an upward trend in the birth rate testify to a nation that believes again in its future.

Today's Russia remains a land of contrasts: between old and new, east and west, town and country, between its public and private faces. And nowhere are they more striking than in central Moscow, where the luxury shops that have replaced the old state department store, GUM, confront Lenin's Mausoleum across Red Square, while the fearsome Lubyanka, now home to Russia's state security service, looks out onto a modest stone monument dedicated to those who died in Soviet prison camps. Funded by individual donations, this is the closest thing Russia has to a national monument to the estimated 15–30 million victims of the *Gulag*. A true reckoning with the past is still ahead.

The changes that Russia has experienced within one generation help to explain why it sometimes comes across as oversensitive, self-absorbed, and clumsily defensive about its imperfections in democracy and law. But its periodic snarls can be deceptive. The Russia that is emerging into the twenty-first century is more prosperous, more secure within its borders, and more at ease with itself than for many a year – perhaps even for more than a century.

PART I

CONTEXT

RUSSIA – FACTS AND FIGURES

Official name: Rossiyskaya Federatsiya (Russian Federation).

Form of government: federal multiparty republic with a bicameral legislative body (Federal Assembly comprising the Federation Council: 172 members[1]; State Duma: 450).

Head of state: President.

Head of government: Prime Minister.

Capital: Moscow.

Official language: Russian.

Official religion: none.

Monetary unit: ruble (RUB).

Demography

Population (2007): 141,378,000.

Density (2007): persons per sq mile 21.4, persons per sq kilometre 8.3.

Urban-rural (2007)[2]: urban 73.0%; rural 27.0%.

Sex distribution (2004): male 46.49%; female 53.51%.

Age breakdown (2006)[2]: under 15, 14.9%; 15–29, 24.7%; 30–44, 21.5%; 45–59, 21.9%; 60–69, 8.4%; 70 and over, 8.6%.

Population projection: (2010) 139,390,000; (2020) 132,242,000.

Ethnic composition (2002): Russian 79.82%; Tatar 3.83%; Ukrainian 2.03%; Bashkir 1.15%; Chuvash 1.13%; Chechen 0.94%; Armenian 0.78%; Mordvin 0.58%; Belarusian 0.56%; Avar 0.52%; Kazakh 0.45%; Udmurt 0.44%; Azerbaijani 0.43%; Mari 0.42%; German 0.41%; Kabardinian 0.36%; Ossetian 0.35%; Dargin 0.35%; Buryat 0.31%; Sakha 0.31%; other 4.83%.

Religious affiliation (2005): Christian 58.4%, of which Russian Orthodox 53.1%, Roman Catholic 1.0%, Ukrainian Orthodox 0.9%, Protestant 0.9%; Muslim 8.2%[3, 4]; traditional beliefs 0.8%; Jewish 0.6%; nonreligious 25.8%; atheist 5.0%; other 1.2%.

Major cities (2006)[2]: Moscow 10,425,075; St Petersburg 4,580,620; Novosibirsk 1,397,015; Yekaterinburg 1,308,441; Nizhny Novgorod 1,283,553; Samara 1,143,346; Omsk 1,138,822; Kazan 1,112,673; Chelyabinsk 1,092,958; Rostov-na-Donu 1,054,865; Ufa 1,029,616; Perm 993,319.

Households (2004): Total households 51,209,000; average

household size 2.8; distribution by size (1995): I person 19.2%; 2 persons 26.2%; 3 persons 22.6%; 4 persons 20.5%; 5 persons or more 11.5%.

Vital statistics

Birth rate per 1,000 population (2006): 10.3 (world average 20.3); (2005) within marriage 70.0%, outside marriage 30.0%.

Death rate per 1,000 population (2006): 15.2 (world average 8.6).

Natural increase rate per 1,000 population (2006): −4.9 (world average 11.7).

Total fertility rate (average births per childbearing woman; 2006): 1.38.

Marriage/divorce rates per 1,000 population (2006): 7.8/4.5.

Life expectancy at birth (2005): male 58.9 years; female 72.4 years.

Major causes of death per 100,000 population (2006): circulatory diseases 860; malignant neoplasms (cancers) 200; accidents, poisoning, and violence 191, of which suicide 30, transport accidents 27, alcohol poisoning 20; diseases of the digestive system 62; diseases of the respiratory system 58; infectious and parasitic diseases 25. Adult population (ages 15–49) living with HIV (2005): 1.1% (world average 1.0%).

Social indicators

Educational attainment (2002). Percentage of population age 15 and over having no formal schooling 2.1%;

primary education 7.7%; some secondary 18.1%; complete secondary/basic vocational 53.0%; incomplete higher 3.1%; complete higher 16.0%, of which advanced degrees 0.3%.
Quality of working life (2006). Average workweek (2004): 40 hours. Annual rate per 100,000 workers of: injury or accident 290; industrial illness 16.0; death 11.8. Average working days lost to labour strikes per 1,000 employees 0.2.
Social participation. Eligible voters participating in last national election (2003): 55.7%. Trade union membership in total workforce (2003): c. 45%[5].
Social deviance. Offence rate per 100,000 population (2006) for: murder and attempted murder 19.4; rape and attempted rape 6.3; serious injury 36.2; theft 1,180.4. Incidence per 100,000 population of: alcoholism (1992) 1,727.5; substance abuse (2000) 25.6; suicide (2006) 30.0. Material well-being (2002): durable goods possessed per 100 households: automobiles 27; personal computers 7; television receivers 126; refrigerators and freezers 113; washing machines 93; VCRs 50; motorcycles 26; bicycles 71.

National economy
Public debt (external, outstanding; 2005): US$75,359,000,000.
Budget (2006). Revenue: RUB 6,276,300,000,000 (VAT 24.1%; taxes on natural resources 17.8%; corporate taxes 8.1%; single social tax 5.0%). Expenditures: RUB 4,281,300,000,000 (transfers 21.4%; defence 15.9%; social and cultural services 14.4%; law enforcement 12.9%; debt service 3.9%).

Gross national income (2006): US$956,557,000,000 (US$6,679 per capita).

Production (in metric tons except as noted). Agriculture, forestry, fishing (2006): wheat 45,006,300, potatoes 38,572,640, sugar beets 30,861,230, barley 18,153,550, sunflower seeds 6,752,860, oats 4,880,270, cabbages 4,073,240, corn (maize) 3,668,560, rye 2,965,060, tomatoes 2,414,860, carrots and turnips 1,918,370, onions 1,788,750, apples 1,617,000, cucumbers 1,423,210, peas 1,157,640; livestock (number of live animals) 21,473,926 cattle, 16,074,449 sheep, 13,454,876 pigs; roundwood (2005) 186,500,000 cu m, of which fuelwood 25%; fisheries production (2005) 3,305,698 (from aquaculture 3%); aquatic plants production (2005) 50,507 (from aquaculture, negligible). Mining and quarrying (2005): nickel 315,000[6] [world rank: 1]; mica 101,500 [world rank: 1]; platinum-group metals 123,000 [world rank: 2]; gem diamonds 21,400,000 carats [world rank: 2]; industrial diamonds 10,400,000 carats [world rank: 3]; vanadium 9,000[6] [world rank: 3]; iron ore (2004) 56,200,000[6] [world rank: 5]; cobalt 5,000[6] [world rank: 5]; copper ore 675,000[6] [world rank: 6]; gold 165,000 kg [world rank: 6]; tin 3,000[6] [world rank: 7]; molybdenum 3,000[6] [world rank: 7]. Manufacturing (value added in US$'000,000; 2004): refined petroleum products 14,329; iron and steel 11,801; food products 8,933; chemicals and chemical products 7,709; nonferrous base metals 7,600; beverages 4,446; transportation equipment 4,255; general purpose machinery 3,369; cement, bricks, and ceramics 3,266;

fabricated metal products 1,949; wood products (excluding furniture) 1,922; printing and publishing 1,648; paper products 1,508; textiles and wearing apparel 1,374; rubber products 1,359; electrical equipment 1,165; tobacco products 1,055.

Energy production (consumption): electricity (kWhr; 2006–07) 989,017,000,000 ([2005] 940,000,000,000); hard coal (metric tons; 2006–07) 237,700,000 ([2004] 144,978,000); lignite (metric tons; 2006–07) 70,300,000 ([2004] 75,460,000); crude petroleum (barrels; 2006–07) 3,482,900,000 ([2005] 1,022,000,000); petroleum products (metric tons; 2004) 175,486,000 (94,312,000); natural gas (cu m; 2006–07) 865,524,000,000 ([2005] 402,100,000,000).

Population economically active (2006): total 74,146,000; activity rate of total population 52.0% (participation rates: ages 15–64, 73.0%; female 49.4%; unemployed 7.2%).

Land use as % of total land area (2003): in temporary crops 7.5%, in permanent crops 0.1%, in pasture 5.6%; overall forest area (2005) 47.9%.

Household income and expenditure: average household size (2004): 2.8; income per household: RUB 52,400 (US$1,692); sources of monetary income (2006): wages 66.4%[7], transfers 13.2%, self-employment 11.2%, property income 7.2%, other 2.0%; expenditure (2002): food 41.7%, clothing 13.3%, housing 6.2%, furniture and household appliances 5.7%, alcohol and tobacco 3.2%, transportation 2.7%.

Selected balance of payments data. Receipts from (US$'000,000) tourism (2005) 5,466; remittances (2006) 3,308; foreign direct investment (FDI; 2001–05 average) 8,842. Disbursements for (US$'000,000): tourism (2005)

17,804; remittances (2006) 11,438; FDI (2001–05 average) 8,541.

Foreign trade[8]

Imports (2006): US$137,548,000,000 (machinery, apparatus, and transportation equipment 47.7%; chemicals and chemical products 15.8%; food, beverages, and tobacco 15.7%; nonferrous metals and iron and steel 7.7%). Major import sources (2006): Germany 13.4%; China 9.4%; Ukraine 6.7%; Japan 5.7%; Belarus 5.0%; USA 4.7%; France 4.3%; Italy 4.2%; Kazakhstan 2.8%.

Exports (2006): US$301,976,000,000 (fuels and lubricants 65.9%; nonferrous metals and iron and steel 16.4%; machinery, apparatus, and transportation equipment 5.8%; chemicals and chemical products 5.6%; wood and paper products 3.1%). Major export destinations (2006): The Netherlands 11.9%; Italy 8.3%; Germany 8.1%; China 5.2%; Ukraine 5.0%; Turkey 4.8%; Belarus 4.3%; Switzerland 4.0%; Poland 3.8%; UK 3.4%; Finland 3.0%; Kazakhstan 3.0%.

Transport

Railways (2005): length (2007[2]) 85,000 km; passenger-km 171,600,000,000; metric ton-km cargo 1,858,000,000,000. Roads (2007[2]): total length 854,000 km (paved 85%). Vehicles (2002): passenger cars 22,342,000; trucks and buses (1999) 5,021,000. Air transport (2006–07): passenger-km 97,510,000,000; metric ton-km cargo 2,980,000,000.

Communications

Daily newspapers (2004[9]): circulation 15,075,000
Television (2003): receivers 50,599,000
Telephones (2005): landlines 40,100,000
Mobile telephones (2005[10]): 120,000,000
Personal computers (2005): 17,400,000
Internet (2006): users 25,689,000
Broadband (2006[10]): 2,900,000

Education (2006–07)

Primary (age 6–13) and secondary (age 14–17):
schools 61,042; teachers 1,537,000; students
14,798,000; student/teacher ratio 9.6.
Vocational, teacher training: schools 2,847; teachers
148,000; students 2,514,000; student/teacher ratio 18.3.
Higher: schools 1,090; teachers 409,000; students
7,310,000; student/teacher ratio 17.9.

Health

Health (2006): physicians 690,000[2] (1 per 206 persons);
hospital beds 1,575,000[2] (1 per 90 persons); infant
mortality rate per 1,000 live births 10.2.
Food (2005): daily per capita caloric intake 3,363
(vegetable products 79%, animal products 21%); 170% of
FAO recommended minimum requirement.

Military

Total active duty personnel (November 2006): 1,027,000
(army 38.5%, navy 13.8%, air force 15.6%, strategic
deterrent forces 7.8%, command and support 24.3%)[11].

Military expenditure as percentage of GDP (2005): 4.1%;
per capita expenditure US$217.

Internet resources for further information

Federal State Statistics Service http://www.gks.ru/eng/
default.asp

Central Bank of the Russian Federation http://www.cbr.ru/eng

Notes

1 Based on 86 federal districts as of mid-July 2007.
2 January 1.
3 Muslim population may be as high as 16%.
4 Shī'i make up c. 8% of all Muslims.
5 Mostly based on a claimed membership of 28,000,000 in the Federation of
  Independent Trade Unions of Russia, the successor to the former labour
  movement.
6 Metal content.
7 Includes unreported wages and salaries.
8 Imports cost, insurance, and freight, exports free on board.
9 Refers to top 20 dailies only.
10 Subscribers.
11 An additional 415,000 personnel in paramilitary forces include railway troops,
   special construction troops, federal border guards, interior troops, and other
   federal guard units.

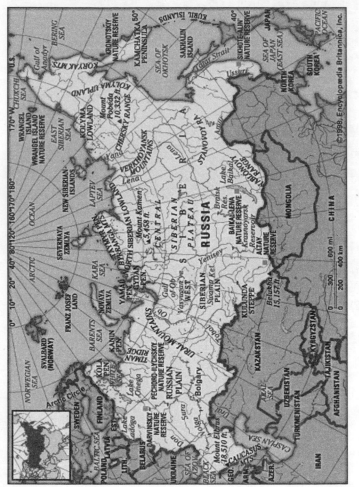

Russia: physical and geographical

I

THE PLACE AND THE PEOPLE

Overview

The Russian Federation stretches over a vast expanse of eastern
Europe and northern Asia. Once the pre-eminent republic of the
Union of Soviet Socialist Republics, Russia became an indepen-
dent country after the dissolution of the Soviet Union in 1991.

Russia is a land of superlatives. By far the world's largest
country, it covers nearly twice the territory of Canada, the second-largest. It spans 11 time zones and incorporates a great range
of environments and landforms, from deserts to semi-arid steppes,
to deep forests and Arctic tundra. Russia contains Europe's longest
river, the Volga, and largest lake, Ladoga, and it is home to the
world's deepest lake, Baikal; it also registers the world's lowest
recorded temperature outside the North and South poles.

The inhabitants of Russia are diverse. Most are ethnic
Russians, but there are also more than 120 other ethnic
groups present, speaking many languages and following
disparate religious and cultural traditions. Most of the

Russian population is concentrated in the European portion of the country, especially in the fertile region surrounding Moscow, the capital. Moscow and St Petersburg (formerly Leningrad) are the two most important cultural and financial centres in Russia and are among the most picturesque cities in the world. Russians are also populous in Asia, however; from the seventeenth century, and particularly throughout much of the twentieth century, a steady flow of ethnic Russians and Russian-speaking people moved eastward into Siberia, where cities such as Vladivostok and Irkutsk now flourish.

Russia's climate is extreme, with forbidding winters that have several times famously saved the country from foreign invaders. Although the climate adds a layer of difficulty to daily life, the land offers a generous source of crops and materials, including vast reserves of oil, gas, and precious metals. That richness of resources has not translated into an easy life for most of the country's people, however: much of Russia's history has been a grim tale of the very wealthy and powerful few ruling over a great mass of their poor and powerless compatriots. Serfdom endured well into the modern era; the years of Soviet communist rule (1917–91), especially the long dictatorship of Joseph Stalin, saw subjugation of a different and more exacting sort.

From the mid-sixteenth century until the early twentieth century an autocratic tsar ruled Russia. In 1917 the Russian Revolution ousted the tsar and established a Russian republic, which, in 1922, became a union republic. During the post-Second World War era, Russia was a central player in international affairs, locked in a Cold War struggle with the United States. In 1991, following the dissolution of the Soviet Union, Russia joined with several other former Soviet republics to form a loose coalition, the Commonwealth of Independent

States (CIS). Although the demise of Soviet-style communism and the subsequent collapse of the Soviet Union brought profound political and economic changes, including the beginnings of the formation of a large middle class, for much of the post-communist era Russians had to endure a generally weak economy, high inflation, and a complex of social ills that served to lower life expectancy significantly. Despite such profound problems, Russia showed promise of achieving its potential as a world power once again, as if to exemplify a favourite proverb coined in the nineteenth century by Austrian statesman Klemens, Prince of Metternich: "Russia is never as strong as she appears, and never as weak as she appears."

Russia can boast a long tradition of excellence in every aspect of the arts and sciences. Pre-revolutionary Russian society produced the writings and music of such giants of world culture as Anton Chekhov, Aleksandr Pushkin, Leo Tolstoy, Nikolay Gogol, Fyodor Dostoyevsky, and Pyotr Ilyich Tchaikovsky. The 1917 Revolution and the changes it brought were reflected in the works of such noted figures as the novelists Maksim Gorky, Boris Pasternak, and Aleksandr Solzhenitsyn, and the composers Dmitry Shostakovich and Sergey Prokofiev. The late Soviet and post-communist eras witnessed a revival of interest in once-forbidden artists such as the poets Vladimir Mayakovsky and Anna Akhmatova, as well as ushering in new talents such as the novelist Viktor Pelevin and the writer and journalist Tatyana Tolstaya.

The Country

Extending nearly halfway around the northern hemisphere and covering much of eastern and north-eastern Europe and all of northern Asia, Russia has a maximum east–west width of some 5,600 miles (9,000 km) and a north–south extent of 1,500 to 2,500 miles (2,500 to 4,000 km). Bounded to the north and east by the Arctic and Pacific oceans, the country has small frontages in the north-west on the Baltic Sea at St Petersburg and at the detached Russian *oblast* (region) of Kaliningrad, which also abuts Poland and Lithuania. To the south it borders North Korea, China, Mongolia, Kazakhstan, Azerbaijan, and Georgia; to the south-west and west it borders Ukraine, Belarus, Latvia, and Estonia, as well as Finland and Norway.

There is an enormous variety of landforms and landscapes within this vast area. Arctic deserts lie in the extreme north, giving way southwards to the tundra and then to the forest zones, which cover about half of the country and give it much of its character. South of the forest zone lie the wooded steppe and the steppe, beyond which are small sections of semi-desert along the northern shore of the Caspian Sea. Much of Russia lies at latitudes where the winter cold is intense and where evaporation can barely keep pace with the accumulation of moisture, giving rise to abundant rivers, lakes, and swamps. Permafrost covers some 4 million square miles (10 million square km), making settlement and road building difficult across large regions.

On the basis of geologic structure and relief, Russia can be divided into two main parts – western and eastern – roughly along the line of the Yenisey River. These sections comprise six relief regions: the Kola-Karelian region, the Russian Plain, the Ural Mountains, the West Siberian Plain, the Central Siberian Plateau, and the mountains of the south and east.

Karelia, the smallest of Russia's relief regions, lies in the north-western part of European Russia between the Finnish border and the White Sea. Karelia is a low, ice-scraped plateau, for the most part below 650 feet (200 metres); low ridges and knolls alternate with lake- and marsh-filled hollows. The Kola Peninsula is similar, but the small Khibiny mountain range rises to nearly 4,000 feet (1,200 metres). Mineral-rich ancient rocks lie at or near the surface in many places.

The Russian Plain (also called the East European Plain) makes up the largest part of one of the great lowland areas of the world, extending from the western border eastwards to the Ural Mountains, and from the Arctic Ocean to the Caucasus Mountains and the Caspian Sea. About half of this vast area lies at less than 650 feet (200 metres) above sea level. North of Moscow lie morainic ridges, which stand out above low, poorly drained hollows interspersed with lakes and marshes. South of Moscow there is a west–east alternation of rolling plateaus and extensive plains. In the west the Central Russian Upland separates the lowlands of the upper Dnieper River valley from those of the Oka and Don rivers, beyond which the Volga Hills rise gently before descending abruptly to the Volga River. East of the Volga is the large Caspian Depression, parts of which lie more than 90 feet (25 metres) below sea level. The Russian Plain also extends southward through the Azov–Caspian isthmus (in the North Caucasus region) to the foot of the Caucasus Mountains, the crest line of which forms the boundary between Russia and the Transcaucasian states of Georgia and Azerbaijan; just inside this border is Mount Elbrus, which at 18,510 feet (5,642 metres) is the highest point in Russia.

Though the Ural Mountains form the traditional boundary between Europe and Asia, in terms of travel and transportation they do not present a significant challenge. The north–south spine of the Urals extends about 1,300 miles (2,100 km) from the Arctic coast to the border with Kazakhstan. The highest peak, Mount Narodnaya, reaches 6,217 feet (1,895 metres), but the system is largely composed of a lower series of broken, parallel ridges; several low passes cut through the system, particularly in the central section between Perm and Yekaterinburg, which carry the main routes from Europe into Siberia. Many districts contain mineral-rich rocks.

Russia's most extensive region, the West Siberian Plain, is the most striking single relief feature of the country and quite possibly of the world. Covering an area well in excess of 1 million square miles (2.6 million square km), one-seventh of Russia's total area, it stretches about 1,200 miles (1,900 km) from the Urals to the Yenisey, and 1,500 miles (2,400 km) from the Arctic Ocean to the foothills of the Altai Mountains. The region is characterized by vast floodplains and some of the world's largest swamps, particularly in the northern half. Slightly higher and drier territory is located south of latitude 55 N, where the bulk of the region's population is concentrated.

The Central Siberian Plateau, which takes up most of the area between the Yenisey and Lena rivers, comprises a series of sharply dissected plateau surfaces ranging in elevation from 1,000 to 2,300 feet (300 to 700 metres). Towards its northern edge rise the Putoran Mountains and on the southern side the Eastern Sayan and Baikal mountains; to the north it descends to the North Siberian Lowland, an eastward extension of the West Siberian Plain. Farther north the Byrranga Mountains reach 3,760 feet (1,146 metres) on the Taymyr Peninsula, which extends into the Arctic Ocean. On its eastern side the Central Siberian Plateau gives way to the low-lying Central Yakut Lowland.

Russia's remaining territory, to the south and east, constitutes about one-fourth of the country's total area and is dominated by a complex series of high mountain systems. These include the Altai Mountains, which lie on the border with Kazakhstan and Mongolia; the area around Lake Baikal; the Stanovoy, Dzhugdzhur, Kolyma, Verkhoyansk, and

Chersky ranges in the east; and a volcanic zone on the Kamchatka Peninsula. The mountainous zone continues on narrow Sakhalin Island, which is separated from the Siberian mainland by the Tatar Strait.

The Russian landscape is known as much for its many and massive rivers as for its geological variety. Five main drainage basins may be distinguished: the Arctic, Pacific, Baltic, Black Sea, and Caspian. The Arctic basin is drained by three gigantic Siberian rivers: the Ob (2,268 miles [3,650 km]), the Yenisey (2,540 miles [4,090 km]), and the Lena (2,734 miles [4,400 km]). These rivers provide transport arteries from the interior to the Arctic sea route, although they are blocked by ice for long periods every year. South-eastern Siberia is drained by the large Amur system into the Pacific. The Dnieper, of which only the upper reaches are in Russia, and the 1,162-mile-long (1,870 km) Don flow south to the Black Sea, and a small north-western section drains to the Baltic. The longest European river is the Volga. Rising in the Valdai Hills north-west of Moscow, it follows a course of 2,193 miles (3,530 km) to the Caspian Sea. Outranked only by the Siberian rivers, the Volga drains an area of 533,000 square miles (1,380,000 square km). The rivers of the Russian Plain, separated only by short overland portages and supplemented by several canals, have long been important transport arteries; indeed, the Volga system carries two-thirds of all Russian waterway traffic.

In addition to its numerous rivers, Russia contains some 2 million freshwater and saltwater lakes. In the European section the largest are Ladoga and Onega in the north-west, with surface areas of 6,830 (inclusive of islands) and 3,753 square miles (17,690 and 9,720 square km), respectively; others are Peipus, on the Estonian border, and the Rybinsk Reservoir on the Volga north of Moscow. What are described as narrow lakes, some

100 to 200 miles (160 to 320 km) long, are located behind barrages (dams) on the Don, Volga, and Kama. In Siberia similar artificial lakes are located on the upper Yenisey and its tributary the Angara, where the Bratsk Reservoir is among the world's largest. All of these are dwarfed by Lake Baikal, the largest body of fresh water in the world. Some 395 miles (636 km) long and with an average width of 30 miles (50 km), Baikal has a surface area of 12,200 square miles (31,500 square km) and a maximum depth of roughly 5,315 feet (1,620 metres). There are also innumerable smaller lakes found mainly in the ill-drained low-lying parts of the Russian and West Siberian plains, especially in their more northerly parts.

Russia's climate has historically been both a blessing – in times of war, most famously during Napoleon's 1812 invasion – and a heavy burden in terms of the difficulties it imposes on everyday life. The country's vast size and compact shape – the great bulk of the land is more than 250 miles (400 km) from the sea, while certain parts lie as much as 1,500 miles (2,400 km) away – produce a dominance of continental regimes. The great mountain barriers to the south and east shut out the potentially gentler influences from the Indian and Pacific oceans, and the absence of relief barriers on the western and northern sides leaves the country open to Atlantic and Arctic influences. All these factors, combined with the country's northerly latitude, mean that in effect there are only two seasons, winter and summer; spring and autumn are brief periods of rapid change from one extreme to the other. Harsh winter cold is characteristic of most of Russia: the frost-free period exceeds six months only in the North Caucasus, and varies with latitude from five to three months in the European section and from three to less than two months in Siberia. The world's lowest minimum January temperature outside Antarctica, –96 F (–71 C), was recorded at Oymyakon in eastern Siberia.

The main characteristics of precipitation throughout Russia are its modest to low total amounts and the pronounced summer maximum. Snow falls in virtually the entire country. The duration of snow cover varies with both latitude and altitude, ranging from 40 to 200 days across the Russian Plain and from 120 to 250 days in Siberia.

Climate, soils, vegetation, and animal life are closely inter-related, and variations among these within Russia form a series of broad latitudinal environmental belts. Moving roughly from north to south are zones of Arctic desert, tundra, taiga, mixed and deciduous forest, wooded steppe, and steppe.

Russia's Arctic desert is completely barren land, often ice-covered, with little or no vegetation. This area is confined to the islands of Franz Josef Land, much of the Novaya Zemlya and Severnaya Zemlya archipelagos, and the New Siberian Islands. Tundra, on the other hand, covers nearly one-tenth of Russian territory. This treeless, marshy plain occupies a narrow coastal belt in the extreme north of the European Plain, widening to a maximum of about 300 miles (500 km) in Siberia. Tundra soils are extremely poor, highly acidic, and frozen for much of the year. During the summer thaw, drainage is inhibited by the presence of permafrost beneath the thawed surface layer. Vegetation includes mosses, lichens, and stunted birch, larch, and spruce. Apart from reindeer, which are herded by the indigenous population, the main animal species are the Arctic foxes, musk oxen, beavers, lemmings, snowy owls, and ptarmigan.

South of the tundra, the vast taiga (boreal forest) zone is the largest of Russia's environmental regions, and the world's largest timber reserve. It occupies the Russian and West Siberian plains north of latitude 56 to 58 N, together with most of the territory east of the Yenisey River. In the western section forests of spruce and fir alternate with shrubs and grasses interspersed with pine on lighter soils; in the east these are present too, but the larch predominates. Only small areas have been cleared for agriculture, though coniferous forest is not continuous; there are large stands of birch, alder, and willow, and, in poorly drained areas, huge stretches of swamp and peat bog. The taiga is also rich in fur-bearing animals, such as sables, squirrels, martens, foxes, and ermines, and home to many elks, bears, muskrat, and wolves.

As conditions become warmer with decreasing latitude, deciduous species appear in greater numbers and eventually become dominant. Oak and spruce are the main trees, but there are also growths of ash, aspen, birch, elm, hornbeam, maple, and pine. The mixed and deciduous forest belt is widest along Russia's western border and narrows toward the Urals, but much of this zone has been cleared for agriculture, particularly in the European section. As a result, the wildlife is less plentiful, but roe deer, wolves, foxes, and squirrels are common.

Farther south still is the wooded steppe, which, as its name suggests, is transitional between the forest zone and the steppe proper. Forests of oak and other species (now largely cleared for agriculture) in the European section and birch and aspen across the West Siberian Plain alternate with areas of open grassland that become increasingly extensive toward the south. The wooded steppe eventually gives way to the true steppe, which occupies a belt some 200 miles (320 km) across and extends from southern Ukraine through northern Kazakhstan to the Altai. Russia has a relatively small share of the Eurasian Steppe, mainly in the North Caucasus and lower Volga regions, though pockets of wooded steppe and steppe also occur in basins among the mountains of southern Siberia. The natural steppe vegetation is characterized by turf grasses such as bunch-grass, fescue, bluegrass, and agropyron, with drought-resistant species common in the south. Much of the steppe vegetation, particularly in the west, has been replaced by grain cultivation, in no small part because of the region's chernozem, or black earth, a highly fertile soil of low acidity and high humus content. Typical rodents of the zone include the marmot and other such burrowing animals, and various mouse species. Skunks, foxes, and wolves are common, and antelope inhabit the south. The most common birds are bustards, eagles, kestrels, larks, and grey partridge.

The People

Although ethnic Russians constitute more than four-fifths of the country's total population, Russia is a diverse, multiethnic society. More than 120 ethnic groups, many with their own national territories, speaking some 100 languages, live within Russia's borders.

Many of the minority groups are small – in some cases consisting of fewer than a thousand individuals – and only the Tatars, Ukrainians, Chuvash, Bashkir, Chechens, and Armenians have more than a million members each. The diversity of peoples is also reflected in the country's numerous minority republics and autonomous administrative units. In most of these divisions, however, the eponymous nationality (which gives its name to the division) is outnumbered by Russians. Since the early 1990s ethnicity has underlain numerous conflicts, notably in Chechnya and Dagestan, within and between these units; many national minorities have demanded more autonomy and, in a few cases, even complete independence.

While linguistically the population of Russia can be divided into various groups – the Indo-European, the Altaic, the Uralic, and the Caucasian – the Russian language, a Slavic language of the Indo-European group, predominates and is homogeneous throughout Russia. This unifying factor can largely be explained historically. The Slavs emerged as a recognizable group in eastern Europe between the third and eighth centuries AD, and the first Slav state, Kievan Rus, arose in the ninth century. After the Tatar (Mongol) invasions the centre of gravity shifted to Moscow, and from the sixteenth century the Russian empire expanded to the Baltic, Arctic, and Pacific, numerically overwhelming the indigenous peoples. Today, East Slavs – mainly Russians but including some Ukrainians and Belarusians – constitute an overwhelming majority of the total population and are prevalent throughout the country. But Russian is not the country's only Indo-European language: the Ossetes of the Caucasus speak an Indo-Iranian language, and ethnic Germans and Jews (recognized as an ethnolinguistic group rather than a religious one) also employ their own languages in everyday life.

The Altaic group is dominated by Turkic speakers. They live mainly in the Central Asian republics, but there is an important cluster of Turkic speakers between the middle Volga and southern Urals, comprising the Bashkir, Chuvash, and Tatars. A second cluster, in the North Caucasus region, includes the Balkar, Karachay, Kumyk, and Nogay. There are also numerous Turkic-speaking groups in southern Siberia between the Urals and Lake Baikal: the Altai, Khakass, Shor, Tofalar, and Tuvans. The Sakha (Yakut) live mainly in the middle Lena basin, and the Dolgan are concentrated in the Arctic. Manchu-Tungus languages are spoken by the Evenk, Even, and other small groups that are widely dispersed throughout eastern Siberia. The Buryat, who live in the Lake Baikal region, and the Kalmyk, who live primarily to the west of the lower Volga, speak Mongolian tongues.

The Uralic group, which is widely disseminated in the Eurasian forest and tundra zones, has complex origins. Finnic peoples inhabit the European section: the Mordvin, Mari (formerly Cheremis), Udmurt (Votyak) and Komi (Zyryan), and the closely related Komi-Permyaks live around the upper Volga and in the Urals, while Karelians, Finns, and Veps inhabit the north-west. The Mansi (Vogul) and Khanty (Ostyak) are spread thinly over the lower Ob basin. The Samoyedic group also has few members dispersed over a vast area: the Nenets in the tundra and forest tundra from the Kola Peninsula to the Yenisey, the Selkup around the middle Ob, and the Nganasan mainly in the Taymyr Peninsula.

There are numerous small groups of Caucasian speakers in the North Caucasus region of Russia. Abaza, Adyghian, and Kabardian (Circassian) are similar languages but differ sharply from the languages of the Nakh group (Chechen and Ingush) and of the Dagestanian group (Avar, Lezgian, Dargin, Lak, Tabasaran, and a dozen more).

Several Paleo-Siberian groups share a common mode of life in far eastern Siberia but differ linguistically from the other language groups and from each other. The Chukchi, Koryak, and Itelmen (Kamchadal) belong to a group known as Luorawetlan, which is distinct from the Eskimo-Aleut group. The languages of the Nivkh (Gilyak) along the lower Amur and on Sakhalin Island, of the Yukaghir of the Kolyma Lowland, and of the Ket of the middle Yenisey are completely isolated, though it is likely that Yukaghir is a relative of the Uralic languages. How to preserve its linguistic heritage is one of Russia's current challenges, in that few of the languages of the smaller indigenous minorities are taught in schools, and so may disappear over the course of the next two generations.

Settlement in Town and Country

Any discussion of Russia's urban–rural divide also must address the population disparity between the European portion of the country and Siberia, the latter of which constitutes three-quarters of the country's territory but contains only about one-fifth of its population. Despite large-scale migrations from west to east, beginning in the 1890s and continuing throughout the next century – including the forced deportations at various times of criminals, political prisoners, and ethnic minorities – today the bulk of the country's population still lives in the main settled belt of European Russia, extending between St Petersburg (north-western Russia), Kemerovo (Siberia), Orsk (southern Urals), and Krasnodar (northern Caucasus).

About one-fourth of Russia's population as a whole lives in rural areas. Population densities in the rural areas of European Russia range from 25 to 250 persons per square mile, with the higher concentrations occurring in the wooded steppe. East of the Urals, across the southern part of the West Siberian Plain, rural densities are considerably lower, rarely exceeding 65 persons per square mile, and beyond the Yenisey settlements are highly dispersed. Thanks partly to industrialization and partly to changing political circumstances, in the second half of the twentieth century rural depopulation was a clear trend, especially in the European section: in the last decades of the century, the rural population there fell by about 25 per cent overall, though it grew in what is now the Southern federal district. Because migration out of rural areas was particularly prevalent among the young, many rural areas are now inhabited primarily by the elderly.

The bulk of the rural population lives in large villages associated with the collective and state farms (*kolkhozy* and *sovkhozy*, respectively) established by the former Soviet regime. These farms have carried on the long-established Russian tradition of communal farming from nucleated settlements. Individual farms started to reappear in the post-Soviet years. By 1995 there were nearly 300,000 private farms, though in the next decade the numbers stagnated or declined. Private farms, however, still produce a tiny fraction of agricultural output.

Since the mid-nineteenth century, industrialization and economic development have led to a substantial increase in urbanization. Nearly three-fourths of Russia's population now live in what are classified as urban areas. In the cities, particularly Moscow, population densities are comparable with other European cities. Moscow, the largest metropolis, has twice the population of its nearest rival, St Petersburg, which in turn dwarfs Russia's other major cities, such as Chelyabinsk, Kazan, Nizhny Novgorod (formerly Gorky), Novosibirsk, Omsk, Perm, Rostov-na-Donu, Samara (formerly Kuybyshev), Ufa, and Yekaterinburg (formerly Sverdlovsk).

Several major urban concentrations have developed in the main industrial regions. St Petersburg (the tsarist capital) stands alone as the northernmost metropolis, whereas Moscow and Nizhny Novgorod are part of the large urbanized central industrial region, which has a score of large cities, numerous smaller towns, and an urban population that constitutes about one-fifth of Russia's total. In the Ural Mountains region, the towns are more widely spaced and include numerous small mining and industrial centres, as well as a number of towns with more than 250,000 inhabitants, which altogether amount to an urban population about half that of the Moscow region. The only slightly less populous Volga region has towns strung out along the riverbanks, with a particularly dense concentration in the vicinity of Samara. European Russia also includes a portion of the Donets Basin (Donbass) industrial zone, arbitrarily split by the Russia–Ukraine boundary; this area's largest city is Rostov-na-Donu, but there are numerous smaller centres.

The main urban concentration east of the Urals is in the Kuznetsk Basin (Kuzbass), which is a centre for mining and industry. Major cities also occur at widely separated points along the length of the Trans-Siberian Railway, including, from west to east, Omsk, Novosibirsk, Krasnoyarsk, Irkutsk, Ulan-Ude, Chita, Khabarovsk, and Vladivostok. A few very isolated cities are located in the far north, notably the ports of Murmansk and Arkhangelsk, and mining centres such as Vorkuta and Norilsk. Resort towns are a feature of the North Caucasus region, including Sochi (on the Black Sea), Pyatigorsk, and Mineralnye Vody. Elsewhere, the capitals of provinces and other administrative divisions are the main towns, having grown to considerable size as the organizing centres for their territories.

During the 1990s Russia began experiencing a negative population growth rate. A primary reason for this was a decline in the fertility rate (particularly of ethnic Russians) similar to that in Japan and in many western European countries. There was also a steep drop in life expectancy beginning in the early 1990s, a result of inadequacies in the health-care system and poor nutrition; high smoking and alcoholism rates and environmental pollution were also considered contributing factors. Declines in life expectancy were more pronounced among men and resulted in a growing gap between the number of men and women in the country.

Until the 1990s migration from the European sector to Siberia was the primary cause of regional variations in population growth rates. For example, in the 1980s, when Russia's population increased by about 7 per cent, growth exceeded 15 per cent in much of Siberia but was less than

2 per cent in parts of western Russia. During the 1990s, however, eastern Siberia (at least according to official statistics) suffered a dramatic population decline, a result of substantial outmigrations caused by the phase-out of heavy government subsidies, upon which it was heavily dependent.

The long-declining Russian birth rate has led to a progressive aging of the population. At the beginning of the twenty-first century, for example, less than one-fifth of the population of Russia was below the age of 15, while the proportion of those aged 60 and above was approaching one-fifth. (The proportion of children was generally higher, and that of the elderly lower, among the non-Russian ethnic groups, which have maintained a somewhat higher birth rate.) Russia's aging population and overall drop in fertility rates have led many demographers to foresee a long-term labour shortage in the country.

PART 2

HISTORY

2

RUSSIA BEFORE AND AFTER THE REVOLUTION

Russia from Its Beginnings

The Russian state has its origins in Kievan Rus (tenth to thirteenth centuries), the first Slavic state, which included the cities of Kiev, Novgorod, and Smolensk. It was crushed by the invading Tatars (Mongols) in 1237–40, and a new centre grew at Moscow. The Grand Principality of Moscow, or Muscovy, a medieval principality under the leadership of a line of princes known as the Rurik dynasty, was transformed from a small settlement into the dominant political unit in north-eastern Russia. Its grand princes included Ivan III (Ivan the Great) and Ivan IV (the Terrible), in 1547 first of the rulers of Moscow to be crowned tsar of all Russia. The rule of the Rurik dynasty came to an end in the late sixteenth century.

Following the reign of Boris Godunov (tsar of Russia 1598–1605) and the 15 chaotic years known as the Time of Troubles (1598–1613), the first of the Romanov line of tsars came to power. They ruled for three centuries, during which time Russia rose to

IVAN III, KNOWN AS
IVAN THE GREAT (1440–1505)

Grand prince of Moscow (1462–1505)

Ivan led successful military campaigns against the Tatars in the south (1458) and east (1467–9). He subdued Novgorod (1478) and gained control of most of the remainder of the Russian lands by 1485. He also renounced Moscow's subjection to the khan of the Golden Horde (1480) and won a final victory over the khan's sons in 1502. Stripping the boyars (a closed aristocratic class that ruled alongside the grand prince at that time) of much of their authority, he laid the administrative foundations of a centralized Russian state.

become one of the most powerful states in Europe. The dynasty included Peter the Great, Catherine the Great, and Alexander II. Russia remained under autocratic control until 1917, when the Russian Revolution ousted Nicholas II, the last tsar. A Russian republic was established, which in 1922 became a union republic.

The Nineteenth Century

Some time in the middle of the nineteenth century, Russia entered a phase of internal crisis that in 1917 would culminate in revolution. Its causes were not so much economic as political and cultural. There were three main players in the political arena: the tsar, the peasantry (which, excluding the working class, its subdivision, made up some 80 per cent of the empire's population), and the intelligentsia.

The tsar was absolute and unlimited in his authority.

IVAN IV, KNOWN AS
IVAN THE TERRIBLE (1530–84)

Grand prince of Moscow (1533–84)
and first tsar of Russia (1547–84)

Ivan IV, grandson of Ivan III, was crowned tsar in 1547 after a long regency (1533–46). He embarked on wide-ranging reforms, including a centralized administration, church councils that systematized the church's affairs, and the first national assembly (1549). He also instituted reforms to limit the powers of the boyars. After conquering Kazan (1552) and Astrakhan (1556), he engaged in an unsuccessful war to control Livonia, fighting against Sweden and Poland (1558–83). After the defeat and the suspected treason of several Russian boyars, Ivan formed an *oprichnina*, a territory separate from the rest of the state and under his personal control. With a large bodyguard, he withdrew into his own entourage and left Russia's management to others. At the same time, he instituted a reign of terror, executing thousands of boyars and ravaging the city of Novgorod. During the 1570s he married five wives in nine years, and, in a fit of rage, he murdered his son Ivan, his only viable heir, in 1581.

Effectively shutting out the population from participation in government, he was subject to neither constitutional restraints nor parliamentary institutions: he was above the law and the army, one of whose main tasks was maintaining internal order. Imperial Russia developed to a greater extent than any contemporary country a powerful and ubiquitous security police. It was a crime to question the existing system or to organize for any purpose whatsoever without government permission.

BORIS GODUNOV (c. 1551–1605)

Tsar of Russia (1598–1605)

After serving in the court of Ivan IV, Godunov was named guardian to Ivan's mentally and physically infirm son Fyodor I, and became the virtual ruler of Russia as Fyodor's chief adviser from 1584. When Fyodor's young brother Dmitry died mysteriously in 1591, Godunov was suspected of having had him put to death. When Fyodor died without heirs in 1598, an assembly of clergy and gentry elected Godunov tsar. A capable ruler, he instituted many reforms, but continuing boyar opposition and a general famine (1601–3) eroded his popularity. A pretender known as the False Dmitry led an army into Russia, and on Boris's sudden death, resistance broke down. The country lapsed into the Time of Troubles (1606–13), a period of political crisis that lasted until Michael Romanov was elected tsar.

MICHAEL (1596–1645)

Tsar of Russia (1613–45)
and founder of the Romanov dynasty

A young nobleman elected as tsar after the chaotic Time of Troubles, Michael allowed his mother's relatives to direct the government early in his reign. They restored order to Russia and made peace with Sweden (1617) and Poland (1618). In 1619 his father, Philaret, released from captivity in Poland, returned to Russia and became co-ruler and Russian Orthodox patriarch of Moscow. Michael's father dominated the government, increasing contact with western Europe and strengthening central authority and serfdom. After his death in 1633, Michael's maternal relatives once again held sway.

PETER I, KNOWN AS
PETER THE GREAT (1672–1725)

Tsar of Russia (1682–1725)

Peter reigned jointly (1682–96) with his half-brother
Ivan V and alone from 1696. Interested in progressive
influences from western Europe, he visited several
countries there (1697–8). After returning to Russia, he
introduced western technology, modernized the
government and military system, and transferred the
capital to the new city of St Petersburg (1703). He
further increased the power of the monarchy at the
expense of the nobles and the Orthodox Church. Some
of his reforms were implemented brutally, with
considerable loss of life. Suspecting that his son, Alexis,
was conspiring against him, he had Alexis tortured to
death in 1718. He pursued foreign policies to give
Russia access to the Baltic and Black seas, engaging in
war with the Ottoman empire (1695–96) and with
Sweden in the Second Northern War (1700–21). His
campaign against Persia (1722–3) secured for Russia the
southern and western shores of the Caspian Sea.

In 1721 Peter was proclaimed emperor; his wife
succeeded him as the empress Catherine I. For raising
Russia to a recognized place among the great European
powers, Peter is widely considered one of the
outstanding rulers and reformers in Russian history, but
he has also been decried by nationalists for discarding
much of what was unique in Russian culture, and his
legacy has been seen as a model for Soviet leader Joseph
Stalin's brutal transformation of Russian life.

CATHERINE II, KNOWN AS
CATHERINE THE GREAT (1729–96)

German-born empress of Russia (1762–96)

The daughter of an obscure German prince, Catherine (born Sophie Friederike Auguste) was chosen at the age of 14 to be the wife of the future Peter III. The marriage was a complete failure. Because her neurotic husband was incapable of ruling, the ambitious Catherine saw the possibility of eliminating him and governing Russia herself. After Peter became emperor in 1762, she conspired with her lover Grigory Orlov to force Peter to abdicate (he was murdered soon after) and have herself proclaimed empress. In her 34-year reign she led Russia into full participation in European political and cultural life. With her ministers she reorganized the administration and law of the Russian empire and extended Russian territory, adding Crimea and much of Poland. Though she had once intended to emancipate the serfs, she instead strengthened the system she had once condemned as inhuman.

Yet while tsarist Russia was absolutist, to maintain its status as a great power it promoted industrial development and higher education, which were inherently dynamic. The result was perpetual tension between government and society, especially its educated element, known as the intelligentsia, which was unalterably opposed to the status quo. Radical intellectuals tried in the 1860s and 1870s to stir the peasants and workers to rebellion. Having met with no response, they adopted methods of terror, which culminated in 1881 in the assassination of Alexander II. The government reacted with repressive measures, which kept unrest at bay in the short term.

NICHOLAS I (1796–1855)

Tsar of Russia (1825–55)

Nicholas, the son of Tsar Paul I, was trained as an army officer. In 1825 he succeeded his brother Alexander I as emperor and suppressed the Decembrist revolt. His reign came to represent autocracy, militarism, and bureaucracy. To enforce his policies, he created such agencies as the Third Section (political police). In foreign policy, Nicholas quelled an uprising in Poland (1830–1) and aided Austria against a Hungarian uprising (1849). His designs on Constantinople led to war with Turkey (1853) and drew other European powers into the Crimean War. He was succeeded by his son Alexander II.

ALEXANDER II (1818–1881)

Tsar of Russia (1855–81)

Alexander succeeded to the throne at the height of the Crimean War, which revealed Russia's backwardness on the world stage. In response, he undertook drastic reform, improving communications, government, and education, and, most importantly, emancipating the serfs (1861). His reforms reduced class privilege and fostered humanitarian progress and economic development. Though sometimes described as a liberal, Alexander was in reality a firm upholder of autocratic principles, and an assassination attempt in 1866 strengthened his commitment to conservatism. A period of repression after 1866 led to a resurgence of revolutionary terrorism, and in 1881 he was killed in a plot sponsored by the terrorist organization People's Will.

ALEXANDER III (1845–94)

Tsar of Russia (1881–94)

Alexander assumed the throne after the assassination of his father, Alexander II. The internal reforms he instituted were designed to correct what he saw as the too-liberal tendencies of his father's reign. He thus opposed representative government and ardently supported Russian nationalism. His political ideal was a nation containing a single nationality, language, religion, and form of administration, and accordingly he instituted programmes such as the Russification of national minorities in the Russian empire and the persecution of non-Orthodox religious groups.

Growing discontent exploded in the Russian Revolution of 1905, an uprising that was instrumental in convincing Nicholas II to attempt the transformation of the Russian government into a constitutional monarchy. Despite concessions made by Nicholas to cede some of his authority (in 1906 his October Manifesto promised the country a legislative parliament), the prestige of the tsar was weakened further by the First World War and the humiliating defeats that the Russian army suffered at the hands of the Germans. On the home front, economic mismanagement led to food shortages – although Russia produced more than enough to feed itself – while the exceptionally severe winter of 1916–17 only added to the misery of the populace.

The 1917 Revolution

The Russian Revolution of 1917 actually comprised two revolutions: the first, in February (March, New Style), overthrew

NICHOLAS II (1868–1918)

Tsar of Russia (1894–1917)

Son of Alexander III, Nicholas received a military education and succeeded his father as tsar in 1894. He was an autocratic but indecisive ruler and was devoted to his wife, Alexandra, who strongly influenced his rule. His interest in Asia led to construction of the Trans-Siberian Railway and also helped cause the disastrous Russo-Japanese War (1904–5).

After the Russian Revolution of 1905, Nicholas agreed reluctantly to a representative Duma but restricted its powers, and made only token efforts to enact its measures. His prime minister, Pyotr Stolypin, attempted reforms, but Nicholas, increasingly influenced by Alexandra and by the mystic Grigory Rasputin, opposed him; Stolypin was assassinated by a revolutionary in 1911. After Russia suffered setbacks in the First World War, Nicholas ousted the popular Grand Duke Nicholas as commander-in-chief of Russian forces and assumed command himself, at the bidding of Alexandra and Rasputin. His absence from Moscow and Alexandra's mismanagement of the government caused increasing unrest and culminated in the Russian Revolution of 1917.

Nicholas abdicated in March 1917 and was detained with his family by Georgy Y. Lvov's provisional government. Plans for the royal family to be sent to England were overruled by the local Bolsheviks (the majority wing of the Russian Social-Democratic Workers' Party). Instead Nicholas and his family were sent to the city of Yekaterinburg, where they were executed in July 1918.

RUSSIAN REVOLUTION OF 1905

Unsuccessful uprising in Russia
against the tsarist regime

After several years of mounting discontent, a peaceful demonstration was crushed by Tsar Nicholas II's troops in the Bloody Sunday massacre of January 1905. General strikes followed in St Petersburg and other industrial cities. The revolt spread to non-Russian parts of the empire, including Poland, Finland, and Georgia. Anti-revolutionary groups, including the Black Hundreds, opposed the rebellion with violent attacks on socialists and pogroms against Jews.

By October 1905, general strikes had spread to all the large cities, and the workers' councils or soviets, often led by the Mensheviks (the minority wing of the Russian Social-Democratic Workers' Party), became revolutionary governments. The strikes' magnitude convinced Nicholas II, advised by Sergey Witte, to issue the October Manifesto, promising an elected legislature. The concessions satisfied most moderates, though the more ardent revolutionaries refused to yield, and pockets of resistance in Poland, Georgia, and elsewhere were harshly suppressed as the regime restored its authority. While most of the revolutionary leaders, including Leon Trotsky, were arrested, the revolution forced the tsar to institute reforms such as a new constitution and an elected legislative body (Duma), though he failed to adequately implement various promised reforms.

the imperial government, and the second, in October (November, New Style), placed the Bolsheviks in power. (Until 1918 Russia still used the Julian or "Old Style" calendar, dating the beginning of the year from December 25; in that year, the Gregorian or "New Style" calendar was adopted, as it had been by most other western countries, in many cases for more than 300 years. The adoption of the new calendar resulted in the loss of 13 days, so that February 1, 1918, became February 14.)

The February Revolution of 1917 was spontaneous, leaderless, and fuelled by deep resentment over the economic and social conditions that had prevailed in imperial Russia under Tsar Nicholas. Hardly a hand was raised in support of the imperial order, and with the defection of the military, the tsar could not survive. After Nicholas's abdication in March, most Russians rejoiced, but a political vacuum was created that needed immediate attention. A Provisional Government was formed and was to remain in office until a democratic parliament, the Constituent Assembly, convened in January 1918. In practice, however, authority was from the outset exercised by the Petrograd (formerly St Petersburg) Soviet, or "Council", a body that claimed to represent the nation's workers and soldiers, but actually was convened and run by an executive committee of radical intellectuals nominated by the socialist parties. Similar soviets sprang up in other cities.

This dual power prevailed because the Provisional Government was undermined by war, economic collapse, and its own incompetence. The government seemingly spoke for the country, but in reality it represented only the middle class; the soviets represented the workers and peasants. Moreover, being a temporary administration, the government postponed all hard decisions – what should be done about land seizures by the peasants, for example – for the Constituent Assembly.

VLADIMIR ILYICH LENIN (1870–1924)

Founder of the Russian Communist Party, leader of the Russian Revolution of 1917, and architect and builder of the Soviet state

Growing up in a middle-class family, Vladimir Ilyich Ulyanov, as Lenin was born, was strongly influenced by his eldest brother, Aleksandr, who was hanged in 1887 for conspiring to assassinate the tsar. He studied law and became a Marxist in 1889 while practising law. He was arrested as a subversive in 1895 and exiled to Siberia, where he married Nadezhda Krupskaya. They lived in western Europe after 1900. At the 1903 meeting in London of the Russian Social-Democratic Workers' Party, Lenin emerged as the leader of the Bolshevik faction. In several revolutionary newspapers that he founded and edited, he put forth his theory of the party as the vanguard of the proletariat, a centralized body organized around a core of professional revolutionaries; his ideas, later known as Leninism, would be joined with Karl Marx's theories to form Marxism-Leninism, which became the communist worldview.

With the outbreak of the Russian Revolution of 1905, Lenin returned to Russia, but he resumed his exile in 1907 and continued his energetic agitation for the next ten years. He saw the First World War as an opportunity to turn a war of nations into a war of classes, and he returned to Russia with the Russian Revolution of 1917 to lead the Bolshevik coup that overthrew the provisional government of Aleksandr Kerensky.

As revolutionary leader of the Soviet state, Lenin

signed the Treaty of Brest-Litovsk with Germany (1918) and repulsed counter-revolutionary threats in the Russian Civil War. It was largely because of his inspired leadership that the Soviet government managed to survive. He guided the formation and strategy of the Workers' and Peasants' Red Army, and ensured there were sufficient resources to sustain it. But above all it was his political leadership that saved the day for the Soviets. By proclaiming the right of the peoples to self-determination, including the right to secession, he won the active sympathy, or at least the benevolent neutrality, of the non-Russian nationalities within Russia. Indeed, his perceptive, skilful policy on the national question enabled Soviet Russia to avoid total disintegration and to remain a huge multinational state. By making the industrial workers the new privileged class, favoured in the distribution of rations, housing, and political power, he retained the loyalty of the proletariat. His championing of the peasants' demand that they take all the land from the gentry, church, and crown without compensation won over the peasants, without whose support the government could not survive.

In ill health from 1922, Lenin died of a stroke in 1924.

Another fatal mistake was its continued prosecution of the war.

By this time Russia's complex political make-up had crystallized into two main parties, both offshoots of the Social Democrats (the Russian Social-Democratic Workers' Party). This party had followed the classic doctrines of Karl Marx and Friedrich Engels, according to which the development of capitalism inevitably created a radicalized proletariat that would in time stage a revolution and introduce socialism. The Mensheviks, the more moderate socialists, held that Russia had to pass through its capitalist phase before the socialist one could appear. The Bolsheviks wanted the transition period to be short. Their firebrand leader, Vladimir Ilyich Lenin (1870–1924), was a fanatical revolutionary who organized a relatively small but totally devoted and highly disciplined party bent on seizing power. Lenin had the advantage that, from his base during the First World War in neutral Switzerland, where he had agitated for Russia's defeat, he had attracted the attention of the Germans, who shrewdly supplied him with the money necessary to organize his party and build up a press. A

COMMUNIST PARTY OF THE SOVIET UNION (CPSU)

Major political party of Russia and the Soviet Union from the Russian Revolution of 1917 to 1991

The CPSU arose from the Bolshevik wing of the Russian Social-Democratic Workers' Party. Also known as the All-Union Communist Party (1925–52), from 1918 to the 1980s the CPSU was a monolithic, monopolistic ruling party that dominated the Soviet Union's political, economic, social, and cultural life. The constitution and other legal documents that supposedly regulated the government were actually subordinate to the CPSU, which also dominated communist parties abroad. Mikhail Gorbachev's efforts to reform the country's economy and political structure weakened the party, and in 1990 it voted to surrender its constitutionally guaranteed monopoly of power. The Soviet Union's dissolution in 1991 marked the party's formal demise.

third grouping that struggled for power in this period was formed by the Socialist Revolutionaries, the main agrarian party.

Lenin quickly sensed the weakness of the Provisional Government and the inherent instability of "dual power". He returned to Russia in April 1917, hoping to launch a revolution immediately. The majority of his followers, however, doubted it would succeed: they were vindicated in July 1917 when a putsch led by the Bolsheviks badly misfired. They were near success when the government released information on Lenin's dealings with the Germans, which caused angry troops to disperse the rebels and end the uprising. Abandoning his followers, Lenin again left the country, seeking refuge in Finland.

The Bolsheviks remained a minority in the soviets until autumn, by which time the Provisional Government had lost popular support, and many were rallying to Lenin's battle cry, "All power to the soviets!" Increasing war-weariness and the breakdown of the economy overtaxed the patience of the workers, peasants, and soldiers, who demanded immediate and fundamental change. Leon Trotsky, a recent convert to Bolshevism, became chairman of the Petrograd Soviet, the country's most important, and immediately turned it into a vehicle for the seizure of power. The result was the so-called October Revolution (November), a classic *coup d'état* carried out by a small group of conspirators – in complete contrast to the spontaneous events of February 1917. The Bolshevik Central Committee made the decision to seize power at a clandestine meeting held on the night of October 10 (October 23). In the meantime they built up an armed force to carry out the coup. Since the Bolsheviks were the only organization with an independent armed force, they took over the Military Revolutionary Committee and used it to topple the government. During the night of October 24–5, Bolshevik Red

LEON TROTSKY (1879–1940)

Russian communist leader

Born to Russian Jewish farmers, Lev Davidovich Bronshtein joined an underground socialist group and was exiled to Siberia in 1898 for his revolutionary activities. He escaped in 1902 with a forged passport using the name Trotsky. He fled to London, where he met Vladimir Lenin. In 1903, when the Russian Social-Democratic Workers' Party split, Trotsky became a Menshevik, allying himself with Lenin's opponents. He returned to St Petersburg to help lead the Russian Revolution of 1905. Arrested and again exiled to Siberia, he wrote *Results and Prospects*, setting forth his theory of "permanent revolution". He escaped to Vienna in 1907, worked as a journalist in the Balkan Wars (1912–13), and moved around Europe and the United States until the Russian Revolution of 1917 brought him back to St Petersburg (then Petrograd). There he became a Bolshevik and was elected leader of the workers' soviet.

Trotsky played a major role in the overthrow of the provisional government and the establishment of Lenin's communist regime. As commissar of war (1918–24) Trotsky rebuilt and brilliantly commanded the Red Army during the Russian Civil War. Although favoured by Lenin to succeed him, Trotsky lost support after Lenin's death (1924) and was forced out of power by Joseph Stalin. After a campaign of denunciation, he was expelled from the Politburo (1926) and Central Committee (1927), then banished from Russia (1929). He lived in Turkey and France, where he wrote his memoirs and a history of the revolution. Under Soviet pressure, he was forced to move around Europe, and he eventually found asylum in 1936 in Mexico, where, having been falsely accused in the purge trials as the chief conspirator against Stalin, he was murdered in 1940 by a Spanish communist.

Guards peacefully occupied strategic points in Petrograd. On the morning of October 25, Lenin, re-emerging from his hideaway, issued a declaration in the name of the Military Revolutionary Committee that the Provisional Government had been overthrown and all power had been assumed by the soviets. The declaration referred neither to the Bolsheviks nor to socialism – unsurprisingly, the inhabitants of the city had no inkling of how profound a change had occurred.

Although Lenin and Trotsky had carried out the October coup in the name of soviets, they intended from the beginning to concentrate all power in the hands of the ruling organs of the Bolshevik Party. The resulting novel arrangement – the prototype of all totalitarian regimes – vested actual sovereignty in the hands of a private organization, called "the Party", which, however, exercised it indirectly, through state institutions. Bolsheviks held leading posts in the state: no decisions could be taken and no laws passed without their consent. The legislative organs, centred in the soviets, merely rubber-stamped Bolshevik orders. The state apparatus was headed by a cabinet called the Council of People's Commissars, chaired by Lenin, all of whose members were drawn from the elite of the party. This governmental structure was to last until the convocation of an elected Constituent Assembly in January 1918. However, when it became clear that the

Bolsheviks did not hold a majority, Lenin disbanded the assembly. If the October Revolution was accepted as democratic – supported by a majority of the population – then it ceased to be so soon after this event.

Lenin's hand was strengthened by his conclusion of the Brest–Litovsk armistice (December 1917) and treaty (March 1918) with the Central Powers. Though the terms were harsh – Russia lost territories inhabited by more than one-quarter of its citizens and providing more than one-third of its grain harvest – the treaty saved the Bolshevik regime: for the next eight months it received critical diplomatic and financial support from Germany that enabled it to beat back political opponents.

In March 1918 the Bolshevik Party was renamed the Russian Communist Party in order to distinguish it from Social Democratic parties in Russia and Europe, and to separate the followers of Lenin from those affiliated with the non-revolutionary Socialist International. The party was directed by a Central Committee. To streamline work, from March 1919 onwards its management was entrusted to the Secretariat, the Organizational Bureau (Orgburo), and the Political Bureau (Politburo). The Secretariat and Orgburo dealt largely with personnel matters, while the Politburo combined legislative and executive powers.

Meanwhile, after the country's withdrawal from the First World War, only part of Russia – Moscow, Petrograd, and much of the industrial heartland – was under Bolshevik control. Ukraine slipped under German influence, the Mensheviks held sway in the Caucasus, and much of the countryside belonged to the Socialist Revolutionaries. Given the Bolshevik desire to dominate the whole of Russia and the rest of the former tsarist empire, civil war was inevitable.

The Civil War and the Creation of the USSR

From 1918 to 1920 Russia was torn by a civil war that cost millions of lives and untold destruction. In the context of the Russian Revolution, the term "civil war" had two distinct meanings. It described the repressive measures applied by the Bolsheviks against those who refused to recognize their power seizure and defied their decrees, such as peasants who refused to surrender grain. It also defined the military conflict between the communists' Red Army and various "White" armies formed on the periphery of Soviet Russia for the purpose of overthrowing the communists. Both wars went on concurrently. The struggle against domestic opponents was to prove even more costly in human lives and more threatening to the new regime than the efforts of the Whites.

In the summer of 1918 the fortunes of the Bolsheviks were at their lowest ebb. Not only had they to contend with rebellious peasants and hostile White armies supported by the Allies, but they lost such support as they had once had among the workers: in elections to the soviets held in the spring of 1918 they were everywhere defeated by rival socialist parties. They dealt with the problem by expelling the Socialist Revolutionaries and Mensheviks from the soviets and forcing re-elections until they obtained the desired majorities.

The Bolsheviks' growing unpopularity moved them to resort to unbridled terror. The Cheka (a forerunner of the notorious KGB), or political police, was formed in December 1917 to protect communist power. By the end of the civil war the Cheka had become a powerful force. In the first half of 1918 it carried out not a few summary executions. In July, on Lenin's orders, the ex-tsar and his entire family were murdered in the basement of a house in Yekaterinburg (called Sverdlovsk between 1924 and 1991), where they had been held prisoner. The formal "Red Terror" began in September 1918. The pretext was a nearly successful attempt on the life of Lenin by a Socialist Revolutionary, Fannie Kaplan. As soon as he recovered from what could have been fatal wounds, Lenin ordered the Cheka to carry out mass executions of suspected opponents. Thousands of political prisoners held without charges were shot.

The civil war in the military sense was fought on several fronts. The first White force, known as the Volunteer Army, formed in the winter of 1917–18 in the southern areas inhabited by the Cossacks. Another army was created in western Siberia; several smaller White armies came into being in the north-west, the north, and the far east. These anti-communist armies were often led by former imperial officers, and all were in varying measures supported by the United Kingdom with money and war matériel. There were also the anti-communist "Greens" and the anarchists, who were strongest in Ukraine; the anarchists' most talented leader was Nestor Makhno. The Allied intervention was initially inspired by the desire to reactivate the Eastern Front of the First World War, but after the Armistice it lost its clear purpose, and it was continued on the insistence of Winston Churchill, who saw in Bolshevism a permanent threat to democracy and world peace. Neither the American nor the French contingents on Russian soil engaged in combat, and they were withdrawn after the Armistice. The British stayed on until the autumn of 1919, doing occasional fighting but mainly providing aid to the White armies.

The Red Army was formed in February 1918, and Trotsky became its leader. He was to reveal great leadership and military skill, fashioning a rabble into a formidable fighting force. The Bolsheviks had been slow in forming a professional army, largely because they feared the prospect of arming peasants, whom they viewed as class enemies. At first they relied mainly on partisans and Latvian volunteers. In the autumn of 1918, however, they decided to proceed with the formation of a regular army manned by conscripts. Command over the troops and the formulation of strategic decisions was entrusted to professional officers of the ex-tsarist army, some 75,000 of whom were drafted. To prevent defections and sabotage, the orders of these officers were subject to approval by Bolshevik political commissars assigned to them. Officer families were treated as hostages. At the height of the civil war the Red Army numbered almost 5 million people.

The decisive battles of the civil war took place in the summer and autumn of 1919. Admiral Aleksandr Kolchak, leader of the White forces in Siberia, launched in the spring a drive on Moscow and approached the shores of the Volga, when he was stopped by a numerically superior Red force and thrown back. His army disintegrated later in the year, and he himself was captured and shot without trial, possibly on Lenin's orders (February 1920). Of all the White generals, Anton Denikin came closest to victory. In October 1919 his Volunteer Army, augmented by conscripts, reached Oryol, 150 miles (250 kilometres) south of Moscow. In their advance, Cossacks in White service carried out frightful pogroms in Ukraine in which an estimated 100,000 Jews lost their lives. Denikin's lines were stretched thin, and he lacked reserves. He advanced recklessly because he had been told by Britain that unless he took Moscow, the country's new capital, before the onset of winter, he would receive no more assistance. In battles waged in October and November the Red Army decisively crushed the Whites and sent them fleeing pell-mell to the ports of the

JOSEPH STALIN (1879–1953)

Soviet politician and dictator

The son of a Georgian cobbler, Iosif Vissarionovich Dzhugashvili studied at a seminary but was expelled for revolutionary activity in 1899. He joined an underground revolutionary group and sided with the Bolshevik faction of the Russian Social-Democratic Workers' Party in 1903. A disciple of Vladimir Lenin, he served in minor party posts and was appointed to the first Bolshevik Central Committee (1912). He remained active behind the scenes and in exile (1913–17) until the Russian Revolution of 1917 brought the Bolsheviks to power. Having adopted the name Stalin (from Russian *stal*, "steel"), he served as commissar for nationalities and for state control in the Bolshevik government (1917–23). He was a member of the Politburo, and in 1922 he became secretary-general of the party's Central Committee.

After Lenin's death (1924), Stalin overcame his rivals, including Leon Trotsky, Grigory Zinovyev, Lev Kamenev, Nikolay Bukharin, and Aleksey Rykov, and took control of Soviet politics. In 1928 he inaugurated the five-year plans that radically altered Soviet economic and social structures and resulted in the deaths of many millions. In the 1930s he contrived to eliminate threats to his power through the purge trials and through widespread secret executions and persecution.

On the eve of the Second World War Stalin signed the German-Soviet Non-Aggression Pact (1939); he attacked Finland, and annexed parts of eastern Europe to strengthen his western frontiers. When Germany invaded Russia (1941), Stalin took control of military operations. He allied Russia with Britain and the United States; at the Tehran, Yalta, and Potsdam conferences he demonstrated his negotiating skill. After the war he consolidated Soviet power in eastern Europe and built up the Soviet Union as a world military power. He continued his repressive political measures to control internal dissent; increasingly paranoid, at the time of his death he was preparing to mount another purge after the so-called Doctors' Plot.

Noted for bringing the Soviet Union into world prominence, at terrible cost to his own people, Stalin left a legacy of repression and fear as well as industrial and military power. In 1956 he and his personality cult were denounced by Soviet leader Nikita Khrushchev.

Black Sea. By mid-1920 the Reds had consolidated their hold on the country.

In part the Bolshevik triumph can be attributed to superior organization and better understanding of the political dimensions of the civil war. But in the ultimate analysis it was due mainly to the insurmountable advantages that they enjoyed. The Reds controlled the heartland of what had been the Russian empire, inhabited by some 70 million Russians, while their opponents operated on the periphery, where the population was sparser and ethnically mixed. In nearly all engagements the Red Army enjoyed great preponderance in numbers. It also enjoyed superiority in military hardware: since most of Russia's defence industries and arsenals were located in the centre of the country, it inherited vast stores of weapons and ammunition from the tsarist army. The Whites, by contrast, were almost wholly dependent on foreign aid.

One of the most significant results of the Bolshevik victory was the reintegration of those borderland areas inhabited by non-Russians that had been separated from Russia at the time of the 1917 Revolution. Although the Bolsheviks originally had encouraged this separatist process, advancing the slogan of "national self-determination", once in power, they moved decisively to reconquer these territories – realizing that Ukraine, for example, was vital for the economic viability of Russia. Except for those regions that enjoyed strong British or French backing – Finland, the Baltic area, and Poland – by 1921 the Red Army had occupied all the independent republics of the defunct Russian empire, including Georgia, Armenia, and Azerbaijan. Lenin's original nationality policy had been based on the assumption that nations would choose to stay in a close relationship with Russia, but this proved not to be the case. Many republics wanted to be independent in order to develop their own brand of national communism. The comrade who imposed Russian dominance was, ironically, Joseph Stalin, a Georgian. As commissar for nationalities, he sought to ensure that Moscow rule prevailed.

In 1922 Bolshevik-controlled Moscow proclaimed the creation of the Union of Soviet Socialist Republics, composed of Russia, Belorussia (now Belarus), Ukraine, and the Transcaucasian Federation. The first USSR constitution was formally adopted in January 1924. In 1925 the All-Union Communist Party, later the Communist Party of the Soviet Union (CPSU), was formed. Nominally a league of equals, the USSR was from the beginning dominated by Russians. The federated state structure was a facade to conceal the dictatorship of the Russian Communist Party, the true locus of power.

For Lenin and his associates Russia itself, however, was no more than a springboard from which to launch a global civil war. They feared that if the revolution remained confined to backward, agrarian Russia it would perish under the combined onslaught of the foreign "bourgeoisie" and the domestic peasantry. In their view it was essential to carry the revolution abroad to the industrial countries of the West, whose workers, they believed, were anxious to stop fighting one another and topple their exploiters. To organize and finance this effort, they formed in March 1919 the Third International, or "Comintern". This organization was a branch of the Russian Communist Party, and it decreed that communist parties abroad were to be accountable to Moscow and not to their domestic constituencies.

Hoping to exploit the political and economic turmoil afflicting central Europe after the Allied victory, Moscow sent agents with ample supplies of money to stir up unrest. By the early 1920s the Comintern succeeded in forming in most European countries, especially France and Italy, Communist Party affiliates that it used as pressure groups. The idea of world revolution, however, had to be postponed indefinitely, which compelled the Bolshevik leadership to concentrate on building in Russia an isolated communist state. Ironically, the methods of government that they devised, centred on the one-party monopoly and known since the early 1920s as "totalitarian", were emulated not by elements sympathetic to communism but by nationalistic radicals hostile to it, such as Benito Mussolini in Italy and Adolf Hitler in Germany.

Creating a Communist Economy

While the Bolsheviks were fighting the Russian Civil War, they had initiated a series of unprecedented measures intended to destroy all vestiges of private property and inaugurate a centralized communist economy. These measures, which in 1921 received the name "War Communism", had two primary objectives. One was political: as Marxists, the Bolsheviks believed that private ownership of the means of production provided the basis of political power. By nationalizing it, they undermined the opposition. They further acted in the conviction that a centralized and planned economy was inherently more efficient than a capitalist one, and would in no time turn Soviet Russia into the most productive country in the world.

War Communism entailed four sets of measures: (1) the nationalization of all the means of production and transportation, (2) the abolition of money and its replacement by barter tokens, as well as by free goods and services, (3) the imposition on the national economy of a single plan, and (4) the introduction of compulsory labour. In 1918 all but the smallest industrial enterprises were nationalized. Agricultural land, the main source of national wealth, was for the time being left at the disposal of peasant communes, with the understanding that sooner or later it would be collectivized. Private ownership of urban real estate was abolished, as was inheritance. The state (in effect, the Bolshevik Party) became the sole owner of the country's productive and income-yielding assets. Management of this wealth was entrusted to a gigantic bureaucratic organization, the Supreme Council of the National Economy, whose purpose was to allocate human and material resources in the most rational manner.

Money was effectively destroyed by the unrestrained printing of banknotes, which led, as intended, to an extraordinary inflation: by January 1923 prices in Soviet Russia, compared with 1913, had increased 100 million times. Ordinary citizens, along with the rich, lost their life savings. Barter and the issuance by government agencies of free goods replaced normal commercial operations. Private trade, whether wholesale or retail, was forbidden. All adult citizens were required to work wherever ordered. The independence of trade unions was abolished, and the right to strike against the nationalized enterprises outlawed.

The policies of War Communism brought about an unprecedented economic crisis. In 1920, when the civil war was for all practical purposes over, industrial production was about one-quarter of what it had been in 1913, and the number of employed workers had fallen by roughly one-half. Productivity per worker was one-quarter of the 1913 level. Most painful was the decline in the production of grain. Compelled to surrender all the grain that government officials decided they did not require for personal consumption, fodder, or seed, and forbidden to sell on the open market, the peasants kept reducing their sown acreage. Such reductions, combined with declining yields caused by shortages of fertilizer and draught animals, led to a steady drop in grain production: in 1920 the cereal harvest in central Russia yielded only two-thirds of the 1913 crop. In the cities bread rations were reduced to one or two ounces a day.

It required only one of the periodic droughts that customarily afflict Russia to bring about a massive famine: this happened in early 1921. There was a catastrophic plunge in foodstuff production in the areas that traditionally supplied the bulk of grains. At the height of the famine some 35 million people suffered from severe malnutrition. The hungry resorted to eating grass and, occasionally, to cannibalism. The losses would have been still more disastrous were it not for assistance provided by the American Relief Administration, headed by the future US president Herbert Hoover, which, with moneys from the US Congress and voluntary contributions, fed most of the starving. Even so, the human casualties of the 1921 famine are estimated at 5.1 million.

The New Economic Policy, 1921–8

The economic policies of War Communism led inevitably to clashes with the labour force, which had understood socialism as industrial self-management. With the threat and reality of hunger ever present, forced requisitioning was resisted and strikes became endemic, especially in Petrograd. This general situation, coupled with revolt in Tambov province in 1920, forced Lenin to change his War Communism policy – while he and the Bolshevik leadership were willing to slaughter the mutinous sailors of the Kronshtadt naval base in March 1921, they could not survive if the countryside turned against them. A tactical retreat from enforced socialism was therefore deemed necessary, a move that was deeply unpopular with the Bolshevik rank and file. The New Economic Policy (NEP) was inaugurated at the 10th Party Congress, one of the periodic gatherings of party delegates that determined major policies, in March 1921. The key sectors of the economy – heavy industry, communications, and transport – remained in state hands, but light and consumer-goods industries were open to the entrepreneur.

Generally speaking, the NEP had the intended economic results. The peasants, now allowed to control their property, began to work their holdings profitably. Small traders began to take over the transfer of rural food products to the towns. In the towns small consumer-goods producers began to turn out the products for which the peasants now had an incentive to pay. Overall, the entire country soon began to return to economic normality. Precise figures are still incompletely researched (over the 1920s they are defective mainly for various intrinsic reasons; in the 1930s and later, because of massive falsification), but the speed and extent of the recovery were phenomenal. Roughly speaking, the 1922 crop was already up to three-quarters of normal. Industry, it is true, only reached a quarter of its pre-war production, and most of this was in light industry, such as textiles.

Yet over the whole NEP period the disproportion between agricultural and industrial progress was seen as a major problem, producing what Trotsky described at the 12th Party Congress in 1923 as the "scissors crisis", from the shape of the graph of (comparatively) high industrial and low agricultural prices. The original "scissors crisis" was a short-lived phenomenon, due mainly to the government setting prices of agricultural goods too low, and it disappeared when this was remedied. But the party was still faced with the challenge of building up heavy industry. This could be funded, for the most part, only by "primitive socialist accumulation" of resources from the peasant sector, whether by fiscal or by other means.

Thus the NEP was in general regarded as no more than a temporary retreat that would have to be made good as soon as the economy had to some degree recovered. In the Communist Party as a whole the policy was accepted only with reluctance, out of perceived necessity, and by the end of the decade the economic debate would be won by those who favoured rapid industrialization and forced collectivization.

Culture and Ideology

Determined not only to change drastically the political and economic order but also to create a new type of human being, the Bolsheviks attached great importance to every aspect of culture, especially education and religion.

The Bolsheviks suppressed political dissidence by shutting down hostile newspapers and subjecting all publications to preventive censorship. In 1922 they set up a central censorship office, known for short as Glavlit, with final authority over printed materials as well as the performing arts. The 1920s also saw the formation of the Agitation and Propaganda Section of the Central Committee Secretariat, known as *agitprop* for short. Affiliated to the Communist Party, this department aimed to determine the content of all official information, overseeing political education in schools, watching over all forms of mass communication, and mobilizing public support for party programmes. Many artists – writers, dramatists, film-makers – were engaged to this end, and every unit of the Communist Party, from the republic to the local-party level, had an agitprop section; at the local level, agitators (party-trained spokespeople) were the chief points of contact between the party and the public.

In literary and artistic matters, however, as long as Lenin was alive, the regime showed a degree of tolerance absent from other spheres of Soviet life. Aware that the overwhelming majority of intellectuals rejected them, and yet wishing to win them over, the Bolsheviks permitted writers and artists creative freedom as long as they did not engage in overt political dissent. Trotsky popularized the term "fellow travellers" for writers who, without joining the communists, were willing to cooperate with them and follow their rules. As a result, the early 1920s saw a degree of innovation in literature and the arts that contrasted vividly with the regime's political rigidity. Among the few writers and artists who joined the Bolsheviks were the Futurists, led by the poet Vladimir Mayakovsky, who closely followed the models set by their Italian counterparts, and the "constructivists", Russian analogues of the German Bauhaus group. In the theatre and cinema, experiments in staging and montage, greatly influenced by Max Reinhardt and D. W. Griffith, were in vogue. Even so, many of Russia's best writers and artists, finding conditions at home insufferable, chose to emigrate. Others withdrew into their private world and gradually ceased to publish or exhibit.

To destroy what they considered the "elitist" character of Russia's educational system, the communists carried out revolutionary changes in its structure and curriculum. All schools, from the lowest to the highest, were nationalized and placed in the charge of the Commissariat of Enlightenment. Teachers lost the authority to enforce discipline in the classroom. Open admission to institutions of higher learning was introduced to assure that anyone who desired, regardless of qualifications, could enrol. Tenure for university professors was abolished, and the universities lost their traditional right of self-government. Fields of study deemed potentially subversive were dropped in favour of courses offering ideological indoctrination. These reforms thoroughly disorganized the educational system, and in the early 1920s many of them were quietly dropped. Party controls, however, remained in place and in the following decade were used by Stalin to impose complete conformity.

The Bolsheviks, in common with other socialists, regarded religious belief as gross superstition, and they were determined to eliminate it by a combination of repression, ridicule, and scientific enlightenment. A decree issued on January 20, 1918 (February 2), formally separated church from state, but it went far beyond its declared purpose by prohibiting religious bodies from engaging in instruction and from collecting dues from their members. Since the state nationalized all church property, the clergy were left destitute. In the spring and summer of 1922 numerous incidents of resistance occurred, in consequence of which priests were arrested and numerous believers killed. On Lenin's orders show trials were staged in Moscow, Petrograd, and other cities, in which some priests were sentenced to death and prison terms. A splinter "Living Church", composed of renegade priests and operating under instructions from the Cheka, was created to serve the interests of the state.

Lenin concentrated on the Orthodox establishment because of its traditional links with the monarchy and its hold on the Russian population. But he did not spare the other faiths. A trial of Catholic priests resulted in death sentences and the closure of churches. Synagogues were also desecrated, and Jewish holidays subjected to public derision. Muslim religious institutions suffered the least because of Lenin's fear of alienating the colonial peoples of the Middle East, on whose support he counted against the western imperial powers.

The Stalin Era

The first phase of Bolshevik power came to an end with the death of Lenin in January 1924. Lenin's partial, then total, disablement had provided a transitional period for a party leadership to emerge and for policies to be argued. But the leaders on to whom Lenin's heritage devolved were divided. Personal ambition and politico-ideological disagreement resulted in a series of factional fights that constituted the political history of the newly formed USSR over the next six years. The major division was between those who thought that the Russian Revolution could not survive on its own and that therefore the main effort should be in supporting revolution abroad, and those, Stalin most prominent among them, who now proclaimed the slogan "Socialism in One Country".

On the face of it, Trotsky was the natural heir to Lenin, since it was Trotsky who had organized the October 1917 coup and managed the Red Army in the Civil War. A superb orator and lively writer, he had an international reputation. His chances of succeeding Lenin, however, were more apparent than real. Trotsky had joined the Bolshevik party late (August 1917); he thus never belonged to its "Old Guard". He was personally unpopular for his arrogance and unwillingness to work as a member of a team. His Jewishness was no asset in a country in which Jews were widely blamed for the devastations wrought by communism. Last but not least, bored by the routine of paperwork, he was a poor administrator.

Although far less known, Stalin was much better positioned to succeed Lenin. Intellectually unprepossessing, a dull speaker and lacklustre writer, he operated behind the scenes. Having realized early that the centralized system of government that Lenin had created vested extraordinary power in the party machine, Stalin avoided the spotlight and instead concentrated on building up cadres loyal to him. By 1922 he was in a unique position to manipulate policies to his own ends by virtue of the fact that he alone belonged to both the Politburo, which set policy, and the Secretariat, which managed personnel. To thwart Trotsky he entered into alliances that dominated the Politburo and isolated their common rival. At the time of the 15th Party Congress in 1927, Trotsky and his faction were expelled from the party; many Trotskyites were exiled to Siberia or Central Asia, among them Trotsky himself.

Collectivization

Stalin's position as secretary general of the party's Central Committee, from 1922 until his death, provided the power base for his dictatorship. Having achieved a majority in the Politburo, and despite further power struggles – the fear of political rivals was an insecurity that was to dog him throughout his life – Stalin could now turn to the wider struggle, his mission to put socialism into tangible effect. In 1928 he thus abandoned Lenin's quasi-capitalist New Economic Policy in favour of headlong state-organized industrialization under a succession of five-year plans, supported by a socialized agriculture. This was, in effect, a new Russian revolution more devastating in its effects than those of 1917.

The burden fell most heavily on the peasantry, since Stalin's first concern was to persuade them to sell their grain surplus and feed the cities. With little economic knowledge and unreliable statistics, the party was suspicious of the market mechanism and moreover believed that the peasantry was divided into classes with different and opposed interests. The rich "kulaks", it was held, were implacable enemies of socialism. The "middle peasants", constituting the great majority, vacillated but could be brought to the proletarian side. And the "poor peasants", together with the "village proletarians", were reliable allies.

Although this idea of a rich exploiting kulak class was false, policies towards kulaks became harsher. During 1929 many fines were imposed, and dispossessions and even deportations took place. By the end of the year the official policy became "the liquidation of the kulak as a class". Over the following three years, many were arrested en masse, shot, exiled, or absorbed into the rapidly expanding network of Stalinist concentration camps and worked to death under atrocious conditions.

Convinced that only collectivization would make grain available to the authorities, Stalin compelled some 25 million rustic households to amalgamate into kolkhozes, collective or state farms, within a few years. Large grain quotas and crippling fines were imposed on the individual peasants. From mid-1929 decisions on the extent and speed of proposed collectivization were changed almost monthly, becoming ever more extreme. The First Five-Year Plan as approved in April–May 1929 envisaged 5 million peasant households collectivized by 1932–3; this figure was doubled by November and doubled again during December. By the turn of the year it was decreed that collectivization should be completed in Ukraine by the autumn of 1930 and in the other main grain areas by the spring of 1931. One of the most destructive effects of collectivization was in Kazakhstan, where a nomad herding population was forced, largely on ideological grounds, into permanent settlements, for which no economic basis existed. About one-quarter of a million managed to escape over the Chinese border. But, of roughly 4 million Kazakhs, more than a million, possibly more, perished. Elsewhere, resistance was met with attacks by troops and OGPU (political police) units.

The immediate result of the collectivization measures was a catastrophic decline in agricultural output across the country as a whole. Collectivization also imposed great hardship on the peasants, partly because they were left with no surplus on which to live, and partly because of their mass slaughter of farm animals to prevent their livestock being taken by the kolkhoz. Official figures given in 1934 showed a loss of 26.6 million head of cattle (42.6 per cent of the country's total) and 63.4 million sheep (65.1 per cent of the total), and this is probably an understatement of the facts.

The government's reaction to the decline in output was to base its requirements for delivery of grain from the kolkhozes not on actual production but rather on what became the basis of Soviet agricultural statistics until 1953 – the "biological yield". This was based on the estimated size of the crop in the fields before harvesting; it was typically more than 40 per cent higher than the reality. And in 1932 even this tenuous link to the facts failed: the figure was distorted by merely multiplying acreage by optimum yield. The grain requisitions made on this basis were ruthlessly enforced by activist squads. Such action left the peasant with a notional but non-existent surplus. As a result, over the winter of 1932–3, a major famine swept the grain-growing areas. Some 4 to 5 million people died in Ukraine, and another 2 to 3 million in the North Caucasus and the lower Volga area. Both the "dekulakization" terror of 1930–2 and the terror-famine of 1932–3 were particularly deadly in Ukraine. During this period about 1.7 million tons (1.5 million metric tons) of grain were exported, enough to have provided some two pounds (one kilogram) a head to 15 million people over three months. There is no doubt that the party leadership knew exactly what was happening and used famine as a means of terror, and revenge, against the peasantry.

Industrialization

Crash industrialization was imposed at the same time as agricultural collectivization, since Stalin had convincingly argued that a slow socialization was impossible. From 1928 to 1929 he began to implement a programme of faster industrialization – in part to sharpen the class struggle with the errant elements of the peasantry.

To this effect a planned economy was to be introduced with, as its first task, the direction of all possible resources into intensive industrialization. The First Five-Year Plan had not been finalized by the time it was announced in April–May 1929, though it had been expected to come into operation six months earlier. In its initial form it prescribed goals for 50 industries and for agriculture, and provided some relation between resources and possibilities, but over the period that followed it was treated mainly as a set of figures to be scaled upward. The industrial growth rate originally laid down was 18–20 per cent (in fact, this had already been achieved, at least on paper). Later in the year Stalin insisted on nearly doubling this rate. The plan was thereafter a permanent feature of Soviet life: the First Five-Year Plan was followed by a series of others. The plan was both the basis of a set of real governmental and economic actions and a concept – organizational, ideological, inspirational, and, it might almost be said, transcendental.

Understanding of the economic side of the industrialization drive of the 1930s was long confused by two factors. The first was the claim by the communists that they were implementing a rational and fulfillable plan. The second, which came later, was the claim that they had in fact secured unprecedented increases in production.

Part of Stalin's industrialization scheme was the movement of people from the country to the towns. Between 1929 and 1932 some 12.5 million new hands were reported to have entered urban work, 8.5 million of them from the countryside (though it was ruled that kulaks should not be given jobs in the factories). These are striking figures, though they did not change the USSR into an urbanized country in the western sense. Even in 1940 just over two-thirds of the population were classified as rural and just under one-third as urban. It was not until the early 1960s that the population became equally urban and rural.

At the end of 1932 it was announced that the First Five-Year Plan had been successfully completed. In fact none of the targets had been reached, or even approached. Extravagant claims were made and continued to be issued until the late 1980s. It was only then revealed by Soviet economists that the true rate of growth in production over the period (including that of the Second Five-Year Plan, slightly less strongly stressing heavy industry, which now followed) was only about 3.5 per cent per annum, about the same as that of Germany over the same span of time. Nevertheless, during this period a number of important industrial enterprises were completed, though there was much waste as well. Some undertakings were ill-considered: the Baltic–White Sea Canal, supposedly completed in 1933, employed some 200,000–300,000 forced labourers but proved almost useless. On the other hand, the great Dneproges dam was a generally successful hydroelectric project on the largest scale. The same can be said of the Magnitogorsk foundries and other great factories. The characteristic fault was "giantism", the party's inclination to build on the largest and most ostentatious scale. One result was that there were continual organizational problems. More crucial was that the main concern was that production figures must always be at, or beyond, the limits of capacity, so that maintenance and infrastructure were neglected, with deleterious long-term results.

Moreover, even if the crash programmes had been intrinsically sound, the party had not had time to prepare adequate technical and managerial staff or to educate the new industrial proletariat. And few genuine economic incentives were available: in 1933 workers' real wages were about one-tenth of what they had been in 1926–7. Hence, everything had to be handled on the basis of myth and coercion rather than through rationality and cooperation. It is impossible to estimate such intangibles as the level of genuine enthusiasm among the Komsomols (the young members of the Communist Party) sent into the industrial plants or how long such enthusiasm lasted. But there was certainly an important element of genuine enthusiasts, and the remainder were at least obliged to behave as such.

From October 1930 a series of regressive measures were introduced into labour relations: a decree was issued forbidding the free movement of labour, unemployment relief was abolished on the grounds that there was "no more unemployment", and a single day's unauthorized absence from work became punishable by instant dismissal. Punitive measures against negligence were announced, followed by a decree holding workers responsible for damage done to instruments or materials. On August 7, 1932, the death penalty was introduced for theft of state or collective property; this law was immediately applied on a large scale. Finally, on December 27, 1932, came the reintroduction of the internal passport, which had been denounced by Lenin as one of the worst stigmas of tsarist backwardness and despotism.

Further signs of the increasing restriction of personal freedoms emerged in these years, as changes became apparent in official attitudes toward the intelligentsia and technical experts. It was felt that the new communist specialists in every field were now well enough equipped to take over from their bourgeois predecessors. The result was a tightening of state control of all intellectual endeavour, and a rigid enforcement of soviet ideological criteria in every sphere of culture, science, and philosophy. The summer of 1928 saw the public trial in Moscow of 53 engineers on charges of sabotage in the so-called Shakhty Case. The theme, repeated in endless propaganda over the following years, was that bourgeois specialists could not be trusted. Large numbers were subsequently arrested. By 1930 more than half of the surviving engineers had no proper training. In all institutes and academies, ideological hacks were intruded to ensure Marxist, or rather Stalinist, purity of theory and practice. Similar repressive measures were exercised in the arts.

The Purges

In late 1934, just when the worst excesses of Stalinism seemed to have spent themselves, Stalin launched a new campaign of political terror against the very Communist Party members who had brought him to power; his pretext was the assassination on December 1 of his leading colleague and potential rival, Sergey Kirov, in Leningrad (as Petrograd had been renamed in 1924, following Lenin's death). That Stalin himself had arranged Kirov's murder – as an excuse for the promotion of mass bloodshed – was strongly hinted by Nikita Khrushchev in a speech denouncing Stalin at the 20th Party Congress in 1956.

Over the next four years the centre of political life in the Soviet Union was the exposure and suppression of ever-increasing circles of alleged plotters against the regime, all of them linked in one way or another with the Kirov case – with the aim, presumably, to secure Stalin's personal power base. The country was submitted to an intensive campaign against hidden "enemies of the people". This manifested itself both in a series of public, or publicized, trials and in a massive terror operation against the population as a whole. The most brutal stage of the purges came with the appointment in September 1936 of Nikolay Ivanovich Yezhov as chief of the Soviet security police or NKVD (People's Commissariat of Internal Affairs). During this phase, known as the Yezhovshchina, special extra-legal tribunals were set up, in particular the notorious NKVD "troikas", which sentenced hundreds of thousands of people to death in their absence. The mass graves of the victims remained secret until the late 1980s.

The Communist Party itself was devastated. The industrial, engineering, and economic cadres, including those of the railways, were heavily purged. The army also suffered heavy losses. The officer corps as a whole lost about half its members. The cultural world suffered equally: several hundred writers were executed or died in camps, including such figures as Osip Mandelshtam, Boris Pilnyak, and Isaak Babel. The same applied in all the professions. Plots were discovered in the State Hermitage Museum, in the Pulkovo Astronomical Observatory, and throughout academe. Nor was the general public spared. In all, some 5 million people were arrested, of whom no more than 10 per cent survived. The *Yezhovshchina* was in fact one of the most brutal terrors in recorded history. The effects were long-lasting.

The purges necessitated a further social and economic component of the Stalinist system: the expansion and development of labour camps, or the *Gulag* (an abbreviation of the Russian words for Chief Administration of Corrective Labour Camps), which housed political prisoners and criminals.

A system of forced labour had begun in Russia soon after the Bolshevik Revolution, and was established by decree on April 15, 1919. It underwent a series of administrative and organizational changes in the 1920s, ending with the founding of the *Gulag* in 1930 under the control of the secret police, OGPU (later, the NKVD and the KGB). But expansion was rapid: in the late 1920s the *Gulag* had a total inmate population of about 100,000; by 1936, mopping up "political" prisoners from Stalin's collectivization of agriculture, among others, the total had risen to 5 million, a number that was probably equalled or exceeded every subsequent year until Stalin died, in 1953. In the mid-1930s the camps were located largely in the Arctic (such as Kolyma and Vorkuta) but also in Kazakhstan and elsewhere.

Besides rich or resistant peasants arrested during collectivization, persons sent to the *Gulag* included purged Communist Party members and military officers, German and other Axis prisoners of war (during the Second World War), members of ethnic groups suspected of disloyalty, Soviet soldiers and other citizens who had been taken prisoner or used as slave labourers by the Germans during the war, suspected saboteurs and traitors, dissident intellectuals, ordinary criminals, and many utterly innocent people who were hapless victims of Stalin's purges.

Inmates filled the *Gulag* in three major waves: in 1929–32, the years of the collectivization of Soviet agriculture; in 1936–8, at the height of Stalin's purges; and in the years immediately following the Second World War. The *Gulag* was largely unknown in the West until the publication in 1973 of Aleksandr Solzhenitsyn's *Gulag Archipelago*. Solzhenitsyn claimed that between 1928 and 1953 "some forty to fifty million people served long sentences in the Archipelago". Figures supposedly compiled by the *Gulag* administration itself (and released by Soviet historians in 1989) show that a total of 10 million people were sent to the camps in the period from 1934 to 1947. The *Gulag* reached its height in the years of collectivization of Soviet agriculture (1929–32), during Joseph Stalin's purges (1936–8), and immediately after the Second World War. At its extreme it consisted of many hundreds of camps, with the average camp holding 2,000–10,000 prisoners. Most of these camps were "corrective labour colonies" in which prisoners felled timber, laboured on general construction projects (such as the building of canals and railways), or worked in mines. Most prisoners laboured under the threat of starvation or execution if they refused. It is estimated that the combination of very long working hours, harsh climatic and other working conditions, inadequate food, and summary executions killed off at least 10 per cent of the *Gulag*'s total prisoner population each year. Western scholarly estimates of the total number of deaths in the *Gulag* in the period from 1918 to 1956 range from 15 to 30 million.

The *Gulag* started to shrink soon after Stalin's death: hundreds of thousands of prisoners were amnestied from 1953 to 1957, by which time the camp system had returned to its proportions of the early 1920s. Several times the *Gulag* was officially disbanded; its activities were absorbed by various economic ministries, and the remaining camps were grouped in 1955 under a new body, GUITK ("Chief Administration of Corrective Labour Colonies").

Life in a typical camp is incisively described in Aleksandr
Solzhenitsyn's *One Day in the Life of Ivan Denisovich* and
The Gulag Archipelago (see also Chapter 3).

Ethnic Minorities

Stalin's nationality policy had promoted native cadres and
cultures, but this changed in the late 1920s. Stalin appears to
have perceived that the non-Russians were becoming dangerously self-confident and self-assertive, and he reversed his
policy by the mid-1930s. The Soviet constitution of 1936 in
effect rearranged the political and nationality map. The
boundaries of many autonomous republics and *oblasts* were
fashioned in such a way as to prevent non-Russians from
forming a critical mass – Moscow's fear was that they would
circumvent central authority. For example, Tatars found
themselves in the Tatar (Tatarstan) and Bashkir (Bashkiriya)
autonomous republics, although Tatars and Bashkirs spoke
essentially the same language. Tatars also inhabited the region
south of Bashkiriya and northern Kazakhstan, but this was not
acknowledged, and no autonomous republic was established.
On security grounds, Stalin also deported some entire small
nationality groups, many with their own territorial base, such
as the Chechen and Ingush, from 1944 onwards. Altogether,
more than 50 nationalities, embracing about 3.5 million
people, were deported to various parts of the Soviet Union.
The vast majority of these were removed from European
Russia to Asiatic Russia, as Moscow played off the various
nationalities to its own advantage. This policy was to have
disastrous long-term consequences for Russians, because they
were seen as imperialists bent on Russifying the locals. With
industrial expansion Russians spread throughout the union as

well: by 1991 there were 25 million living outside the Russian republic, including 11 million in Ukraine. President Boris Yeltsin, in apologizing for these deportations, later identified them as a major source of inter-ethnic conflict in Russia in the late twentieth century.

The Second World War and Its Aftermath

During the Second World War Stalin emerged, after an unpromising start, as the most successful of the supreme leaders thrown up by the combatant nations. In August 1939, after first attempting to form an anti-Hitler alliance with the western powers, he concluded a pact with Hitler, which encouraged the German dictator to attack Poland and begin the war. Anxious to strengthen his western frontiers while his new but palpably treacherous German ally was still engaged in the west, Stalin annexed eastern Poland, Estonia, Latvia, Lithuania, and parts of Romania; he also attacked Finland and extorted territorial concessions. In May 1941 Stalin, recognizing the growing danger of German attack on the Soviet Union, appointed himself chairman of the Council of People's Commissars (head of the government); it was his first governmental office since 1923.

Stalin's pre-war defensive measures were exposed as incompetent by the German blitzkrieg that surged deep into Soviet territory after Hitler's unprovoked attack on the Soviet Union of June 22, 1941. Khrushchev later claimed that Stalin was shocked into temporary inactivity by the onslaught, but, if so, he soon rallied and appointed himself supreme commander-in-chief. When the Germans menaced Moscow in the winter of 1941, he remained in the threatened capital, helping to organize a great counter-offensive. The battle of Stalingrad (in the following winter) and the battle of Kursk (in the summer of 1943) were also won by the Soviet Army under Stalin's supreme direction, turning the tide of invasion against the retreating Germans, who capitulated in May 1945. As war leader, Stalin maintained close personal control over the Soviet battle-fronts, military reserves, and war economy. At first over-inclined to intervene with inept telephoned instructions, as did Hitler, the Soviet generalissimo gradually learned to delegate military decisions.

Stalin participated in high-level Allied meetings, including those of the "Big Three" with Winston Churchill and Franklin D. Roosevelt at Tehran (1943) and Yalta (1945). A formidable negotiator, he outwitted these foreign statesmen; his superior skill was acclaimed by Anthony Eden, then British foreign secretary.

On the home front after the war, the primacy of Marxist ideology was harshly reasserted. Stalin's chief ideological hatchet man, Andrey Zhdanov, a secretary of the Central Committee, began a reign of terror in the Soviet artistic and intellectual world; foreign achievements were derided, and the primacy of Russians as inventors and pioneers in practically every field was asserted. The Jewish Anti-Fascist Committee set up during the war was dissolved, and its leader, the actor and theatrical producer Solomon Mikhoels, was murdered by the MGB (Ministry of State Security). "Rootless cosmopolitans" with Jewish names, mostly critics and playwrights, were attacked in a new propaganda drive, and many were arrested. In August 1952 came the secret "Crimean Case", in which leading Yiddish writers and others were executed. In 1951 a purge began in Georgia, directed against the closest followers of Lavrenty Beria, formerly Stalin's Commissar for Internal Affairs and himself responsible for purging many of Stalin's opponents during the Second World War. His followers were jailed in the "Mingrelian Affair", which was still being processed when Stalin died; it seems also to have been linked to the Jewish "plotters". Hopes for domestic relaxation, widely aroused in the Soviet Union during the war, were thus sadly disappointed.

The Cold War and Stalin's Final Years

Following the surrender of Nazi Germany in May 1945 the uneasy wartime alliance between the Allies and the Soviets began to unravel. This developed into the so-called Cold War between the United States and the Soviet Union and their respective allies. The rivalry that developed between the two blocs was waged on political, economic, and propaganda fronts, and had only limited recourse to weapons.

By 1948 the Soviets had installed left-wing governments in the countries of Eastern Europe that had been liberated by the Red Army. The Americans and the British feared the permanent Soviet domination of Eastern Europe, and the threat of Soviet-influenced communist parties coming to power in the democracies of western Europe. The Soviets, on the other hand, were determined to maintain control of Eastern Europe in order to safeguard against any possible renewed threat from Germany, and they were intent on spreading communism worldwide, largely for ideological reasons. The Cold War had solidified by 1947–8, when US aid provided under the Marshall Plan to western Europe had brought those countries under American influence and the Soviets had installed openly communist regimes in Eastern Europe.

In 1948 the defection from the Soviet camp of Yugoslavia under the leadership of Marshal Tito struck a severe blow to world communism as a Stalin-dominated monolith. To prevent other client states from following Tito's example, Stalin instigated local show trials, manipulated like those of the purges of the 1930s in Russia, in which satellite communist leaders confessed to Titoism (the revisionist form of communism practised by Tito); many were executed.

The Cold War reached its peak in 1948–53. In this period the Soviets unsuccessfully blockaded the western-held sectors of West Berlin (1948–9); the United States and its European allies formed the North Atlantic Treaty Organization (NATO), a unified military command to resist the Soviet presence in Europe (1949); the Soviets exploded their first atomic warhead (1949), thus ending the American monopoly on the atomic bomb; the Chinese communists came to power in mainland China (1949); and the Soviet-supported communist government of North Korea invaded US-supported South Korea in 1950, setting off an indecisive Korean War that lasted until 1953. Stalin died in that year, and the burden of continuing the Cold War was a legacy he left to his successors.

Stalin arguably made a greater impact on the lives of more individuals than any other figure in history. While the destruction and misery he unleashed are undeniable, he achieved the industrialization of a country which, when he assumed complete control in 1928, was still notably backward by comparison with the leading industrial nations of the world. By 1937, after less than a decade's rule, he had increased the Soviet Union's total industrial output to the point where it was surpassed only by that of the United States. This, coupled with the Soviet Union's major role in defeating Hitler in the Second World War, helped to establish the USSR as the world's second most powerful industrial and military unit after the United States.

Stalin's particular brilliance was, however, narrowly specialized and confined within the single crucial area of creative political manipulation, where he remains unsurpassed. He was the first to recognize the potential of bureaucratic power. By interlinking various levels of authority – the Communist Party, ministries, legislative bodies, trade unions, political police, and armed forces, among others – he was able to weld together a power base that gave him a quarter of a century's virtually unchallenged rule.

3

POST-STALIN RUSSIA TO THE FALL OF COMMUNISM, 1953–91

The Khrushchev Era, 1953–64

The power struggle for leadership that followed Joseph Stalin's death in 1953 was won by Nikita Khrushchev. His landmark decisions in foreign policy and domestic programmes markedly changed the direction of the Soviet Union, bringing detente with the West and a relaxation of rigid controls within the country.

NIKITA KHRUSHCHEV (1894–1971)

Soviet leader

The son of a miner, Khrushchev joined the Communist Party in 1918. In 1934 he was elected to its Central Committee, and in 1935 he became first secretary of the Moscow party organization. He participated in Joseph Stalin's purges of party leaders. In 1938 he became head of the Ukrainian party and in 1939 was made a member of the Politburo. After Stalin's death in 1953, he emerged from a bitter power struggle as the party's first secretary, and Nikolay Bulganin became premier.

In 1955, on his first trip outside the Soviet Union, Khrushchev showed his flexibility and the brash, extraverted style of diplomacy that would become his trademark. At the 20th Party Congress in 1956, he delivered a secret speech denouncing Stalin for his "intolerance, his brutality, his abuse of power". Thousands of political prisoners were released. Poland and Hungary used de-Stalinization to reform their regimes: Khrushchev allowed the Poles relative freedom, but he crushed the Hungarian Revolution by force (1956) when Imre Nagy attempted to withdraw from the Warsaw Pact.

Opposition within the party crystallized in 1957, but Khrushchev secured the dismissal of his enemies and in 1958 assumed the premiership himself. Asserting a doctrine of peaceful coexistence with capitalist nations, he toured the United States in 1959, but a planned Paris summit with President Eisenhower in 1960 was cancelled after the U-2 Affair, when the Soviet Union shot down a US reconnaissance plane. In 1962 Khrushchev attempted to place Soviet missiles in Cuba; in the ensuing Cuban missile crisis he retreated. Ideological differences and the signing of the Nuclear Test-Ban Treaty (1963) led to a split with the Chinese. Agricultural failures that necessitated importation of wheat from the West, the China quarrel, and his often arbitrary administrative methods led to his forced retirement in 1964.

Khrushchev, who rose under Stalin as an agricultural specialist, was a Russian who had grown up in Ukraine. During his reign Ukrainians prospered in Moscow. He took it for granted that Russians had a natural right to instruct less fortunate nationals. This was especially evident in the non-Slavic republics of the USSR and in eastern and south-eastern Europe. His nationality policies reversed the repressive policies of Stalin. He grasped the nettle of the deported nationalities and rehabilitated almost all of them; the accusations of disloyalty made against them by Stalin were declared to be false. This allowed many nationalities to return to their homelands within Russia, the Volga Germans being a notable exception. (Their lands had been occupied by Russians who, fearing competition from the Germans, opposed their return.) The Crimean Tatars were similarly not allowed to return to their home territory. Their situation was complicated by the fact that Russians and Ukrainians had replaced them in the Crimea, and in 1954 Khrushchev made Ukraine a present of the Crimea. Khrushchev abided by the nationality theory that suggested that all Soviet national groups would come closer together and eventually coalesce; the Russians, of course, would be the dominant group. The theory was profoundly wrong. There was in fact a flowering of national cultures during Khrushchev's administration, as well as an expansion of technical and cultural elites.

Khrushchev sought to promote himself through his agricultural policy. As head of the party Secretariat (which ran the day-to-day affairs of the party machine) after Stalin's death, he could use that vehicle to promote his campaigns. *Pravda* ("Truth"), the party newspaper, served as his mouthpiece. His main opponent in the quest for power, Georgy M. Malenkov, was skilled in administration and headed the government. *Izvestiya*

("News"), the government's newspaper, was Malenkov's main media outlet. Khrushchev's agricultural policy involved a bold plan to rapidly expand the sown area of grain. He chose to implement this policy on virgin land in the North Caucasus and west Siberia, lying in both Russia and northern Kazakhstan. The Kazakh party leaders were not enamoured of the idea, since they did not want more Russians in their republic. The Kazakh leadership was therefore dismissed, and the new first secretary was a Malenkov appointee; he was soon replaced by Leonid Brezhnev, a Khrushchev protégé who eventually replaced Khrushchev as the Soviet leader. Thousands of young communists descended on Kazakhstan to grow crops where none had been grown before.

Khrushchev's so-called "secret speech" about the excesses of Stalin's one-man rule, attacking the late Soviet ruler's "intolerance, his brutality, his abuse of power", at the 20th Party Congress in 1956 had far-reaching effects on both foreign and domestic policies. Through its denunciation of Stalin, it substantially destroyed the infallibility of the party. The congress also formulated ideological reformations, which softened the party's hardline foreign policy. De-Stalinization had unexpected consequences, especially in 1956 in eastern and south-eastern Europe, where unrest became widespread. The Hungarian uprising in that year was brutally suppressed, with Yury V. Andropov, Moscow's chief representative in Budapest, revealing considerable talent for double-dealing. (He had given a promise of safe conduct to Imre Nagy, the Hungarian leader, but permitted, or arranged for, Nagy's arrest.) The events in Hungary and elsewhere stoked up anti-Russian fires.

Khrushchev invested heavily in and set great store by rocketry, and successes in space exploration under his regime brought Russia great acclaim. On August 26, 1957, the USSR had startled the world by announcing the successful firing of its first intercontinental ballistic missile. On October 4 of the same year, the first space satellite, Sputnik 1, was launched, followed on November 3 by Sputnik 2, with the dog Laika on board. So great was Khrushchev's faith in rocketry that he began to regard ground forces as less important and even to cut the size of the military. He also tried to translate the USSR's advances in rocketry into tangible diplomatic success, threatening the West with Soviet missiles if it dared to think of attacking. The strategy misfired, however: the result was to stimulate even greater western defence spending and thereby involve the Soviet Union in an expensive arms race that it could not win.

Before the escalation of the arms race, Khrushchev's rule witnessed another crucial development in the Cold War. While from 1953 to 1957 tensions relaxed somewhat, the stand-off remained. It became increasingly apparent that the United States and the Soviet Union were avoiding direct military confrontation in Europe, engaging in actual combat operations only to keep allies from defecting to the other side or to overthrow them after they had done so. This rationale can be seen in the Soviet Union sending troops to preserve communist rule in East Germany (1953) and Hungary (1956); for its part, the United States helped overthrow a left-wing government in Guatemala (1954). In 1955 a unified military organization among the Soviet-bloc countries, the Warsaw Pact, was formed, and West Germany was admitted into the six-year-old NATO that same year. East–West relations deteriorated in 1958–62, particularly during the civil war in the Congo in the early 1960s and over the building of the Berlin Wall in 1961.

In October 1962 the development of intercontinental ballistic missiles by both the United States and the Soviet Union brought the two superpowers to the brink of nuclear war. When the Soviets began secretly installing missiles in Cuba that could be used to launch nuclear attacks on US cities, the US Navy blockaded Cuba; the Soviet ground commanders were then given the authority to launch a missile attack, without approval from Moscow, if they perceived that an American invasion was under way. Eventually Khrushchev backed off, and an agreement was reached to withdraw the missiles. The Chinese severely criticized Khrushchev for giving in to the United States and capitalism, and relations between China and the USSR, already uneasy, became worse as a result.

In the following year the two superpowers signed the Nuclear Test-Ban Treaty, which banned above-ground nuclear weapons testing. But the crisis also hardened the Soviets' determination never again to be humiliated by their military inferiority, and they began a build-up of both conventional and strategic forces that the United States was forced to match for the next 25 years.

While Khrushchev had failures and triumphs in foreign policy, he was often viewed in the West as eccentric and blunt, traits that sometimes negated his own diplomacy. On one occasion he appeared at the United Nations and emphasized a point in his speech by banging a shoe on his desk. Such conduct tended to reinforce certain western prejudices about oafish, peasant behaviour by Soviet leaders, and harmed the Russian image abroad. Khrushchev's forthright remarks occasionally caused massive unrest in the world. He told the United States, "We will bury you," and boasted that his rockets could hit a fly over the United States, statements that added to the alarm of Americans, who subsequently increased their defence budget.

As the Soviet defence burden increased, living standards in Russia improved only slowly. Here Khrushchev was often his own worst enemy. He launched many industrial and agricultural initiatives, but the net result was an overall decline of growth rates. US specialists calculated that between 1961 and 1965 the annual increase of gross national product (GNP) in the USSR slowed to 5 per cent, industrial output to 6.6 per cent, and agricultural growth to 2.8 per cent. Since the population growth was about 1.4 per cent annually, this meant that there was no tangible improvement in the diet available. Khrushchev correctly perceived that the party apparatus was a major barrier to economic progress. In an effort to revitalize the apparatus he split it into separate industrial and agricultural branches in November 1962, but discovered that industrial and local political networks had developed, which made it very difficult for the central authority to impose its will. This reform made Khrushchev deeply unpopular and accelerated his departure from high office, while economic problems continued to plague the union.

Khrushchev was a patriot who had a sincere desire to improve the lot of all Soviet citizens. Under his leadership there was a cultural thaw, and Russian writers who had been suppressed began to publish again. Western ideas about democracy began to penetrate universities and academies. These were to leave their mark on a whole generation of Russians, most notably Mikhail Gorbachev, who was to become the last leader of the Soviet Union. Khrushchev had effectively led the Soviet Union away from the harsh Stalin period. Under his rule Russia continued to dominate the union, but there was considerably more concern for minorities.

The Brezhnev Era, 1964–82

After Khrushchev came the triumvirate of Leonid I. Brezhnev, Aleksey N. Kosygin, and N. V. Podgorny. The first was the party leader, the second headed the government, and the third became chairman of the Presidium of the Supreme Soviet, a ceremonial position. By the late 1960s Brezhnev was clearly the dominant leader. His strengths were in manipulating party and government cadres, but he was weak on policy ideas. He ensured that there was an unprecedented stability of cadres within the Communist Party and the bureaucracy, thereby creating conditions for the rampant spread of corruption in the Soviet political and administrative structures. Under Brezhnev, Russia dominated the union as never before, and the republic accounted for about three-fourths of the Soviet GNP. In the mid-1970s the USSR reached its apogee: it acquired nuclear parity with the United States and was recognized as a world superpower. Detente flourished in the 1970s but was disrupted by the Soviet invasion of Afghanistan in December 1979.

The economy, at first in the hands of Kosygin, needed attention. He found that the central direction of the economy became more and more difficult to achieve. There were many reforms, but all to no avail. The economy had become very complex, but there was no mechanism, in the absence of the market, to coordinate economic activity in the interests of society. A bureaucratic market took over. Bureaucrats and enterprises negotiated the acquisition of inputs and agreed where the final product should go. The goal of every enterprise was to become a monopoly producer. The core of this system was the military-industrial complex, which accounted for the top quarter of output and had first call on resource allocation.

LEONID BREZHNEV (1906–82)

Soviet leader

Brezhnev worked as an engineer and director of a technical school in Ukraine and held local posts in the Communist Party; he became regional party secretary in 1939. In the Second World War he was a political commissar in the Red Army and rose to major general (1943). In the 1950s he supported Nikita Khrushchev and became a member of the Politburo, though in 1964 he was the leader of a coalition that ousted Khrushchev, and soon he emerged as general secretary of the party (1966–82). He developed the Brezhnev Doctrine, which asserted the right of Soviet intervention in such Warsaw Pact countries as Czechoslovakia (1968).

In the 1970s Brezhnev attempted to normalize relations with the West and to promote detente with the United States. He was made marshal of the Soviet Union in 1976 and chairman of the Presidium of the Supreme Soviet in 1977, becoming the first to hold the leadership of both the party and the state. He greatly expanded the Soviet Union's military-industrial complex, but in so doing he deprived the rest of the Soviet economy. Despite frail health, he retained his hold on power to the end.

On the positive side, the rapid expansion of the chemical, oil, and gas industries boosted exports so that Russia earned most of the union's hard-currency income. The middle class grew in size, as did its average salary, which more than doubled in two decades. Ownership of consumer goods, such as refrigerators and cars, became a realistic expectation for a growing part of the population. Until the early 1970s the availability of medical care, higher education, and improved accommodation reached levels unprecedented in the Soviet context.

These successes and a few others – some defence sectors and the space industry, and the sale of Russia's natural resources – allowed the Soviet regime to evade undertaking necessary but potentially politically dangerous structural economic reforms. According to US estimates for the years 1966–70 and 1976–80, the Soviet economy went into sharp decline in terms of industrial growth, agricultural output, and investment. Agricultural performance was even worse than the figures implied: over the years 1971–5 there was negative growth annually of 0.6 per cent, despite huge investments in agriculture, with one ruble in three going into agriculture and agriculture-related industry. The result was large annual imports of grain, paid for in US dollars. This was made possible by the explosion of oil prices in the 1970s, which saw the terms of trade turn in favour of the Soviet Union. Unfortunately the oil bonanza was wasted, and little use was made of foreign technology. After the initial improvement in living standards came stagnation or decline. The black market grew to plug the holes of the planned economy. Along with this went corruption, which had filtered down from the political elites; it eventually became pervasive. Increasing defence expenditure at a time of slowing economic growth led to cuts in investment. Education and medical and social services suffered most. At the end of the Brezhnev era the medical care of the population was a disgrace. In sum, by the early 1980s, continued economic stagnation posed a serious threat to the world standing of the USSR and to the regime's legitimacy at home.

ANDREY SAKHAROV (1921–89)

Russian nuclear physicist and human rights advocate
Sakharov worked with I. Y. Tamm (1895–1971) to develop the Soviet Union's first hydrogen bomb, but in 1961 he opposed Nikita Khrushchev's plan to test a 100-megaton hydrogen bomb in the atmosphere. In 1968 he published in the West "Progress, Coexistence, and Intellectual Freedom", which called for nuclear arms reduction and criticized Soviet repression of dissidents. He and his wife, Yelena G. Bonner, continued to advocate civil liberties and reform in the Soviet Union.

In 1975 Sakharov received the Nobel Prize for Peace but was forbidden to travel to Oslo to receive it. In 1980 he was exiled to the closed city Gorky (now Nizhny Novgorod); his wife was exiled there in 1984. They were released in 1986 and returned to Moscow. Elected to the Congress of People's Deputies in April 1989, Sakharov had his honours restored and saw many of the causes for which he had fought and suffered become official policy under Mikhail Gorbachev.

It was in the Brezhnev era, thanks largely to the publication in 1973 of *The Gulag Archipelago, 1918–1956* by the dissenting novelist Aleksandr Solzhenitsyn, that the extent and horror of the *Gulag* system of labour camps was fully revealed. Reaction to this work, whose title likens the camps scattered through the Soviet Union to an island chain, was immediate, and provoked outrage and public criticism of Russia's policies.

Also during the 1970s the state gradually lost its monopoly on information control. A counterculture influenced by western pop music, especially rock, spread rapidly. Russian youth had become enamoured of western pop stars, and the advent of the audiocassette made it easier to experience their music. The widespread teaching of foreign languages further facilitated access to outside ideas. By the end of the Brezhnev era, the Russian intelligentsia had rejected Communist Party values. The party's way of dealing with uncomfortable critics – such as Solzhenitsyn – was to deport them. These exiles then became the voice of Russian culture abroad. The academician Andrey Sakharov could not be imprisoned, for fear of western scientists cutting off contact with the Soviet Union, but he was exiled until 1986 to the closed city of Gorky (now Nizhny Novgorod).

The 1960s and 1970s were also a period when the Cold War bipolar struggle between the Soviet and American blocs gave way to a more complicated pattern of international relationships in which the world was no longer split into two clearly opposed spheres of influence. A major split had occurred between the Soviet Union and China in 1960 and this widened over the years, shattering the unity of the communist bloc. In the meantime, western Europe and Japan achieved dynamic economic growth in the 1950s and 1960s, reducing their relative inferiority to the United States. Less powerful countries had more room to assert their independence, and often showed themselves resistant to superpower coercion or cajoling.

The 1970s saw an easing of Cold War tensions as evinced in the SALT (Strategic Arms Limitation Talks) I and II agreements of 1972 and 1979 respectively, in which the USA and USSR set limits on their antiballistic missiles and on their strategic missiles capable of carrying nuclear weapons. This was followed by a period of renewed Cold War tensions in the early 1980s as the two superpowers continued their massive arms build-up and competed for influence in the Third World. But the Cold War began to break down in the late 1980s during the administration of Soviet leader Mikhail S. Gorbachev (see below and Chapter 4).

The Gorbachev Era, 1985–91

When Brezhnev died in 1982, most elite groups understood that the Soviet economy was in trouble. Owing to senility, Brezhnev had not been in effective control of the country during his last few years, and Kosygin had died in 1980. The Politburo was dominated by old men, and they were overwhelmingly Russian. Non-Russian representation at the top of the party and the government had declined over time. Yury V. Andropov and then Konstantin Chernenko led the country from 1982 until 1985, but their administrations failed to address critical problems. Andropov believed that the economic stagnation could be remedied by greater worker discipline and by cracking down on corruption. He did not consider the structure of the Soviet economic system itself to be a cause of the country's growing economic problems.

When Gorbachev became head of the Communist Party in March 1985 he was clear about his policy preferences. In a speech on December 10, 1984, he spoke of the need to effect "deep transformations in the economy and the whole system of social relations", to carry through the policies of *perestroika* ("restructuring" of economic management), the "democratization of social and economic life", and *glasnost* ("openness"). His goal was to set in motion a revolution controlled from above. He did not wish to undermine the Soviet system, only to make it more efficient. The leading role of the party and the

MIKHAIL GORBACHEV (b. 1931)

Soviet official, general secretary of the Communist Party of the Soviet Union (1985–91), and president of the Soviet Union (1990–1)

After earning a law degree from Moscow State University (1955), Gorbachev rose through the ranks to become a full Politburo member (1980) and general secretary of the Communist Party of the Soviet Union (1985–91). His extraordinary reform policies of *glasnost* and *perestroika* were resisted by party bureaucrats; to reduce their power, Gorbachev changed the Soviet constitution in 1988 to allow multi-candidate elections, and removed the monopoly power of the party in 1990. He cultivated warmer relations with the United States, and in 1989–90 he supported the democratically elected governments that replaced the communist regimes of eastern Europe. In 1990 he was awarded the Nobel Prize for Peace.

Russia's economic and political problems led to a 1991 coup attempt by hardliners. In alliance with Boris Yeltsin, president of the Russian republic, Gorbachev quit the Communist Party, disbanded its Central Committee, and shifted political powers to the Soviet Union's constituent republics. Events outpaced him, and the various republics formed the Commonwealth of Independent States under Yeltsin's leadership. On December 25, 1991, Gorbachev resigned the presidency of the Soviet Union, which ceased to exist that same day.

PERESTROIKA ("RESTRUCTURING")

Programme instituted in the Soviet Union by Mikhail Gorbachev in the mid-1980s to restructure Soviet political and economic policy

Gorbachev proposed reducing the direct involvement of the Communist Party leadership in the country's governance and increasing the local governments' authority. Seeking to bring the Soviet Union up to economic par with capitalist countries such as Germany, Japan, and the United States, he decentralized economic controls and encouraged enterprises to become self-financing. The economic bureaucracy, fearing loss of its power and privileges, obstructed much of his programme.

central direction of the economy were to stay. He thus pursued an economic policy that aimed to increase economic growth while increasing capital investment, which was to improve the technological basis of the Soviet economy as well as promote certain structural economic changes. His goal was simple: to bring the Soviet Union up to par economically with the West. This had been the aim of Russian leaders since the first great wave of modernization and westernization was unleashed in the early eighteenth century.

Thus *perestroika* concentrated initially on economic reform. Enterprises were encouraged to become self-financing, cooperatives were set up by groups of people as businesses, and land could be leased to allow family farming. Machine building was given preference as light and consumer goods took second place. There was to be more technical innovation and worker discipline. Yet all this produced few positive results,

GLASNOST ("OPENNESS")

Soviet policy of open discussion of political and social issues

Glasnost was instituted by Mikhail Gorbachev in the late 1980s and began the democratization of the Soviet Union. *Glasnost* also permitted criticism of government officials and allowed the media freer dissemination of news and information.

and in fact led to a fall in the consumer goods available, and agriculture did not blossom. Not only was the public hostile to Gorbachev's policies, but the cooperatives resented the heavy taxation and, perhaps most significant, the bureaucrats who ran the economy feared that these new activities would undermine their privileges and power.

Faced with a worsening economic situation, Gorbachev now concluded that deeper structural changes were necessary. He admitted that his first two years of reform had been wasted since he had been unaware of the depth of the crisis when he took over. He now received much advice on how to solve the Soviet Union's economic crisis. There were two basic solutions: the socialist solution and the market solution. Supporters of Nikolay Ryzhkov, Chairman of the Council of Ministers, favoured central planning, more efficient administration, and greater decision-making powers for enterprises and farms. State ownership of the means of production would continue. They called it a "regulated market economy". The radicals advocated a move toward a free-market economy. This involved private ownership of enterprises, land, services, and so on. It also meant the freeing of prices. Gorbachev could not make up his mind and always tried to persuade the two groups to pool their resources and arrive at a compromise. The radicals thought they had convinced Gorbachev in the autumn of 1990 to introduce a 500-day programme that would have implemented a market economy, but he changed his mind and sided with the conservatives. This was a fatal mistake. It left him without a viable economic policy, and the right felt that if they applied enough pressure he would always abandon radical solutions.

One of the reasons Gorbachev shied away from the market was price liberalization. He would not risk sharp price rises because of the fear of social unrest. Despite the abundant evidence of the seriousness of the situation in 1988, the critical year, Gorbachev and other leading communists refused to draw the necessary lessons or to adopt austerity measures. The popular mood was one of spend, spend, spend, and Gorbachev paid only cursory attention to the economy until late 1989. He was never able to construct a viable economic policy or to put in place a mechanism for the implementation of economic policy.

As the second vital plank of his reform efforts Gorbachev launched *glasnost*. He believed that the opening up of the political system – essentially, democratizing it – was the only way to overcome inertia in the political and bureaucratic apparatus, which had a big interest in maintaining the status quo. In addition, he believed that the path to economic and social recovery required the inclusion of people in the political process. *Glasnost* also allowed the media more freedom of expression, and editorials complaining of depressed conditions and of the government's inability to correct them began to appear.

As the economic and political situation began to deteriorate, Gorbachev concentrated his energies on increasing his authority (that is to say, his ability to make decisions). He did not, however, develop the power to implement these decisions. He became a constitutional dictator – but only on paper. His policies were simply not put into practice. When he took office, Yegor Ligachev was made head of the party's Central Committee Secretariat, one of the two main centres of power (with the Politburo) in the Soviet Union. Ligachev subsequently became one of Gorbachev's opponents, making it difficult for Gorbachev to use the party apparatus to implement his views on *perestroika*.

By the summer of 1988, however, Gorbachev had become strong enough to emasculate the Central Committee Secretariat and take the party out of the day-to-day running of the economy. This responsibility was to pass to the local soviets. A new parliament, the Congress of People's Deputies, was convened in the spring of 1989, with Gorbachev presiding. The new body superseded the Supreme Soviet as the highest organ of state power. The Congress elected a new Supreme Soviet, and Gorbachev, who had opted for an executive presidency modelled on the US and French systems, became the Soviet president, with broad powers. This meant that all the republics, including first and foremost Russia, could have a similar type of presidency. Moreover, Gorbachev radically changed Soviet political life when he removed the constitutional article according to which the only legal political organization was the Communist Party of the Soviet Union.

Gorbachev understood that the defence burden, equivalent to perhaps 25 per cent of GNP, was crippling the country. This had led to cuts in expenditure in education, social services, and medical care, which hurt the regime's domestic legitimacy. Moreover, the huge defence expenditure that characterized the Cold War years was one of the causes of Soviet economic decline. Gorbachev therefore transformed Soviet foreign policy. He travelled abroad extensively and was brilliantly successful in convincing foreigners that the USSR was no longer an international threat. His changes in foreign policy led to the democratization of Eastern Europe. With the collapse of communist regimes in the Soviet-bloc countries of Eastern Europe in 1989–90 – and the subsequent rise to power of democratic governments in East Germany, Poland, Hungary, and Czechoslovakia, quickly followed by the unification of West and East Germany under NATO auspices – the Cold War came to a definitive end. On the other hand, Gorbachev's policies deprived the Soviet Union of ideological enemies, which in turn weakened the hold of Soviet ideology over the people.

By 1991 the Russian economy was facing total collapse. The government found it increasingly difficult to intervene decisively. The Law on State Enterprises reduced the power of the ministries, and simultaneously the number of officials was cut back sharply. Those who remained were overwhelmed by the workload. Since there was no effective control from Moscow, rising nationalism, ethnic strife, and regionalism fragmented the economy into dozens of mini-economies. Many republics sought independence, others sovereignty, and they all pursued policies of economic autarchy. Barter was widespread. Ukraine introduced coupons, and Moscow issued ration cards. As calls for faster political reforms and decentralization began to increase, the nationality problem became acute for Gorbachev. Limited force was used in Georgia, Azerbaijan, and the Baltic states to quell nationality problems, though Gorbachev was never prepared to use systematic force in order to re-establish the centre's control. The re-emergence of Russian nationalism seriously weakened Gorbachev as the leader of the Soviet empire.

In 1985 Gorbachev had brought Boris Yeltsin to Moscow to run the city's party machine. Yeltsin came into conflict with the more conservative members of the Politburo and was eventually removed from the Moscow post in late 1987. He returned to public life as an elected deputy from Moscow to the Congress of People's Deputies in 1989. When the Congress elected the Supreme Soviet as a standing parliament, Yeltsin was not chosen, since the Congress had an overwhelmingly communist majority. However, a Siberian deputy stepped down in his favour. Yeltsin for the first time had a national platform. In parliament he pilloried Gorbachev, the Communist Party, corruption, and the slow pace of economic reform. Yeltsin was elected president of the Russian parliament despite the bitter opposition of Gorbachev.

In March 1991, when Gorbachev launched an all-union referendum about the future Soviet federation, Russia and several other republics added some supplementary questions. One of the Russian questions was whether the voters were in favour of a directly elected president. They were, and they chose Yeltsin. He used his new-found legitimacy to promote Russian sovereignty, to advocate and adopt radical economic reform, to demand Gorbachev's resignation, and to negotiate treaties with the Baltic republics, in which he acknowledged their right to independence. Soviet attempts to discourage Baltic independence had led to a bloody confrontation in Vilnius in January 1991, after which Yeltsin called upon Russian troops to disobey orders that would have had them shoot unarmed civilians.

Yeltsin's politics reflected the rise of Russian nationalism. In the later Gorbachev years, the opinion that the 1917 Bolshevik Revolution and establishment of the USSR were mistakes that had prevented Russia from continuing along the historical path travelled by the countries of western Europe, and had made Russia more economically backward vis-à-vis the West, had gained greater acceptance. Russians began to view the Soviet system as one that worked for its own political and economic interests at Russia's expense. There were increasing complaints that the "Soviets" had destroyed the Russian environment and had impoverished Russia in order to maintain their empire and subsidize the poorer republics. Consequently, Yeltsin and his supporters demanded Russian control over Russia and its resources. In June 1990 the Russian republic had declared sovereignty, establishing the primacy of Russian law within the republic. This effectively undermined all attempts by Gorbachev to establish a Union of Sovereign Socialist Republics. Yeltsin appeared to be willing to go along with this vision but, in reality, wanted Russia to dominate the new union and replace the formal leading role of the Soviet Union. The Russian parliament passed radical reforms that would introduce a market economy, and Yeltsin also cut funding to a large number of Soviet agencies based on Russian soil. Clearly, Yeltsin wished to rid Russia of the encumbrance of the Soviet Union and to seek the disbandment of that body.

Collapse of the Soviet Union

An ill-conceived, ill-planned, and poorly executed coup attempt occurred on August 19–21, 1991. Its failure brought an end to the Communist Party and accelerated the movement to disband the Soviet Union. The coup was carried out by hard-line Communist Party, KGB, and military officials attempting to avert a new liberalized union treaty and return to the old-line party values. The most significant anti-coup role was played by Yeltsin, who brilliantly grasped the opportunity to promote himself and Russia. He demanded the reinstatement of Gorbachev as USSR president, but, when Gorbachev returned from house arrest in the Crimea, Yeltsin set out to demonstrate that he was the stronger leader. In a decisive move, Yeltsin banned the Communist Party in Russia and seized all its property. From a strictly legal point of view, this should have been done by court order, not by presidential decree, but the result was that at a stroke Russia systematically laid claim to most Soviet property on its territory.

4

POST-SOVIET RUSSIA

The Yeltsin Presidency, 1991–9

The Union of Soviet Socialist Republics (USSR) legally ceased to exist on December 31, 1991. The Russian republic, renamed the Russian Federation, embarked on the road to democracy and a market economy with no clear conception of how such a transformation would be completed.

Political and Social Changes

Yeltsin's popularity had surged after the key role he played in defeating the attempted coup against Gorbachev in 1991, when the world saw him on television in an unforgettable image, standing atop a tank and calling on the people to defy the plotters. A skilful politician, he was first elected president of the Russian republic in 1991, soon before the formal end of the USSR, and he was re-elected in 1996. Yet his first priority was to preserve his own power and authority. He managed

BORIS YELTSIN (1931–2007)

Russian politician and president of Russia (1990–9)
After attending the Urals Polytechnic Institute, Yeltsin worked at construction projects in western Russia (1955–68). He became Communist Party leader in Sverdlovsk in 1976, and he was an ally of Mikhail Gorbachev. Gorbachev later charged Yeltsin with eliminating corruption in the Moscow party organization, and as first secretary (mayor) of Moscow (1985–7) he proved a determined reformer. His criticism of the slow pace of reform led to a break with Gorbachev, and Yeltsin lost his position. In 1989 he was elected to the new Soviet parliament by a landslide, then became president of the Russian Republic (1990) and resigned from the Communist Party. In 1991 he won the presidency again in the first popular election in Russian history.

When communist hardliners staged a coup against Gorbachev, Yeltsin successfully opposed it, facing down its leaders with a dramatic outdoor speech in Moscow. He led the establishment of the Commonwealth of Independent States (1991) and began to transform Russia's economy into one based on free markets and private enterprise. Hardliners staged an unsuccessful coup against Yeltsin in 1993. When Chechnya unilaterally declared independence, Yeltsin sent troops to fight the rebels (1994). The Chechnya situation and Russia's deepening economic distress lessened his popularity, but he won re-election over a Communist Party challenger in 1996. After suffering a heart attack, he spent several months recovering. Continuing poor health led to his resignation on December 31, 1999. He was succeeded by Vladimir Putin.

both the government and the bureaucracy with a divide-and-rule strategy that encouraged the various factions to compete for influence. Yeltsin also frequently changed his ministers and prime ministers, leading to abrupt changes in policy. Professing to believe that the president should remain above party politics, he declined to establish his own political party or to align himself openly with any party or coalition. But he remained at the heart of the political process, enjoying his favourite role of power broker until his resignation in 1999.

In the immediate aftermath of the collapse of the Soviet Union, the Russian Federation continued to be governed under its Soviet-era constitution. The office of president had been added to the constitution of the Russian Soviet republic in 1991. However, the constitution did not clearly give supreme power to either the legislative or the executive branch, leading to constitutional conflicts between the two. The breach was exacerbated by personality clashes between Yeltsin and the parliamentary leadership, and by the government's preoccupation with financial stabilization and economic reform, apparently heedless of the social needs of the public. Complicating Yeltsin's difficulties was the fact that many members of the Congress of People's Deputies had vested interests in the economic and political structure of the communist era. The leader of the parliament, Ruslan Khasbulatov, and Yeltsin both sought support from regional elites by promising subsidies and greater local control. Their struggle reached a climax in March 1993, when Yeltsin was stripped of the decree-making powers that he had been granted after the attempted coup of August 1991.

Yeltsin was not prepared to accept total defeat. He announced that a referendum would be held on April 25, 1993, over who "really ruled" Russia. He also ruled that any acts passed by parliament that contradicted presidential decrees would be null and void. But Yeltsin's ministers, including Prime Minister Viktor Chernomyrdin, only half-heartedly supported this move, and Yeltsin eventually had to back down. Nonetheless, it was agreed that a referendum would be held. Four questions, drafted by the Congress to maximize Yeltsin's embarrassment, were put to the Russian people: (1) Do you trust the President of the Russian Federation, Boris Nikolayevich Yeltsin? (2) Do you approve of the socio-economic policies implemented by the President of the Russian Federation and the government of the Russian Federation since 1992? (3) Do you consider it essential to hold pre-term elections for the presidency of the Russian Federation? and (4) Do you consider it essential to hold pre-term elections for the People's Deputies of the Russian Federation? The Constitutional Court ruled that the first two questions were non-binding and that the latter two needed the backing of at least half of all eligible voters (and not just half of the actual ballots cast). With Yeltsin's camp using the slogan "Da, da, nyet, da" ("Yes, yes, no, yes"), the result was a victory for Yeltsin. However, as only 43 per cent of eligible voters backed early parliamentary elections, Yeltsin was forced to continue his uneasy relationship with the Congress.

In the summer of 1993 both Yeltsin and the parliament drafted versions of a new post-Soviet constitution. Inevitably, the drafts were incompatible, but an increasing number of regional leaders supported the Congress's version. In September 1993 Yeltsin issued a series of presidential decrees that dissolved the parliament and imposed presidential rule until after elections to a new parliament and a referendum on a new draft constitution were held in December. The parliament declared Yeltsin's decree illegal, impeached him, and swore

VIKTOR CHERNOMYRDIN (b. 1938)

Prime minister of Russia (1992–8)

Born in Cherny-Otrog in 1938, Viktor Chernomyrdin, who joined the Communist Party of the Soviet Union in 1961, acquired extensive experience as an industrial administrator, having served as deputy chief engineer and director of a natural gas plant in Orenburg in the 1970s. He went to Moscow in 1978 to work for the Central Committee of the CPSU, and in 1982 he was appointed deputy minister of the Soviet natural-gas industry. In 1985 Mikhail Gorbachev promoted him to serve as minister of the gas industry. In this post in 1989 Chernomyrdin converted the Ministry of Gas into a state-owned corporate complex called Gazprom, which was one of the few profitable large-scale enterprises in the declining Soviet economy. He remained chairman of the board of Gazprom during the dissolution of the Soviet Union and the creation of the Russian Federation in 1991. In June 1992 he became a deputy prime minister and minister of fuel and energy in the reformist government of the Russian acting prime minister, Yegor Gaidar. When Russia's Congress of People's Deputies refused to confirm the liberal Gaidar as prime minister, Yeltsin replaced him with Chernomyrdin on December 14, 1992. As a long-time Soviet administrator, Chernomyrdin was more acceptable to the Congress, which confirmed his nomination.

in his vice-president, Aleksandr Rutskoy, as president. Weapons were then handed out to civilians to defend the parliament building, known as the "Russian White House". On September 25, troops and militia loyal to Yeltsin surrounded the building. On October 2 there were armed clashes between troops and supporters of the parliament, who had begun to fill the streets of Moscow. On October 4, Yeltsin declared a state of emergency in Moscow. Shortly thereafter, tanks began firing on the parliamentary building, leading to the surrender and arrest of everyone inside, including Rutskoy. The way was now clear for elections to a new parliament and a referendum on a new constitution in December 1993, which was duly carried.

Yeltsin's new constitution gave the president vast powers. The president appointed the prime minister, who had to be approved by the Duma, the lower house of the new Federal Assembly, and the president could issue decrees that had the force of law as long as they did not contradict federal or constitutional law. The president was also given the power to dismiss the Duma and call for new elections. The prime minister was the vital link connecting the president with the Federal Assembly. Although the prime minister was accountable to the Federal Assembly, in practice he could not remain in office without the confidence of the president – as became clear under the premiership of Chernomyrdin.

In trying to implement Yeltsin's economic policies, Chernomyrdin had steered a middle course between those favouring privatization and other free-market reforms and those advocating the continued support of inefficient Soviet-era state enterprises. He cultivated improved relations with the fractious Congress and brought inflation under control, while Anatoly Chubais and other reformers in the Cabinet oversaw the privatization of the industrial and commercial sectors of the economy. When Yeltsin won re-election to the presidency in 1996, he retained Chernomyrdin as prime minister. In March 1998, however, Chernomyrdin lost his post when

Yeltsin dismissed the entire cabinet, ostensibly for failing to implement reforms energetically enough, and installed a new leadership team to carry out ongoing economic reforms. Chernomyrdin himself had probably also offended Yeltsin by acting too independently and appearing to groom himself to succeed Yeltsin as president.

In the first two Dumas (elected in 1993 and 1995), the Communist Party of the Russian Federation was the single largest party, though it was never close to enjoying a majority. As it had inherited the infrastructure of the dissolved CPSU, it had the most effective nationwide organization. Other parties found it difficult to operate outside the major urban areas. Party loyalties were weak, and deputies jumped from one party to another in the hope of improving their electoral chances. Worrying to many was the success of the ultra-nationalist Vladimir Zhirinovsky's Liberal Democratic Party of Russia, which captured nearly a quarter of the vote in 1993 (though its share of the vote declined thereafter). Nevertheless, despite hostile and even inflammatory rhetoric directed towards Yeltsin and his foreign policy, Zhirinovsky's party generally backed the executive branch. Throughout the 1990s hundreds of parties were founded, but most were short-lived, as their appeal was based solely on the personalities of their founders. The liberal party of acting prime minister Yegor Gaidar, Russia's Choice, floundered once Gaidar was forced out of government at the end of 1992. Chernomyrdin's party, Our Home Is Russia, suffered a similar fate soon after Yeltsin dismissed Chernomyrdin as prime minister.

Despite the public hostility between the Duma and President Yeltsin, compromises were usually hammered out behind the scenes. Yeltsin used the threat of dissolution to secure the

Duma's support for his presidential bills, and deputies could never be confident of re-election in view of the voters' disgust with politicians. During Yeltsin's second term, some deputies tried to initiate impeachment proceedings against him, but they were defeated by the many legal obstacles to such a move.

Throughout the political turmoil of the 1990s, the weakened Russian state failed to fulfil its basic responsibilities. The legal system, suffering from a lack of resources and trained personnel and the absence of a legal code suitable for the new market economy, was near collapse. Low salaries led to a drain of experienced jurists to the private sector; there was also widespread corruption within law enforcement and the legal system, as judges and police officials took bribes to supplement their meagre incomes. The country's public services were also under severe strain. Because of a lack of resources, law-enforcement agencies proved unable to combat rising crime. As medical services collapsed, life expectancy declined and the population started to shrink.

Another consequence of the political and economic changes of the 1990s was the emergence of Russian organized crime. This has taken various forms, including the drug trade and the black market. Armed robbery has been particularly popular and easy because of the widespread availability of arms supplied to nationalist movements by those seeking political destabilization of their own or other countries. By the beginning of the twenty-first century, official Russian crime statistics had identified more than 5,000 organized-crime groups responsible for international money laundering, tax evasion, and assassinations of businessmen and politicians. Throughout most of the Yeltsin administration, shoot-outs between rival groups and the assassinations of organized-crime or business figures filled the headlines of

Russian newspapers, and created further disillusionment among Russians over the course of economic and political reform. The explosive rise in crime shocked most Russians, who had had little direct experience of such incidents in the Soviet era. The assassinations of well-known and well-liked figures, such as human rights advocate Galina Starovoytova, served to underscore the Yeltsin regime's inability to combat crime. The open warfare between organized-crime groups had diminished by the end of the Yeltsin era, not because of effective state action but because of the consolidation of the remaining criminal groups that had emerged victorious from their bloody struggles.

Economic Reforms

The new Russia faced economic collapse. In 1991 alone, gross domestic product (GDP) fell by about one-sixth, and the budget deficit was approximately one-fourth of GDP. The government of Mikhail Gorbachev had printed huge amounts of money to finance both the budget and subsidies to factories and on food at a time when the tax system was collapsing. Moreover, the price controls on most goods had kept their supply well below the levels demanded. By 1991 few items essential for everyday life were available in traditional retail outlets. The entire system of goods distribution was on the verge of disintegration. Since the central-command economy had existed in Russia for more than 70 years, the transition to a market economy proved more difficult for Russia than for the other ex-communist countries of Eastern Europe. The reformists had to balance the necessities of economic reform with the vested interests that had become extremely powerful under communism.

Although Russia's manufacturing sector was one of the world's largest, it was also very inefficient and expensive to support. It was heavily geared toward defence and heavy industrial products. The industrial managers and workforce, though highly educated, lacked the skills needed by a market-based consumer-led economy, and would therefore have to be retrained.

In January 1992 the Yeltsin government removed price controls on most items – the first essential step towards a market-based economy. The immediate goal of getting goods into the stores was achieved, and the long queues typical of the Soviet era disappeared. However, inflation soared and became a daily concern for Russians, whose purchasing power declined as prices for even some of the most basic goods rose. The government was forced to print money to finance the budget and to keep failing factories afloat. By 1993 the budget deficit financed by the printing of money consumed one-fifth of GDP. Consequently, people lost faith in the value of the ruble and started to use US dollars instead. Inflationary pressures were exacerbated by the establishment of a "ruble zone" when the Soviet Union collapsed: many of the former republics continued to issue and use rubles and receive credits from the Russian Central Bank, thereby further devaluing the ruble. In the summer of 1993 the Russian government pulled out of the ruble zone, effectively reducing Russian influence over many of the former Soviet republics.

During the Soviet era the factory had been not only a place of work but often also a source of social services, such as child care, holidays, and housing. If the government allowed many industries to collapse, it would have not only to provide relief for unemployed workers but also to guarantee a whole array of social services – a responsibility it was in no position to assume. Yet the inflation caused by keeping factories afloat undermined popular support for both Yeltsin and economic reform, as many Russians struggled to survive. Factories resorted to paying their workers and their creditors in kind, creating a barter economy. It was not uncommon for workers to go months without being paid or to be paid in, for example, rubber gloves or crockery, either because they made such things themselves or because their factory had received them as payments from its debtors. Meanwhile street markets sprang up where people tried to sell their personal possessions in a desperate effort to maintain their incomes.

In 1995 the government moved to resolve the crisis and end the misery. With loans from the International Monetary Fund (IMF) and the proceeds from the sale of oil and natural gas, it fixed the ruble's exchange rate at a level that the Russian Central Bank was committed to defend. Inflation fell and the economy started to stabilize. Yet the government continued to borrow money on domestic and foreign markets while avoiding serious structural reforms of the economy. It failed to establish an effective tax system, clear property rights, and a coherent bankruptcy law, but continued to support failing industries. As a result the ruble exchange rate proved increasingly expensive to defend, and became the target of speculators. In 1998 the ruble collapsed, and the government defaulted on its debts amid a growing number of bankruptcies. The ruble eventually stabilized and inflation diminished, but living standards hardly improved for most Russians, though a small proportion of them became very wealthy. Moreover, any improvements were confined to Moscow, St Petersburg, and some other urban areas; elsewhere, vast tracts of Russia were gripped by economic depression.

Another element of economic reform was shifting Russian industry into private hands. The reformists hoped that the threat of a return to communism would dwindle once a Russian capitalist class had developed, and believed, like many western economists, that the economy could recover only if enterprises were privatized and then left to fight for survival. As well as allowing privately owned industrial and commercial ventures to start up (using both foreign and domestic sources of investment), the government moved to sell state-owned enterprises to private owners. Initially, the government issued to each citizen a voucher worth 10,000 rubles: Russians could invest their entire vouchers, sell them, or use them to bid for additional shares in specific enterprises. However, the average Russian did not benefit from this rather complicated scheme. By the end of 1992 some one-third of services and trade enterprises had been privatized.

In a second wave of privatization in 1994–5, much of Russian industry was sold at knock-down prices to the friends of "the Family", meaning Yeltsin and his daughter Tatyana Dyachenko and their allies in the government. Natural resource companies were sold at prices well below those recommended by the IMF. From this process emerged the "oligarchs", individuals who, because of their political connections, controlled huge segments of the Russian economy. Many oligarchs bought factories for almost nothing, stripped out and sold their assets, and then closed them, creating huge job losses. By the time Yeltsin left office in 1999, most of the Russian economy had been privatized.

The stripping of the factories played a major role in the public's disenchantment with the development of capitalism in Russia. To many Russians, it seemed that bandit capitalism had emerged. Most people had suffered a fall in living standards, the social services had disintegrated, and the country was engulfed by a wave of crime and corruption. Yeltsin's popularity plummeted.

Ethnic Relations and Russia's "Near-Abroad"

Post-Soviet Russia emerged with formidable ethnic problems. Many of the autonomous ethnic regions that had been part of the Russian empire since before the 1917 Revolution wanted to escape Russian hegemony, and ethnic Russians made up less than four-fifths of the population of the Russian Federation. The term *rossiyanin* was used to denote a citizen of the Russian Federation and was not given any ethnic Russian connotation. However, a committee set up to construct a Russian identity to rally people around the new Russian Federation eventually concluded that national identity could emerge only from the grass roots, and history had shown that attempts to impose an identity from above led to an authoritarian or totalitarian state. The Russian Orthodox Church re-established itself as a force in the moral guidance of reborn Russia, but many minority groups observed religions other than Christianity, notably Islam.

During the Yeltsin years, Russia's numerous administrative regions sought greater autonomy. For example, Tatarstan negotiated additional rights and privileges. The republic of Chechnya declared independence in 1991, but Russia refused to accept the declaration. Chechen nationalism was based on the struggle against Russian imperialism since the early nineteenth century and the living memory of Stalin's massive deportations of the Chechen population in 1944 that had resulted in the deaths of a large segment of the population. In late 1994 Yeltsin sent the army into Chechnya in the aftermath of a botched Russian-orchestrated coup against the secessionist president, Dzhokhar Dudayev.

There were fears that if Chechnya succeeded in breaking away from the Russian Federation, other republics might follow suit. Moreover, Dudayev's Chechnya had become a source of drug dealing and arms peddling. In 1995 Russia gained control of the capital, Grozny, but in 1996 Russian forces were pushed out of the city. Yeltsin, faced with a forthcoming presidential election and great unpopularity because of both the war and economic problems, had General Aleksandr Lebed sign a ceasefire agreement with the Chechens. The Russians subsequently withdrew from the republic, postponing the question of Chechen independence.

When the Soviet Union collapsed, the Commonwealth of Independent States was established to serve as a forum for the former Soviet republics (which Moscow now called the "near-abroad"). The CIS had its origins on December 8, 1991, when the elected leaders of Russia, Ukraine, and Belarus signed an agreement forming a new association to replace the crumbling USSR. The three Slavic republics were subsequently joined by the Central Asian republics of Kazakhstan, Kyrgyzstan, Tajikistan, Turkmenistan, and Uzbekistan, by the Transcaucasian republics of Armenia, Azerbaijan, and Georgia, and by Moldova. (The remaining former Soviet republics of Lithuania, Latvia, and Estonia declined to join the new organization.) The Commonwealth formally came into being on December 21, 1991, and began operations the following month with the city of Minsk in Belarus designated as its administrative centre.

Russia hoped to maintain its influence over most of these former republics; it considered the Caucasus and Central Asia special areas of interest, as was clear from its aid to ethnic Russian separatists in the Dniester region of Moldova and intervention in the Tajik civil war. In addition, the Russian government exerted economic pressure on Ukraine and supported separatist groups in Georgia to attain its ends.

However, Moscow did more to undermine the CIS through its inconsistent policies, lack of organizational leadership, and tendency to work bilaterally with the governments of the newly independent republics. In 1996 Russia and Belarus began a process that, it was proclaimed, would eventually result in the unification of the two countries. However, by the early twenty-first century there was still no sign that unification would occur. Russia's severe economic difficulties limited its ability to provide financial and military assistance to its neighbours (at least until the surge in oil prices in the early twenty-first century) and hence to retain influence over its near-abroad. Russian officials were even wary of allowing in too many imports from the near-abroad for fear that they would further weaken Russian industry.

The collapse of the Soviet Union left some 30 million ethnic Russians outside the borders of the Russian Federation. The largest such populations were in Kazakhstan, Ukraine, and the Baltic countries. These countries feared that Moscow could use the resident ethnic Russian populations to pressure them to adopt policies friendly to Moscow. However, during the 1990s Moscow refrained from following such an approach – sometimes to the great criticism of the Russians living in these areas.

Foreign Affairs

For several years after the collapse of the Soviet Union, Yeltsin placed a high priority on relations with the West, particularly with the United States. But the geopolitical goals of the two countries were not always compatible. Russia opposed the eastward expansion of NATO. Although eventually accepting the inevitability of some such expansion, it tried to thwart the entry of former Soviet republics and to construct a viable bilateral relationship with NATO so as to acquire some influence over it. Russia also attempted to strengthen its links with the European Union. But Washington and Moscow's disagreements over the Balkans – in particular, US support for NATO's armed intervention against the Yugoslav government of Slobodan Milosevic – soured their relations.

The Yeltsin government tried not only to come to terms with Russia's loss of empire and of its superpower status but also to create a foreign policy doctrine reflecting the new global geo-political reality. Its increasing concerns about US world hege-mony led Yevgeny Primakov, who became foreign minister in 1995, to promote a multipolar system of international relations to replace the US-dominated unipolar world. To balance US power, Russia strengthened its relations with China and India; Russia's good relations with Iran and differences in approaches to Iraq further increased tensions in Russian–US relations.

Overall, Russian foreign policy in the 1990s was aimless, contradictory, and confused. Despite Primakov's efforts to give it coherence, Yeltsin himself was erratic in foreign policy, and his divide-and-rule strategy allowed various bureaucratic bodies to fight for control over the direction of Russia's external relations.

Rewriting History

During the Soviet period, history had been written in light of the official ideology of Marxism-Leninism, which stressed the Soviet Union's leading role in the inevitable emergence of world communism. After 1991, aided by the opening of official archives, Russian historians debated whether the events of 1917 were inevitable, and many concluded that the Bolshevik Revolution had thrown Russia off the evolutionary course travelled by other European countries. Tsarist leaders such as Peter I, Catherine II, and Alexander II became positive figures in Russian history. Nicholas II's great love for his family and Russia was recognized. The reburial of the remains of the immediate imperial family (all of whom were executed together in 1918) in the Peter-Paul Fortress in St Petersburg in 1999 brought to a head the partial transformation of Nicholas II's position in Russian history. The Stalinist period and the role of Lenin in the emergence of a totalitarian state after the revolution were re-evaluated; documentary evidence reflecting official thinking during and after the Second World War gave historians an opportunity to reassess the origins of the Cold War. Consequently, much of the conventional wisdom among western historians about Soviet intentions at the time was debunked.

The Putin Leadership, 1999–2008

Toward the end of Yeltsin's presidency, Vladimir Putin began playing a more important role. During the Soviet period, he joined the KGB and worked in East Germany for many years. Fluent in German and proficient in English, Putin worked for the liberal mayor of St Petersburg, Anatoly Sobchak, in the initial post-Soviet period, and ended up in Moscow when Sobchak failed to be re-elected mayor in 1996. In July 1998 Putin became director of the Federal Security Service (FSB), one of the successor organizations of the KGB, and in August 1999 Yeltsin plucked Putin out of relative obscurity for the post of prime minister.

VLADIMIR PUTIN (b. 1952)

Russian president (1999–2008)

Putin served 15 years with the KGB, including six years in Dresden, East Germany. In 1990 he retired from active KGB service and returned to Russia to become pro-rector of Leningrad State University, and by 1994 he had risen to the post of first deputy mayor of St Petersburg. In 1996 he moved to Moscow, where he joined the presidential staff as deputy to Pavel Borodin, the Kremlin's chief administrator. In July 1998 President Boris Yeltsin made Putin director of the Federal Security Service (the KGB's domestic successor). In 1999 Yeltsin appointed Putin prime minister, and on December 31 of that year Yeltsin stepped down as president in Putin's favour. Three months later Putin won a resounding electoral victory, partly the result of his success in the battle to keep Chechnya from seceding.

In his first term Putin asserted central control over Russia's 89 regions and republics, and moved to reduce the power of Russia's unpopular financiers and media tycoons. The period was also marked by frequent terrorist attacks by Chechen separatists. Putin easily won re-election in 2004. His chosen successor, Dmitry Medvedev, was elected president in March 2008.

Separatism

As prime minister, Putin blamed Chechen secessionists for the bombing of several apartment buildings that killed scores of Russian civilians, prompting the Moscow government to send

Russian forces into the republic once again. (Evidence never proved Chechen involvement in these bombings, leading some to believe that the Russian intelligence services played a role in them.) Grozny fell to the Russian forces, Putin's popularity soared, and Yeltsin, having chosen Putin as his successor, resigned the presidency on December 31, 1999. Putin became acting president, and his first official undertaking in this role was to grant Yeltsin a pardon for any offences he might have committed during his administration. In the presidential election of early 2000, Putin easily defeated Communist Party leader Gennady Zyuganov.

Although the Russian military was able to win control of Chechnya, Chechen fighters threatened Russian forces with a prolonged guerrilla war. After two years the fighting abated, and Putin felt confident enough to seek talks with the remaining Chechen leadership. Then in October 2002 Chechen separatists seized a Moscow theatre and threatened to kill all those inside; Putin responded by ordering special forces to raid the theatre, and during the operation some 130 hostages died – mostly as the result of inhaling gas released by the security forces in order to subdue the terrorists. In 2003 Chechen voters approved a new constitution that devolved greater powers to the Chechen government but kept the republic in the federation. The following year the Russian-backed Chechen president was killed in a bomb blast allegedly carried out by Chechen guerrillas.

Despite worries arising from his years working for the intelligence services, many Russians believed that Putin's coolness and decisiveness – which contrasted starkly with Yeltsin's unpredictable behaviour – would restore order and prestige to the country and deal with the Chechen problem. Indeed, Putin reasserted central control over the country's numerous regions by dividing Russia into seven administrative districts, each overseen by a presidential appointee charged with rooting out corruption, monitoring the local governors, and ensuring that Moscow's will and laws were enforced. Putin established the supremacy of Russian Federation law throughout the country, ending the often chaotic contradictions between Russian federal law and that of the regions. Even independent-minded regions such as the republics of Tatarstan and Bashkortostan reluctantly aligned their constitutions in 2002 to that of the Russian Federation.

Foreign Affairs

Putin's foreign affairs priority was to strengthen Russia's security and economic relations with Europe. Nevertheless, after the al-Qaeda attacks of September 11, 2001, on the United States, Putin was the first foreign leader to telephone US President George W. Bush to offer sympathy and help. Moreover, Russia established a council with NATO on which it sat as an equal alongside NATO's 19 members. Russia also reacted calmly when the United States officially abandoned the Anti-Ballistic Missile Treaty in 2002 and established temporary military links with several former Soviet states in Central Asia and Georgia.

However, wary of US unilateralism, Putin strengthened Russian ties with China and India and maintained ties with Iran. In 2002–3 he opposed the US-led military intervention against Iraq, favouring a more stringent inspections regime of Iraq's suspected weapons of mass destruction programme.

Putin brought new life to the CIS by providing relatively active Russian leadership, and strengthened Russia's ties with the Central Asian republics. Under Yeltsin the Russian army had lost much of its effectiveness and technological edge, as revealed by its defeats in the first Chechen war. Putin hoped to increase funding for the armed forces through greater arms sales.

The Oligarchs

Putin also moved against the political and economic power of the infamous oligarchs. Although he could not destroy the business elite, he insisted on certain limits on its conduct. Those oligarchs who criticized Putin during the presidential campaign faced the Kremlin's wrath. In 2001 Vladimir Gusinsky and Boris Berezovsky, two of Russia's richest men, were stripped of their electronic media holdings, and Berezovsky was removed from his position of influence at Russian Public Television. In 2003 Russia's richest man, Mikhail Khodorkovsky, the former head of the oil giant Yukos, was convicted of fraud and tax evasion. This campaign prompted doubts about Putin's commitment to free speech and a free press. Under Yeltsin the oligarchs had used their individual media outlets in their battles with each other and with political figures. Yet some television stations consistently contradicted the reports of government-controlled stations on issues such as corruption and the wars in Chechnya, thereby providing an alternative source to government news sources. Yeltsin never tried to reassert control over the mass media, but Putin moved to close television networks that criticized him, usually by charging their owners with non-payment of taxes and financial mismanagement.

THE KREMLIN

As throughout its history, the Kremlin remains the heart of Moscow. It was established in 1156, and served as the centre of Russian government until 1712 and again after 1918. It has been the symbol of both Russian and Soviet power and authority, as well as being the official residence of the president of the Russian Federation since 1991. Its crenellated brick walls and 20 towers were built in the fifteenth century by Italian architects. The palaces, cathedrals, and government buildings within the walls encompass a variety of styles, including Byzantine, Russian baroque, and classical.

Several capitals of principalities were built around old kremlins, or central fortresses, which generally contained cathedrals, palaces, governmental offices, and munitions stores. They were usually located at a strategic point along a river and separated from the surrounding parts of the city by a wall with ramparts, moat, towers, and battlements.

Political and Economic Reforms

Putin proved adept at constructing a stable relationship with the Duma. Where Yeltsin's automatic hostility to the Communist Party had hobbled his reform programme, Putin was better able to work with the parties, and he secured the passage of bills that reformed the tax, judicial, labour, and bankruptcy systems, provided property rights, adopted national symbols and the flag, and approved arms treaties. In addition, he avoided frequent changes in the cabinet or premiership, thereby promoting policy consistency and political stability that ordinary Russians appreciated. He also attempted to reduce the number of political parties – in particular, regional parties – in Russia by requiring them to have registered offices and at least 10,000 members in at least half of Russia's regions to be eligible to compete in national elections.

Putin believed that the Russian economy's long-term health required deep structural reforms that the Yeltsin administration had avoided, though implementing such reforms proved difficult. He secured the creation of a new tax code that simplified and streamlined the tax system in order to encourage individuals and businesses to pay taxes. As a result the state's rate of tax collection dramatically increased, which, along with a surge in income from the increase in world oil prices, allowed the Russian government to enjoy a budget surplus and to repay some of its external debt. Putin was also keen to attract foreign investment in order to reduce Russia's dependence on western loans (which he believed threatened the country's national interests and long-term economic prospects) and to help finance the development of Russian industry. Russia also sought to increase its exports by promoting the sale of oil, natural gas, and arms. The reforms implemented by Putin – as well as his demeanour – produced political stability and economic vitality not seen in the country during the 1990s. Nevertheless, problems in the economy remained, and many people still lived in poverty.

Putin's presidency also witnessed a change in the way Russians viewed the Soviet past. Whereas under Yeltsin popular histories and general opinion were critical of the Soviet period and nostalgic for pre-revolutionary days, during Putin's tenure aspects of the Soviet age – for example, the victory in the Second World War, Russia's superpower status, and even the Stalinist era – were again glorified (Stalin was described in one teaching manual as "the most successful leader of the USSR"). Despite nostalgia among some communists for the Soviet period and uncertainty among many about the future, by the early twenty-first century Russia seemed poised to set out upon the long path of economic and political development.

Though accused of over-centralizing power in the presidency and curtailing freedoms won when the Soviet Union collapsed, Putin remained popular and was re-elected in 2004 in a landslide. During his second term his popularity continued, and speculation arose that, constitutionally ineligible as he was to run for another term in office because of term limits, he might engineer a constitutional amendment to allow his re-election. Instead, in October 2007 Putin made the surprise announcement that he would head the list of the pro-Putin United Russia Party in parliamentary elections. In December 2007 United Russia won more than three-fifths of the vote and 315 of the Duma's 450 seats. Within days Putin anointed First Deputy Prime Minister Dmitry Medvedev as his successor as president for the 2008 elections. In turn, Medvedev subsequently announced that he would appoint Putin prime minister if his campaign succeeded, thus giving Putin a base to continue his dominance of Russian politics. In March 2008 Medvedev was easily elected president, winning 70 per cent of the vote. Although some outside observers criticized the contest as unfair, most agreed that Medvedev's victory reflected the will of the majority of the Russian people. Medvedev took office on May 7, 2008; Putin was confirmed as prime minister the next day.

DMITRY MEDVEDEV (b. 1965)

Russian president (from 2008)

Dmitry Medvedev was born into a middle-class family in suburban Leningrad (now St Petersburg) in 1965. He attended Leningrad State University, where he received a bachelor's degree in 1987 and a law degree in 1990. In 1991 Medvedev joined the legal team of St Petersburg's newly elected mayor, Anatoly Sobchak, who also had brought future president Vladimir Putin into his administration. Medvedev and Putin worked together in the mayor's office for the next five years.

When Sobchak's term ended, Medvedev returned to academic life, and Putin moved to a position at the Kremlin. After Putin became acting president of Russia in December 1999, he made Medvedev his protege. In 2000 Medvedev headed Putin's presidential election campaign, and following Putin's victory he was named first deputy chief of staff. Later that same year, Medvedev was appointed chairman of the state-owned natural-gas monopoly Gazprom. In 2003 he became Putin's chief of staff, and two years later he was appointed to the newly created post of first deputy prime minister.

Throughout his service under Putin, Medvedev distinguished himself as an able administrator with an eye towards reform. His admiration of western popular culture made some conservatives within the Kremlin uneasy, but much of this criticism was softened after Putin named Medvedev his heir apparent in December 2007. The central message of Medvedev's subsequent

presidential campaign was "Freedom is better than no
freedom", a remark that hinted at an openness to the
West that was uncharacteristic of the Putin years.

Just three months into his presidency, Medvedev was confronted with a growing military conflict between Russia's neighbour Georgia and South Ossetia, a separatist region of Georgia that borders the Russian republic of North Ossetia-Alania. As fighting between Georgian and Ossetian forces escalated in August 2008, Russia sent thousands of troops across the border with the goal of supporting rebels in not only South Ossetia but also Abkhazia, another separatist region within Georgia. Despite a French-brokered ceasefire, hostilities continued, and Russian troops remained in Georgia. The conflict heightened tensions between Russia and the West. In response to condemnation from NATO, which Georgia hopes to join, Russia suspended its cooperation with the Atlantic alliance. In September the Russian government agreed to withdraw its troops from Georgia; however, it planned to maintain a military presence in South Ossetia and Abkhazia, whose independence it had recognized.

THE FSB (FEDERAL SECURITY SERVICE) AND ITS PREDECESSORS

Russian internal security and counterintelligence service
The FSB was created in 1994 as one of the successor
agencies of the Soviet-era KGB (Committee for State
Security). The KGB was the most durable of a series of
security agencies starting with the Cheka (1917), which
was charged with the preliminary investigation of
counter-revolution and sabotage; it quickly assumed

responsibility for arresting, imprisoning, and executing "enemies of the state", including members of the former nobility, the bourgeoisie, and the clergy. Successors of the Cheka included the OGPU (Unified State Political Administration, 1923), whose duties included the administration of "corrective" labour camps and the surveillance of the population, and the NKVD (People's Commissariat of Internal Affairs, 1934), which helped Stalin to consolidate his power by carrying out purges.

The KGB was created in 1954 to serve as the "sword and shield of the Communist Party". For the next 20 years the KGB became increasingly zealous in its pursuit of enemies, harassing, arresting, and sometimes exiling human rights advocates, Christian and Jewish activists, and intellectuals judged to be disloyal to the regime. Among the most famous of its victims were the Nobel laureates Aleksandr Solzhenitsyn and Andrey Sakharov.

During the late 1980s, as the Soviet government and economy were crumbling, the KGB survived better than most state institutions, suffering far fewer cuts in its personnel and budget. The agency was dismantled, however, after the attempted coup in August 1991 against Mikhail Gorbachev, in which some KGB units participated. In early 1992 the internal security functions of the KGB were reconstituted first as the Ministry of Security and less than two years later as the Federal Counterintelligence Service (FSK), which was placed under the control of the president. In 1995 Boris Yeltsin renamed the service the Federal Security Service (FSB) and granted it additional powers, enabling it to enter private homes and to conduct intelligence activities in

Russia as well as abroad in cooperation with the Russian Foreign Intelligence Service (SVR).

Despite early promises to reform the Russian intelligence community, the FSB and the services that collect foreign intelligence and signals intelligence – the SVR and the Federal Agency for Government Communications and Information (FAPSI) – remained largely unreformed and subject to little legislative or judicial scrutiny. Although some limits were placed on the FSB's domestic surveillance activities – for example, spying on religious institutions and charitable organizations was reduced – all the services continued to be controlled by KGB veterans schooled under the old regime. Moreover, few former KGB officers were removed following the agency's dissolution, and little effort was made to examine the KGB's operations or its use of informants.

After appointing Vladimir Putin as its director in 1998, Yeltsin ordered the FSB to expand its operations against labour unions in Siberia and to crack down on right-wing dissidents. As president, Putin increased the FSB's powers to include countering foreign intelligence operations, fighting organized crime, and suppressing Chechen separatists.

The FSB, the largest security service in Europe, is extremely effective at counterintelligence. Human rights activists, however, have claimed that it has been slow to shed its KGB heritage, and there have been allegations that it has manufactured cases against suspected dissidents and used threats to recruit agents. At the end of the 1990s, critics alleged that the FSB had attempted to frame Russian academics involved in joint research with western arms-control experts.

PART 3

CULTURE

5

THE DEVELOPMENT OF THE ARTS IN RUSSIA

Russia's unique and vibrant culture developed, as did the country itself, from a complicated interplay of native Slavic cultural material and borrowings from a wide variety of foreign cultures. This sometimes took place gradually, across several centuries – in the Kievan period, for example (*c.* tenth–thirteenth centuries), when the borrowings were primarily from Eastern Orthodox Byzantine culture. At other times external influences were consciously sought and imported: under Peter I (1682–1725), known as Peter the Great, the cultural heritage of western Europe was deliberately added to the Russian melting pot, and in the 1860s a deliberate programme of "Russification" was introduced, imposing Russian culture on minorities and outlying parts of the empire. Over and above this interplay between foreign and native elements, though not unrelated, was another creative tension, the relationship between high and folk art. Both these sets of relationships were closely linked with Russia's political development.

Several strands from Russia's medieval past stand out as being influential in the culture of modern Russia. One recurring thread was the influence of the Orthodox Church, and in particular church architecture. From the tenth century, when Russia was Christianized, Slavic culture in Kievan Rus was dominated by the church: artistic composition was undertaken almost exclusively by monks, and the early Slavic rulers, like their western European counterparts, expressed their religious piety and displayed their wealth through the construction of stone churches. The earliest of these were in Byzantine style and indeed built by craftsmen from Constantinople, the capital of Byzantium: perhaps the most famous example is the eleventh-century Cathedral of St Sophia, which still stands in Kiev, Ukraine.

The destruction of Kievan Rus by the Tatar (Mongol) invasions of the early thirteenth century led to new political focuses and, inevitably, new cultural influences. By the time Russian political and cultural life began to recover in the fourteenth century, a new centre had arisen, Muscovy (Moscow). In the next century the whole country united under the Grand Dukes of Moscow, and after the fall of Constantinople in 1453 Russian political ideology developed the slogan "Moscow, the third Rome": Russian art became the self-conscious successor to Byzantine art, and Moscow its artistic centre. Although Italian architects were called in to help build the Kremlin, Moscow's citadel, they had to compromise with traditional Russian elements: the Cathedral of the Assumption is very much a Russian church, with its typical bulbous domes and an interior that makes no concession to foreign tastes.

It was this period that saw the flourishing of an art that is truly Russian, no longer dependent on Byzantium, and not yet an integral part of European culture. Central to this was the influence, artistically and intellectually, of the Orthodox Church, which was a beacon of national life during the period of Tatar domination and which continued to play a central role in Russian culture into the seventeenth century. This meant that Russian cultural development in the Muscovite period was quite different from that of western Europe – which at this time was experiencing the secularization of society and the rediscovery of the classical cultural heritage that characterized the Renaissance. It also meant that the most significant cultural achievements of Muscovy were again in the visual arts and architecture, rather than in literature, and in ecclesiastical art in its many forms. The Moscow school of icon painting produced great masters, among them Dionisy and Andrey Rublyov (whose *Old Testament Trinity*, now in Moscow's Tretyakov Gallery, is among the most revered icons ever painted). Russian architects continued to design and build impressive churches, most famously the celebrated Cathedral of St Basil the Blessed on Moscow's Red Square. Built between 1554 and 1560 to commemorate the Russian capture of Kazar, the Tatar capital, St Basil's is a supreme example of the confluence of Byzantine and Asiatic cultural streams that characterizes Muscovite culture. It remains today an icon of Russian identity.

The late seventeenth century witnessed a pendulum swing of cultural awareness and development. The gradual turning of Russia towards western Europe and a weakening of the power of the Orthodox Church gave rise, under Peter I, to an almost total reorientation of Russian culture. Although Peter was not particularly interested in cultural questions, he was energetic and insistent in introducing western cultural and technological traditions to Russia. He personally visited western Europe as part of the so-called "Grand Embassy", comprising about 250

ANDREI RUBLYOV (c. 1360–1430)

Russian painter

Rublyov (or Rublev) was trained wholly in the stylized tradition of Byzantine art, but to the more humanistic approach it had adopted by the fourteenth century he added a truly Russian element, a complete unworldliness that distinguishes his work from that of his predecessors and successors. He assisted Theophanes the Greek in decorating the Cathedral of the Annunciation in Moscow. The greatest of medieval Russian icon painters, he is best known for *The Old Testament Trinity* (c. 1410). He became a monk fairly late in life.

people; one of the aims of the tour was to gather information on the economic and cultural life of Europe. The emperor travelled incognito under the name of Sergeant Pyotr Mikhaylov, and though he spent much of his time studying shipbuilding – his passion – he also visited factories, arsenals, schools, and museums. The result of this visit was a rapid westernization of Russia that altered the daily life of the upper classes and high culture generally. Some of the reforms Peter introduced were brutal and superficial – he decreed that beards should be shorn off and western dress worn – while others were longer-lasting and more influential. He promoted the translation of books from western European languages; the first Russian newspaper, *Vedomosti* ("Records"), appeared in 1703; the Russian Academy of Sciences was instituted in 1724; women came out of seclusion; and from January 1, 1700, a European calendar was introduced, making the Russian calendar conform to European usage with regard to the year, which in

Russia had hitherto been numbered "from the Creation of the World".

These changes were inevitably reflected in literature and the development of the Russian language. With the introduction of new subject matter into Russian literature and cultural life and the influx of foreign expressions, Church Slavonic – descended from Old Church Slavonic, the religious and literary language of Orthodox Slavs throughout the Middle Ages – proved inadequate, and the resulting linguistic chaos required the standardization of literary Russian. In 1758 the poet and scientist Mikhail Lomonosov published *Preface on the Use of Church Books in the Russian Language*, in which he classified Russian and Church Slavonic words, assigning their use to three styles, and correlated these styles with appropriate themes, genres, and tones. Thus the Russian literary language was to be established by a combination of Russian and Church Slavonic. Lomonosov was also instrumental, along with Vasily Trediakovsky, in carrying out far-reaching reforms in versification, developing a system of "classical" metre that prevails in Russian poetry to this day. The writings of the nineteenth-century poet Aleksandr Pushkin gave further impetus to the development of the language. By combining the colloquial and Church Slavonic styles, Pushkin put an end to the considerable controversy that had developed as to which style of the language was best for literary uses.

By the nineteenth century, the absorption of western culture had been so rapid and complete that the first language of the upper nobility was not Russian but French. The very foreignness that adhered to high culture was one reason why a tradition arose in which the sign of Russianness was the defiance of European generic norms. Justifying the self-consciously odd form of *War and Peace*, Leo Tolstoy observed

MIKHAIL VASILYEVICH LOMONOSOV (1711–65)

Russian scientist, poet, and grammarian, considered the first great Russian linguistic reformer

Educated in Russia and Germany, Mikhail Lomonosov established what became the standards for Russian verse in the *Letter Concerning the Rules of Russian Versification*. In 1745 he joined the faculty at the St Petersburg Imperial Academy of Sciences, where he made substantial contributions to the physical sciences. He later wrote a Russian grammar and worked to systematize the Russian literary language, which had been an amalgam of Church Slavonic and Russian vernacular. He also reorganized the academy, founded Moscow State University (which now bears his name), and created the first coloured-glass mosaics in Russia.

that departure from European form is necessary for a Russian writer: "There is not a single work of Russian artistic prose, at all rising above mediocrity, that quite fits the form of a novel, a poem, or a story." This (admittedly exaggerated) view, which became a cliché, helps explain the enormous popularity in Russia of those western writers who parodied literary conventions, as well as the development of Russia's most influential school of literary criticism, Formalism, which viewed formal self-consciousness as the defining quality of "literariness". The sense that culture, literature, and the forms of "civilized" life were a foreign product imported by the upper classes is also reflected in a tendency of Russian thinkers to regard all art as morally unjustifiable, and in a pattern of Russian writers renouncing their own works. While English and French critics were arguing about the merits of different literary schools, Russian critics also debated whether literature itself had a right to exist – a question that reveals the peculiar ethos of Russian literary culture.

The spirit of nationalism that swept across Europe in the nineteenth century did not leave Russia untouched. In turning their backs on inherited western "traditions" nineteenth-century writers, musicians, and artists made a self-conscious return to what were perceived as typically Russian themes, often from folk culture – whether in song or verse – and to the Middle Ages, to source their particular Russian identity. Composers, writers, and dramatists all turned to the Russian Middle Ages for inspiration for Russian themes and characters: Tolstoy's novella *Father Sergius*, Modest Mussorgsky's opera *Boris Godunov*, many of his songs, and his setting of some of Nikolay Gogol's *Zhenitba* ("The Marriage"), and Mikhail Glinka's operas *Life of the Tsar* and *Ruslan and Lyudmila*, as well as Rimsky-Korsakov's series of operas on Russian folk tales, to name only a few.

The political control of the arts became a marked feature of the culture of the Soviet era. Such control was not entirely new – censorship, for example, had flourished in tsarist Russia – but from the late 1920s and under Stalin's iron hand it reached new heights, with more brutally repressive measures for those who failed to conform. Though periods of strict suppression were followed by brief thaws, during the Soviet era most customs and traditions of Russia's imperial past were forbidden expression, and life was strictly controlled and regulated by the state through its vast intelligence network. Stalin's policy of socialist realism, which came to dominate Soviet arts, dictated that individual creativity be subordinated to the political aims of the Communist Party and the state. In practice, it militated against the symbolic, the experimental, and the avant-garde in favour of a literal-minded "people's art" that glorified representative Soviet heroes and idealized Soviet experience. Its effects were felt in literature, film-making, the visual arts, and music.

This repressive policy was facilitated by control of sources of information: propaganda manifested itself quickly after the 1917 Revolution, and most independent publications were eliminated by the early 1920s. What remained were the ubiquitous daily duo of the newspapers *Pravda* ("Truth") and *Izvestiya* ("News"). Radio and television, from the time of their appearance in the Soviet Union, were similarly heavily dominated by the Communist Party apparatus and were seen as primary tools for propaganda. Until the mid-1980s most television programming consisted of either direct or indirect propaganda spiced with high art (such as filmed concerts and plays) and occasional B-movie thrillers. Interestingly, ground-breaking television programming was to play a part in creating the situation in which the Soviet state was destroyed, so that from the mid-1980s, with Mikhail Gorbachev's reforms, the political and social restrictions on cultural activity that had predominated for much of the century were eased and common traditions and folk customs, along with the open practice of religion, were actively encouraged.

6

LITERATURE

From the nineteenth century, literature in Russia enjoyed much greater prestige than in the West. Its achievements were sometimes thought, as the novelist Fyodor Dostoyevsky once declared, to be the justification for the Russian people's very existence. The function, role, and compass of literature were broader than in the West: literature and criticism were expected to offer philosophical, moral, and religious analysis, for example, and literary critics were typically the leaders of Russian intellectual life and political thought. Thus, in the nineteenth – and still more, the twentieth – century, politics and literature were intimately connected, and a writer or critic was often called upon to be a political prophet. (In the nineteenth century, Aleksandr Pushkin emphasized the writer's civic responsibility and exhorted the poet-prophet to "fire the hearts of men with his words".) Inevitably this could lead to conflict with the authorities, whether tsarist or Soviet, and, not infrequently, to exile or emigration, imprisonment, and, in the twentieth century, execution. It also led to a self-consciousness

BOYARS

Male members of the upper class of medieval Russian society and state administration

In Kievan Rus (tenth–twelfth centuries) the boyars belonged to the prince's retinue, holding posts in the army and civil administration and advising the prince in matters of state through a boyar council, or duma. In the thirteenth–fourteenth centuries the boyars constituted a privileged class of rich landowners in north-eastern Russia. In the fifteenth–seventeenth centuries the boyars of Muscovy ruled the country along with the grand prince (later the tsar) and legislated through the boyar council. Their importance declined in the seventeenth century, and the title was abolished by Peter I in the early eighteenth century.

about literature's relation to the cultures of the West, and a strong tendency toward formal innovation and defiance of received generic norms. The combination of formal radicalism and preoccupation with abstract philosophical issues is one of the hallmarks of the Russian classics.

The Nineteenth Century

Pushkin is a natural starting point for any discussion of Russian literature, not only because of his acknowledged genius, the subjects he introduced, and the literary genres he opened up or foreshadowed, but also because of the way he shaped the Russian language itself. His personal literary trajectory can be seen as a microcosm of the various strands of

SERFS

Tenant farmers bound to a hereditary plot of land and to the will of their landlord

Serfs differed from slaves in that slaves could be bought and sold without reference to land, whereas serfs changed lords only when the land they worked changed hands. In western Europe the development of centralized political power, the labour shortage caused by the Black Death, and endemic peasant uprisings in the fourteenth and fifteenth centuries led to the gradual emancipation of serfs. In eastern Europe serfdom became more entrenched during that period; the peasants of the Austro-Hungarian empire were freed in the late 18th century. Russia's serfs were not freed until 1861, during the reign of Alexander II.

Defeat in the Crimean War, change in public opinion, and the increasing number and violence of peasant revolts had convinced Alexander of the need for reform. The final Edict of Emancipation was a compromise and fully satisfied no one, particularly the peasants. It immediately granted personal liberties to the serfs, but the process by which they were to acquire land was slow, complex, and expensive. Though it failed to create an economically viable class of peasant proprietors, its psychological impact was immense.

Russian literature, combining elements of high and low culture, and aristocratic and native folk traditions, and illustrating the political role of the writer and his or her dependent relationship with authority. Even the stories surrounding Pushkin's birth are emblematic: on his father's side he came from an old boyar family; on his mother's he is said to have inherited an Abyssinian princely lineage – it is possible that his maternal grandfather was bought as a slave at Constantinople.

French culture and the French language had been adopted in Russia as a hallmark of culture, and so, like many aristocratic families in early nineteenth-century Russia, Pushkin and his siblings learned first to talk and to read in French. Yet he was also immersed in the much older tradition of the Russian folktale, which he heard mostly from his old nurse, Arina Rodionovna Yakovleva, a freed serf, but also during the summer months that he spent on his grandmother's estate near Moscow, where he talked to the peasants and spent hours alone, living in the dream world of a precocious, imaginative child.

Pushkin was one of the first writers to draw on such traditions in his literary output. Even his first completed major work, the romantic poem *Ruslan and Lyudmila* (1820), though largely written in the style of the narrative poems of Ludovico Ariosto and Voltaire, introduced an old Russian setting and made use of Russian folklore. Over time, the Russian features of his poetry became steadily more marked. His ballad "The Bridegroom" (1825), for instance, with its simple, swift-moving style, is based on motifs from Russian folklore. Others followed: in 1824 he published *The Gypsies* and in 1831 one of his major works, the historical tragedy *Boris Godunov*. His central masterpiece, however, was a novel in verse, *Yevgeny Onegin* (1833), in which he unfolds a panoramic picture of Russian life. The characters it depicts and immortalizes – Onegin, Lensky, Tatyana – are typically Russian and are shown in relationship to the social and environmental forces that mould them.

Fairly early on in his career Pushkin's outspokenness brought him face to face with political authority and repression. In May 1820 he was banished from St Petersburg to a remote southern province. But the fact of exile did not deter him from tackling the burning themes of his day – the struggle of the masses against the ruling classes, headed by the tsar – or from following the "folk-principles" of Shakespeare's plays, writing for the people in the widest sense. Recalled from exile in the autumn of 1826, he was given a personal audience with the new tsar, Nicholas I. During their long conversation the tsar met the poet's complaints about censorship with a promise that in the future he himself would be Pushkin's censor. He also told the poet of his plans to introduce several pressing reforms from above and, in particular, to prepare the way for liberation of the serfs. Pushkin himself believed that the only possible way of achieving essential reforms was from above, "on the tsar's initiative"; these ideas are explored in the great historical poems *Poltava* (1829) and *The Bronze Horseman* (1837), the latter arguably one of the greatest poems in Russian literature.

After returning from exile, Pushkin found himself in an awkward and invidious position. Government censorship had been replaced by the personal censorship of the tsar, and his personal freedoms were curtailed. Yet it was during this period that his genius came to its fullest flowering. His art acquired new dimensions, and almost every one of the works written between 1829 and 1836 opened a new chapter in the history of Russian literature. During this time he wrote the four so-called "little tragedies" – *The Covetous Knight* (1836), *Mozart and Salieri* (1831), *The Stone Guest* (1839), and *Feast in Time of the Plague* (1832) – the short story "The Queen of Spades" (1834); "A Small House in Kolomna" (1833), a comic poem of everyday lower-class life; and many lyrics in widely differing styles, as well as several critical and polemical articles, rough drafts, and sketches.

Pushkin also exerted a profound influence on other aspects of Russian culture, notably opera, but perhaps his most enduring legacy was his reshaping of the Russian literary language. His writings, by combining the colloquial and Church Slavonic styles, put an end to the considerable controversy that had developed as to which style of the language was best for literary uses. The astonishing simplicity of his language formed the basis of the style of the novelists Ivan Turgenev, Ivan Goncharov, and Leo Tolstoy. To the later classical writers of the nineteenth century, Pushkin, the creator of the Russian literary language, stood as the cornerstone of Russian literature: in Maksim Gorky's words, "the beginning of beginnings".

The first quarter of the nineteenth century had been dominated by Romantic poetry. Vasily Zhukovsky's 1802 translation of Thomas Gray's "Elegy Written in a Country Church Yard" ushered in a vogue for the personal, elegiac mode that was soon amplified in the work of Konstantin Batyushkov, Prince Pyotr Vyazemsky, and the young Pushkin. Although there was a call for civic-oriented poetry in the late 1810s and early 1820s, most of the strongest poets followed Zhukovsky's lyrical path. In the 1820s the mature Pushkin went his own way, producing a series of masterpieces that laid the foundation for his eventual recognition as Russia's national poet.

But despite Pushkin's immense influence, during the 1830s poetry gradually gave way to prose-writing, a shift that coincided with a change in literary institutions. The aristocratic salon, which had been the seedbed for Russian literature, was gradually supplanted by the monthly "thick journals", the editors and critics of which became Russia's tastemakers. Also in the 1830s the first publications appeared by Nikolay Gogol, a comic writer of Ukrainian origin, whose grotesquely hilarious oeuvre includes the story "The Nose" and the play *The Government Inspector* (both 1836), and the epic novel *Dead Souls* (1842). Although Gogol was then known primarily as a satirist, he is now appreciated as one of the founders of the great nineteenth-century tradition of Russian realism and a verbal magician whose works seem akin to the absurdists of the twentieth century. One final burst of poetic energy appeared in the late 1830s in the verse of Mikhail Lermontov, who also wrote *A Hero of Our Time* (1840), the first Russian psychological novel.

In the 1840s the axis of Russian literature shifted decisively from the personal and Romantic to the civic and realistic, a shift presided over by the great Russian literary critic Vissarion Belinsky, who believed that literature should be primarily concerned with current social problems. By the end of the 1840s, Belinsky's ideas had triumphed. Early works of Russian realism include Goncharov's anti-romantic novel *A Common Story* (1847) and Dostoyevsky's *Poor Folk* (1846).

From the 1840s until the turn of the twentieth century, the realist novel dominated Russian literature, and in turn was dominated by three literary giants, Turgenev, Dostoyevsky, and Tolstoy. In the early period the favoured method was the "physiological sketch", which often depicted a typical member of the downtrodden classes. Turgenev's beautifully crafted stories in the collection *A Sportsman's Sketches* (1852) describe the life of Russian serfs as seen through the eyes of a Turgenev-like narrator; in fact, his depiction was so powerful that he was credited with convincing Tsar Alexander II of the

NIKOLAY GOGOL (1809–52)

Ukrainian-born Russian humorist, dramatist, and novelist
Gogol tried acting and worked at minor government jobs in St Petersburg before achieving literary success with *Evenings on a Farm near Dikanka* (1831–2). His pessimism emerged in such stories as "Taras Bulba" (1835) and "Diary of a Madman" (1835). His farcical drama *The Government Inspector* (1836) lampooned a corrupt government bureaucracy. From 1836 to 1846 he lived in Italy. During this time he laid the foundations of nineteenth-century Russian realism with his masterpiece, the novel *Dead Souls* (1842), a satire about serfdom and bureaucratic inequities in which he hoped to castigate abuses and guide his compatriots through laughter, and his story "The Overcoat" (1842). His collected stories (1842) received great acclaim. Soon afterward he came under the influence of a fanatical priest who prompted him to burn the manuscript of the second volume of *Dead Souls*. He died a few days later at the age of 42, perhaps of intentional starvation, on the verge of madness.

need to emancipate the serfs. Turgenev followed *Sketches* with a series of novels, each of which was felt by contemporaries to have captured the essence of Russian society. In addition to his subtle descriptions of peasant life, further novels, such as *Rudin* (1856), *On the Eve* (1860), and *Smoke* (1867), focused on *intelligenty* (members of the intelligentsia) and ideology, and, in his most celebrated work, *Fathers and Sons* (1862), on generational and class differences in Russia. Though Turgenev was the first Russian writer to be widely celebrated in the

West, he was reviled in Russia by the radicals, as well as by Tolstoy and Dostoyevsky, for his dedicated westernism, bland liberalism, aesthetic elegance, and tendency to nostalgia and self-pity.

Dostoyevsky was the second nineteenth-century literary giant. In 1849, at the outset of his career, he was arrested and imprisoned in Siberia for his involvement in a socialist reading group, and he rejoined the literary scene only in the late 1850s. During his imprisonment he experienced a religious conversion, and his novels of the 1860s and 1870s are suffused with messianic Orthodox ideas. Many of his works delve into the psychology of men and women at the edge. In *Notes from the Underground* (1864) the hero argues, in a complex series of paradoxes, against determinism, utopianism, and historical laws. In *Crime and Punishment* (1866), a philosophical and psychological account of a murder, Dostoyevsky examines the tendency of members of the intelligentsia to regard themselves as superior to ordinary people and as beyond traditional morality. *The Possessed* (1872), a novel based on Russian terrorism, is famous as the work that most accurately predicted twentieth-century totalitarianism. In *The Idiot* (1868–9) and *The Brothers Karamazov* (1879–80) Dostoyevsky, who is generally regarded as one of the supreme psychologists in world literature, sought to demonstrate the compatibility of Christianity with the deepest truths of the psyche.

Probably even more than Dostoyevsky, Tolstoy has been praised as being the greatest novelist in world literature. The nineteenth-century English critic and poet Matthew Arnold famously expressed the commonest view in saying that a work by Tolstoy is not a piece of art but a piece of life: his novels read as if life were writing directly, without mediation. Tolstoy's techniques reflect his belief that no theory is adequate to

FYODOR DOSTOYEVSKY (1821–81)

Russian novelist

Dostoyevsky gave up an engineering career early in order to write. In 1849 he was arrested for belonging to a radical discussion group: he was sentenced to be shot, but was reprieved at the last moment and spent four years at hard labour in Siberia, where he developed epilepsy and experienced a deepening of his religious faith. Later he published and wrote for several periodicals while producing his best novels. His novels are concerned especially with faith, suffering, and the meaning of life; they are famous for their psychological depth and insight and their near-prophetic treatment of issues in philosophy and politics. His first, *Poor Folk* (1846), was followed the same year by *The Double*. *The House of the Dead* (1862) is based on his imprisonment and *The Gambler* (1866) on his own gambling addiction. Best-known are the novella *Notes from the Underground* (1864) and the great novels *Crime and Punishment* (1866), *The Idiot* (1869), *The Possessed* (1872), and *The Brothers Karamazov* (1880), which focuses on the problem of evil, the nature of freedom, and the characters' craving for some kind of faith. By the end of his life, Dostoyevsky had been acclaimed one of his country's greatest writers, and his works had a profound influence on twentieth-century literature.

explain the world's complexity, which unfolds by "tiny, tiny alterations" fitting no pattern. He denied the existence of historical laws and insisted that ethics is a matter not of rules but of supreme sensitivity to the particular. "True life", he contended, is lived not at moments of grand crisis but at countless ordinary and prosaic moments, which human beings usually do not notice. All these ideas are illustrated and explicitly expressed in *War and Peace* (1865–9), set in the time of the Napoleonic Wars, and in *Anna Karenina* (1875–7), which applies this prosaic view of life to marriage, the family, and work. *Anna Karenina* also contrasts romantic love, which is based on intense moments of passion and may lead to adultery, with the prosaic love of the family, which is based above all on intimacy.

After completing *Anna Karenina*, Tolstoy underwent a religious crisis, which eventually led him to reject his two great novels, formulate a new religion that he thought of as true Christianity, and cultivate a different type of art. To outline his views, he wrote a number of tracts in the 1890s. His only long novel of this period, *Resurrection* (1899), is a tendentious failure. But he produced brilliant novellas, many of which were published posthumously, including *Father Sergius* (written in 1898), in which he seems to reflect on his own quest for sainthood, and *Hadji-Murad* (written in 1904). *The Death of Ivan Ilyich* (1886), which is often considered the greatest novella in Russian literature, conveys the existential horror of sickness and mortality, while describing civilization as a web of lies designed to distract people from an awareness of death.

Apart from these literary giants, the mid-nineteenth century produced a number of other fine prose writers. Among them are Sergey Aksakov (*The Family Chronicle*, 1856, and *Years of Childhood*, 1858), Aleksandr Herzen (*From the Other Shore*, 1851, and *My Past and Thoughts*, 1861–7), Ivan Goncharov (*Oblomov*, 1859), Nikolay Leskov ("Lady Macbeth of the Mtsensk District", 1865), Mikhail Saltykov

LEO TOLSTOY (1828–1910)

Russian writer, one of the world's greatest novelists

The scion of prominent aristocrats, Tolstoy spent much of his life at his family estate of Yasnaya Polyana. After a somewhat dissolute youth, he served in the army and travelled in Europe before returning home and starting a school for peasant children. He was already known as a brilliant writer for the short stories in *Sevastopol Sketches* (1855–6) and the novel *The Cossacks* (1863) when *War and Peace* (1865–9) established him as Russia's pre-eminent novelist. Set during the Napoleonic Wars, the novel examines the lives of a large group of characters, centring on the partly autobiographical figure of the spiritually questing Pierre. Its structure, with its flawless placement of complex characters in a turbulent historical setting, is regarded as one of the great technical achievements in the history of the western novel. His other great novel, *Anna Karenina* (1875–7), concerns an aristocratic woman who deserts her husband for a lover and the search for meaning by another autobiographical character, Levin.

After the publication of *Anna Karenina* Tolstoy underwent a spiritual crisis and turned to a form of Christian anarchism. Advocating simplicity and non-violence, he devoted himself to social reform. His later works include *The Death of Ivan Ilyich* (1886) and *What Is Art?* (1898), which condemns fashionable aestheticism and celebrates art's moral and religious functions. Tolstoy lived humbly on his great estate, practising a radical asceticism and in constant conflict with his wife. In November 1910, unable to bear his situation any longer, he left his estate incognito. During his flight he contracted pneumonia, and he was dead within a few days.

(*The Golovlyov Family*, 1876), and Vsevolod Garshin ("Artists", 1879). But by the early 1880s the hold of the realist novel was waning. Russian poetry had not played a central role in the literary process since the 1830s, and drama, despite the able work of Aleksandr Ostrovsky (1823–1886), was a marginal literary activity for most writers.

The only major prose writer to emerge in the 1880s and 1890s was Anton Chekhov (1860–1904), one of the greatest short story writers in world literature. Chekhov reinterpreted the short story genre within his essentially bourgeois values, stressing the moral necessity of ordinary virtues such as daily kindness, cleanliness, politeness, work, sobriety, paying one's debts, and avoiding self-pity – a rejection of the intelligentsia's demand for political tendentiousness. In his hundreds of stories and novellas Chekhov – a practising doctor – adopts something of a clinical approach to ordinary life. Meticulous observation and broad sympathy for diverse points of view shape his fiction. In his stories, an overt plot subtly hints at other hidden stories, and so the experience of rereading his fiction often differs substantially from that produced by a first reading. In his greatest stories – including "The Man in a Case" (1898), "The Lady with a Lapdog" (1899), "The Darling" (1899), "In the Ravine" (1900), "The Bishop" (written 1902), and "The Betrothed" (written 1903) – Chekhov manages to attain all the power of his great predecessors

MAKSIM GORKY (1868–1936)

Russian writer

Aleksey Maksimovich Peshkov was born in Nizhny Novgorod. After a childhood of poverty and misery he became a wandering tramp. He assumed the name Gorky, meaning "bitter". His early works offered sympathetic portrayals of the social dregs of Russia: they include the outstanding stories "Chelkash" (1895) and "Twenty-Six Men and a Girl" (1899), and the successful play *The Lower Depths* (1902). For his revolutionary activity, he spent the years 1906–13 abroad as a political exile. His works include the autobiographical trilogy *My Childhood* (1913–14), *In the World* (1915–16), and *My Universities* (1923).

Though initially an open critic of Lenin and the Bolsheviks, after 1919 Gorky cooperated with Lenin's government. He lived in Italy from 1921 to 1928. Upon his return to the USSR, he became the undisputed leader of Soviet writers. When the Union of Soviet Writers was established in 1934, he became its first president and helped establish socialist realism. He died suddenly while under medical treatment, possibly killed on the orders of Joseph Stalin.

in a remarkably compact form. Towards the end of his career, Chekhov also became known for his dramatic work, including such pillars of the world theatrical repertoire as *Uncle Vanya* (1897) and *The Cherry Orchard* (first performed 1904). In these, his belief that life is lived at ordinary moments and that histrionics are a dangerous lie found expression in a major innovation, the undramatic drama – or, as it is sometimes called, the theatre of inaction.

IVAN BUNIN (1870–1953)

Russian poet and novelist

Bunin worked as a journalist and clerk while writing and translating poetry, but he made his name as a short-story writer, with such masterpieces as the title story of *The Gentleman from San Francisco* (1916). His other works include the novella *Mitya's Love* (1925), the collection *Dark Avenues, and Other Stories* (1943), fictional autobiography, memoirs, and books on Leo Tolstoy and Anton Chekhov. He was the first Russian awarded the Nobel Prize for Literature (1933) and is among the best stylists in the language.

Chekhov's heirs in the area of short fiction were Maksim Gorky (later the doyen of Soviet letters), who began his career by writing sympathetic portraits of various social outcasts, and the aristocrat Ivan Bunin, who emigrated after the Russian Revolution of 1917 and received the Nobel Prize for Literature in 1933.

The Twentieth Century

The interplay between art and life, literature and politics, came once more to the fore, sometimes in dramatic and bloody fashion, in the twentieth century. By way of example, the poet Nikolay Gumilyov (first husband of the poet Anna Akhmatova) was executed by the Bolsheviks in 1921; Akhmatova's son Lev was twice imprisoned under Stalin; Osip Mandelshtam, considered by many to be the greatest Russian poet of the twentieth century, died in a Soviet prison camp; and among the millions whose lives were taken during the Stalinist purges (see Chapter 2), were the writers Isaak Babel, Daniil Kharms, and Boris Pilnyak, the peasant poet Nikolay Klyuyev, and the theatre director Vsevolod Meyerhold.

Russian literary history in the twentieth century was characterized by major upheavals. The 1917 Revolution and the Bolshevik coup later in the same year created the first major divide between the imperial and post-revolutionary periods, eventually turning "official" Russian literature into political propaganda for the communist state. Mikhail Gorbachev's ascent to power in 1985 and the collapse of the USSR in 1991 marked the second dramatic break, this time between the post-revolutionary and post-Soviet periods. These breaks were sudden rather than gradual and were the product of political forces external to literary history itself.

However, the cross-over period from the 1890s to 1917 was a time of revival, ushering in a new era of Russian poetry and drama, a "Silver Age" that rivalled, and in some respects surpassed, the Pushkinian "Golden Age". In literature generally this was a time of intellectual ferment, in which mysticism, aestheticism, Neo-Kantianism, eroticism, Marxism, apocalypticism, Nietzscheanism, and other movements combined with each other in improbable ways. The civic orientation that had dominated Russian literature since the 1840s was, for the moment, abandoned. The avant-garde's new cry was "art for art's sake", and the new idols were the French symbolists. The symbolists saw art as a way to approach a higher reality. The first wave of symbolists included Konstantin Balmont, who wrote verse that he left unrevised on principle (he believed in first inspiration); Valery Bryusov, who for years was the leader of the movement; Zinaida Gippius, who wrote decadent, erotic, and religious poetry; and Fyodor Sologub, author

Cathedral of St Basil the Blessed in Red Square, Moscow. Constructed between 1554 and 1560 by Ivan the Terrible as a votive offering for his military victories over the khanates of Kazan and Astrakhan.

Red Square, Moscow. Dating from the late fifteenth century, Red Square (*Krasnaya Ploshchad*) adjoins the Kremlin, Russia's centre of government. It has long been a focal point in the social and political history of Russia and the former Soviet Union. It has had several names, but the present name has been used consistently since the later seventeenth century. The Russian word *krasnaya* (now translated as "red") also means "beautiful".

Catherine the Great (1729–96). German-born empress of Russia who reigned from 1762 and led her country into full participation in the political and cultural life of Europe, carrying on the work begun by Peter the Great. With her ministers she reorganized the administration and law of the Russian Empire and extended Russian territory.

Gallery in the Hermitage Museum, St Petersburg. Founded in 1764 by Catherine the Great, the Hermitage adjoined the Winter Palace and served as a private gallery for the art amassed by the empress. It was opened to the public in 1852. Following the Bolshevik Revolution of 1917, the imperial collections became public property.

Demonstrators gathering in front of the Winter Palace in Petrograd (St Petersburg) in January 1917, shortly before the Russian Revolution.

Monument to the Third International, 1920. The most famous work of Ukrainian artist Vladimir Tatlin (1885–1953), this was one of the first buildings conceived entirely in abstract terms and would have been the world's tallest structure at more than 1,300 feet (396 m) tall. The striking design consisted of a leaning spiral iron framework supporting a glass cylinder, a glass cone, and a glass cube, each of which could be rotated at different speeds. It was never built.

Soviet leader Vladimir Iliych Lenin (1870–1924) addressing a crowd in 1920. Lenin was founder of the Russian Communist Party (Bolsheviks), leader of the Bolshevik Revolution (1917), and the architect and first head (1917–24) of the Soviet state. Lenin was the posthumous source of "Leninism", the doctrine codified and conjoined with Karl Marx's works by Lenin's successors to form Marxism-Leninism, which became the communist worldview.

Joseph Stalin (1879–1953). Secretary-general of the Communist Party of the Soviet Union (1922–53) and premier of the Soviet state (1941–53), Stalin dictatorially ruled the Soviet Union for a quarter of a century and transformed it into a major world power.

Aleksandr Pushkin (1799–1837). Russian poet, novelist, dramatist, and short-story writer, Pushkin has often been considered his country's greatest poet and the founder of modern Russian literature. His masterpiece, the novel in verse *Yevgeny Onegin* (1833), is considered by many to be the first great Russian novel.

Leo Tolstoy (1828–1910). Russian author, a master of realistic fiction, and one of the world's greatest novelists, Tolstoy is best known for his two longest works, *War and Peace* (1865–9) and *Anna Karenina* (1875–7), which are commonly regarded as among the finest novels ever written.

Boris Pasternak (1890–1960) with companion Olga Iwinskaja and their daughter Irina in the late 1950s. Pasternak's novel *Doctor Zhivago* (1957) won the Nobel Prize for Literature in 1958 but aroused so much opposition in the Soviet Union that he declined the honour. An epic of wandering, spiritual isolation and love amid the harshness of the Russian Revolution and its aftermath, the novel became an international bestseller but circulated only in secrecy and translation in his own land.

Aleksandr Solzhenitsyn (1918–2008). Russian novelist and historian who was exiled from the Soviet Union in 1974 following the publication, in Paris, of *The Gulag Archipelago*, a literary-historical record of the vast system of prisons and labour camps that came into being shortly after the Bolsheviks seized power and that underwent an enormous expansion under Stalin.

Yury Gagarin (1934–68). Soviet cosmonaut who in 1961 became the first man to travel into space. His spaceflight brought him immediate worldwide fame; he was awarded the Order of Lenin and given the titles of Hero of the Soviet Union and Pilot Cosmonaut of the Soviet Union.

Mikhail Gorbachev (b. 1931) on a state visit to Poland. General secretary of the Communist Party of the Soviet Union from 1985 to 1991 and president of the Soviet Union in 1990–91. His efforts to democratize his country's political system and decentralize its economy led to the downfall of communism and the breakup of the Soviet Union in 1991. Gorbachev was awarded the Nobel Prize for Peace in 1990.

Military parade in Moscow's Red Square in 1985.

Vladimir Putin (b. 1952). Russian intelligence officer and politician who served as president of Russia (1999–2008) and was also the country's prime minister in 1999 and again from 2008.

of melancholic verse and of a novel about a sadistic, homicidal, paranoid schoolteacher. The second wave was dominated by Andrey Bely, whose novel *St Petersburg* (1913–22) is regarded as the masterpiece of symbolist fiction; Aleksandr Blok, whose best-known work is the poem *The Twelve*, which describes 12 brutal Red Guards who turn out to be unwittingly led by Jesus Christ; and the principal theoretician of the symbolist movement, Vyacheslav Ivanov, who wrote mythic poetry conveying a Neoplatonist philosophy.

The symbolists dominated the literary scene until 1910, when internal dissension led to the movement's collapse. Their beliefs and writings were challenged by two different poetic groupings, the Acmeists and Futurists. The Acmeist school of poetry rejected the mysticism and abstraction of Russian symbolism and demanded concrete representation and precise form and meaning, combined with a broad-ranging erudition (classical antiquity, European history and culture, including art and religion). The Acmeists, whose outstanding members included Nikolay Gumilyov, Anna Akhmatova, and Osip Mandelshtam, were associated with the new St Petersburg journal *Apollon* and the poets of the older generation who stood apart from the dominant symbolist poets of the day. The Futurists, on the other hand, wanted to throw all earlier and most contemporary poetry "from the steamship of modernity" and thus to free poetic discourse from the fetters of tradition. The two most important Futurist poets were Velimir Khlebnikov and Vladimir Mayakovsky. Khlebnikov hoped to find the laws of history through numerology and developed amazingly implausible theories about language and its origins; his verse is characterized by neologisms and "trans-sense" language. Mayakovsky epitomized the spirit of romantic bohemian radicalism. Humour, bravado, and self-pity characterize his inventive long poems.

VLADIMIR MAYAKOVSKY (1893–1930)

Leading poet of the Russian Revolution of 1917 and of the early Soviet period

From his youth repeatedly jailed for subversive activity, Mayakovsky began writing poetry during solitary confinement in 1909. On his release he became the spokesman for Futurism in Russia, and his poetry became conspicuously self-assertive and defiant. As a vigorous spokesman for the Communist Party he produced declamatory works saturated with politics and aimed at mass audiences, including "Ode to Revolution" (1918) and "Left March" (1919), and the drama *Mystery Bouffe* (performed 1921). Disappointed in love, increasingly alienated from Soviet reality, and denied a visa to travel abroad, he committed suicide at the age of 36.

In the years immediately after the 1917 Revolution a brief period of relative openness was enjoyed. Many writers turned to prose, particularly the short story and the novella. Some were inspired by the recent revolution and the subsequent Russian Civil War (1918–20): these included Pilnyak (*The Naked Year*, 1922), Babel (*Red Cavalry*, 1926, a formally chiselled and morally complex cycle of linked stories about a Jewish commissar in a Cossack regiment), and Mikhail Sholokhov, who was awarded the Nobel Prize for Literature in 1965. Others described life in the new Soviet Union with varying degrees of mordant sarcasm: the short stories of Mikhail Zoshchenko, the comic novels of Ilya Ilf and Yevgeny Petrov, and the short novel *Envy* (1927) by Yury Olesha fall into this category. Boris

BORIS PASTERNAK (1890–1960)

Russian poet and prose writer

Pasternak studied music and philosophy and after the Russian Revolution of 1917 worked in the library of the Soviet commissariat of education. His early poetry, though avant-garde, was successful, but in the 1930s a gap widened between his work and officially approved literary modes, and he supported himself by doing translations. The novel *Doctor Zhivago* (1957; film, 1965), an epic of wandering, spiritual isolation, and love amid the harshness of the revolution and its aftermath, was a best-seller in the West but until 1987 circulated only in secrecy in the Soviet Union. Pasternak was awarded the Nobel Prize for Literature in 1958, but he was forced to decline it because of Soviet opposition to his work.

Pasternak, a Futurist poet before the revolution, published a cycle of poems, *My Sister – Life* (1922), and the story "Zhenya Luvers's Childhood" (1918).

The lull in the storm was short-lived, however, and it soon became clear that the Bolshevik seizure of power in 1917 would radically change Russian literature. From the mid-1920s, literature became a tool of state propaganda. Officially approved writing (the only kind that could be published) by and large sank to a sub-literary level. Censorship, imprisonment in labour camps, and mass terror were only part of the problem. Writers were not only forbidden to create works that were dissident, formally complex, or objective (a term of reproach), but they were also expected to fulfil the dictates of the Communist Party to produce propaganda on specific, often rather narrow, themes of current interest to it. Writers

OSIP MANDELSHTAM (1891–1938?)

Russian poet and critic

Osip Mandelshtam was a major Russian poet and literary critic. He was born in Warsaw in 1891 and grew up in St Petersburg. His first poems appeared in the avant-garde journal *Apollon* in 1910. It was partly the apolitical stance of Mandelshtam's poetry, together with its heavy intellectual demands, that led to his estrangement from and eventual denunciation by the official Soviet literary establishment. In 1928 a volume of his collected poetry and a collection of literary criticism appeared: these were his last books published in the Soviet Union during his lifetime.

In May 1934 Mandelshtam was arrested for an epigram he had written on Joseph Stalin and was sent into exile. In 1938, the year after his return to Moscow, he was arrested again. In a letter to his wife, Nadezhda, that autumn, he reported that he was ill in a transit camp near Vladivostok. Nothing further was ever heard from him. The Soviet authorities officially gave his death date as 27 December 1938, although he was also reported by government sources to have died "at the beginning of 1939".

were called upon to be "engineers of human souls" helping to produce "the new Soviet man".

The decade beginning with Stalin's ascendancy in the late 1920s was one of unprecedented repression. Censorship became much stricter, and many of the best writers were silenced. In 1932 all independent literary groupings were dissolved and replaced by an institution that had no counterpart in the West,

ANNA AKHMATOVA (1889–1966)

Russian poet

The Russian poet Anna Akhmatova was recognized at her death as the greatest woman poet in Russian literature. Her brief, finely chiselled lyrics brought her fame at the outset of her career, but from the 1920s she was forced into years of silence, emerging again into public life only from the 1940s; publication of much of her work had to wait until the 1960s, and full recognition, at least on an international scale, until the 1980s.

Akhmatova was born in 1889 near Odessa, Ukraine. At 21 she joined the Acmeists, adding to the school her own stamp of elegant colloquialism and the psychological sophistication of a young cosmopolitan woman. During the Soviet period her former husband, Nikolay Gumilyov, was executed, and her son, Lev, and her third husband, Nikolay Punin, were arrested for political deviance in 1935. No volume of her poetry appeared in the Soviet Union until 1940. Her public life became limited to her studies of Pushkin.

In the years following Stalin's death Akhmatova was slowly, if ambivalently, rehabilitated. A slender volume of her poetry, including some of her translations, was published in 1958. What is perhaps her masterpiece, "Poem without a Hero", on which she worked from 1940 to 1962, was not published in the Soviet Union until 1976. She died, near Moscow, in 1966.

MARINA TSVETAYEVA (1892–1941)

Russian poet

After spending most of her youth in Moscow, Tsvetayeva began studies at the Sorbonne in Paris at the age of 16. She published her first poetry collection in 1910. Her verses on the Russian Revolution glorify the anti-Bolshevik resistance, of which her husband was a part. She lived abroad from 1922 to 1939, mostly in Paris, writing varied works including poetry that increasingly reflected nostalgia for her homeland. Many of her best and most typical poetic qualities are displayed in the long verse fairy tale *Tsar-devitsa* (1922; "Tsar-Maiden"). Separated from her husband and daughter and isolated from friends after the evacuation of Moscow, she committed suicide. Though little-known outside Russia, she is considered one of the finest twentieth-century poets in Russian.

the Union of Soviet Writers, which became the state's instrument of control over literature; expulsion from it meant literary death. In 1934 socialist realism was proclaimed the only acceptable form of writing. Henceforth, literature was to be governed by a series of official directives regarding details of style and content in order to ensure that each work offered a "truthful" depiction "of reality in its revolutionary development". Literature had to be "party-minded" and "typical" (that is, avoiding unpleasant, hence "atypical", aspects of Soviet reality), while showing the triumph of fully "positive heroes". Only a few of the works produced in this style have retained some literary interest, notably Fyodor Gladkov's *Cement* (1925), Nikolay Ostrovsky's *How the Steel Was Tempered* (1932–4), and Valentin Katayev's

MIKHAIL SHOLOKHOV (1905–84)

Russian novelist

A native of the Don River region, Sholokhov served in the Red Army and joined the Communist Party in 1932. He is best known for the huge novel *The Quiet Don*, translated in two parts as *And Quiet Flows the Don* (1934) and *The Don Flows Home to the Sea* (1940). A portrayal of the struggle between the Cossacks and Bolsheviks, it was heralded in the Soviet Union as a powerful example of socialist realism and became the most widely read novel in Russia. It became controversial when Aleksandr Solzhenitsyn and others alleged that it was plagiarized from the Cossack writer Fyodor Kryukov (d. 1920). Sholokhov's later novels include *Virgin Soil Upturned* (1932–60). He received the Nobel Prize for Literature in 1965.

Time, Forward! (1932). The moral nadir of Soviet literature was reached in a collaborative volume, *Belomor: An Account of the Construction of the New Canal between the White Sea and the Baltic Sea* (1934). With Gorky as an editor and 34 contributors, the volume praised a project (and the secret police who directed it) that used convict labour and cost tens of thousands of lives.

In addition to official Soviet Russian literature, two kinds of unofficial literature existed. First, a tradition of emigre literature, containing some of the best works of the century, continued until the fall of the Soviet Union. Writing in Russian flourished in communities of anti-communist exiles in Germany, France, Italy, and the United States, with writers as various as the novelists Vladimir Nabokov and Yevgeny

Zamyatin, and the theologian-philosophers Vladimir Niko-layevich Lossky, Sergey Bulgakov, and Nikolay Berdyayev. Second, unofficial literature written within the Soviet Union came to include works circulated illegally in typewritten copies (*samizdat*), works smuggled abroad for publication (*tamiz-dat*), and works written "for the drawer" or not published until decades after they were written ("delayed" literature). Isolation from the West and from its own literary past was another feature of Russian literature at this time. Whereas pre-revolutionary writers had been intensely aware of western trends, for much of the Soviet period access to western literary movements was severely restricted, as was foreign travel. Access to pre-revolutionary Russian writing was also inter-mittent. As a result, Russians periodically had to change their sense of the past, as did western scholars when "delayed" works became known.

From a literary point of view, unofficial literature clearly surpasses official literature. Of Russia's five winners of the Nobel Prize for Literature during the Soviet period, Bunin emigrated after the revolution, Pasternak had his novel *Doctor Zhivago* (1957) published abroad, Solzhenitsyn had most of his works published abroad and was expelled from the Soviet Union, and Joseph Brodsky published all his collections of verse abroad and was forced to emigrate in 1972. Only Mikhail Sholokhov was clearly an official Soviet writer. Emi-gres also included the poets Vladislav Khodasevich and Georgy Ivanov. Marina Tsvetayeva, regarded as one of the great poets of the twentieth century, eventually returned to Russia, where she committed suicide. Nabokov, who later wrote in English, published nine novels in Russian, including *The Gift* (published serially 1937–8) and *Invitation to a Beheading* (1938). And a modern literary genre, the dystopia,

MIKHAIL BULGAKOV (1891–1940)

Playwright, novelist, and short-story writer

Bulgakov was born in Kiev and trained as a doctor, but gave up medicine to write. His first major work was the novel *The White Guard*, serialized in 1925 but never published in book form. A realistic and sympathetic portrayal of the motives and behaviour of a group of anti-Bolshevik White officers during the civil war, it was met by a storm of official criticism for its lack of a communist hero. Bulgakov wrote and staged many popular plays in the years 1925–9, including dramatizations of his own novels, but by 1930 his trenchant criticism of Soviet mores had caused him to be effectively prohibited from publishing. His works, known for their scathing humour, include the novella *The Heart of a Dog* (written 1925), a satire on pseudoscience that did not appear openly in the Soviet Union until 1987, and the dazzling fantasy *The Master and Margarita*, not published in unexpurgated form until 1973.

was invented by Zamyatin in his novel *We* (1924), published only abroad, which describes a future socialist society that has turned out to be not perfect but inhuman.

The work now generally regarded as the finest post-revolutionary novel, Mikhail Bulgakov's grotesquely funny *The Master and Margarita*, was written "for the drawer" (1928–40); it appeared (expurgated) in Russia only in 1966–7 and unexpurgated in 1973. It tells of the Devil and his retinue visiting Soviet Russia, where they play practical jokes of metaphysical and political significance. A novel within the novel gives the "true" version of Christ's encounter with Pilate. The result is a joyful philosophical comedy of enormous profundity. Other masterpieces that did not fit the canons of socialist realism and were not published until many years later include the dark pictures of rural and semi-urban Russia by Andrey Platonov (1899–1951), *The Foundation Pit* (1973) and *Chevengur* (1972).

The need to rally support in the Second World War brought a loosening of Communist Party control. The war itself created the opportunity for a large "second wave" of emigration, thus feeding emigre literature. However, the period from 1946 until the death of Stalin in 1953 was one of severe repression known as the *Zhdanovshchina*, or Zhdanovism, after Andrey Zhdanov, a Politburo member and the director of Stalin's programme of cultural tyranny. During this campaign, attacks on "rootless cosmopolitans" involved anti-Semitism and the rejection of all foreign influences on Russian literature. The Soviet practice of *samokritika* (public denunciation of one's own work) was frequent.

The years from the death of Stalin until the fall of Nikita Khrushchev in 1964 saw several "thaws" separated by "freezes". In 1956 Khrushchev delivered a famous speech denouncing certain Stalinist crimes. From that time on, it was possible for Russians to perceive orthodox communists as people of the past and to regard dissidents not as holdovers from before the revolution but as progressives. New writers and trends appeared in the 1950s and early 1960s. Vibrant young poets such as Brodsky, Yevgeny Yevtushenko, and Andrey Voznesensky exerted a significant influence, and Aleksandr Solzhenitsyn emerged from a Soviet prison camp (*Gulag*) and shocked the country and the world in 1962 with details of his brutal experiences in *One Day in the Life of Ivan*

Denisovich. "Youth" prose on the model of American writer J. D. Salinger appeared as well, particularly in the work of Vasily Aksyonov and Vladimir Voynovich.

By the late 1960s, however, most of these writers had again been silenced. The harsher years under Leonid Brezhnev following Khrushchev's fall opened with the arrest, trial, and imprisonment of two writers, Andrey Sinyavsky (whose pseudonym was Abram Terts) and Yuly Daniel (pseudonym Nikolay Arzhak), for publishing "anti-Soviet propaganda" abroad. In the years that followed, well-known writers were arrested or, in one way or another, expelled from the Soviet Union, thus generating the third wave of emigre literature. Among those who found themselves in the West were Brodsky, Sinyavsky, Solzhenitsyn, Aksyonov, and Voynovich.

That trend in Russian literature towards speaking the truth about moral and political issues was exemplified in the work and life of Solzhenitsyn. Arrested initially for writing a letter in which he criticized Joseph Stalin, Solzhenitsyn spent eight years in prisons and labour camps, followed by three more years in enforced exile. Rehabilitated in 1956, he was allowed to settle in Ryazan, in central Russia, where he became a mathematics teacher and began to write. Encouraged by the loosening of government restraints on cultural life, Solzhenitsyn submitted his short novel *One Day in the Life of Ivan Denisovich* (1962) to the leading Soviet literary periodical, *Novy Mir* ("New World"). Based on Solzhenitsyn's own experiences, *Ivan Denisovich* describes a typical day in the life of an inmate of a forced-labour camp during the Stalin era. The impression made on the public by the book's simple, direct language and by the obvious authority with which it treated the daily struggles and material hardships of camp life was magnified by its being one of the first Soviet literary works of the post-Stalin era to directly describe such a life. The book produced a political sensation both abroad and in the Soviet Union, where it inspired a number of other writers to produce accounts of their imprisonment under Stalin's regime. Interestingly, Khrushchev personally saw to its publication as part of his de-Stalinization campaign.

Solzhenitsyn's period of official favour proved to be short-lived, however. Ideological strictures on cultural activity in the Soviet Union tightened with Khrushchev's fall from power in 1964, and Solzhenitsyn met first with increasing criticism and then with overt harassment from the authorities when he emerged as an eloquent opponent of repressive government policies. Denied the option of official publication, he resorted to *samizdat* literature and publication abroad – and it was this that secured his international literary reputation. Probably his most celebrated work was *The Gulag Archipelago*, published in Paris in 1973 after a copy of the manuscript had been seized in the Soviet Union by the KGB. Various sections of the work describe the arrest, interrogation, conviction, transportation, and imprisonment of the *Gulag*'s victims as practised by the Soviet authorities over four decades. This work, arguably the greatest work of Soviet prose, narrates the history of the Soviet camp system with controlled fury and in an ironic mode reminiscent of the eighteenth-century English historian Edward Gibbon. It is all the more remarkable in that much of the raw material for the book was committed to memory during Solzhenitsyn's imprisonment.

Inevitably, the Soviet press immediately attacked the work and, despite the intense interest in his fate that was shown in the West, Solzhenitsyn was arrested and charged with treason on February 12, 1974. On the following day he was exiled from the Soviet Union. In December he took possession of his

Nobel Prize and later settled in the United States; he returned to Russia from exile only in 1994.

Practically the only valuable writing published between the late 1960s and early 1980s came from the "village prose" writers, who treated the clash of rural traditions with modern life in a realistic idiom: the most notable members of this group are the novelist Valentin Rasputin and the short-story writer Vasily Shukshin. The morally complex fiction of Yury Trifonov, staged in the urban setting (*The House on the Embankment*, 1976), stands somewhat apart from the works of Rasputin and Shukshin that praise Russian rural simplicity. Nevertheless, as with the 1930s and 1940s, the most important literature of this period was first published outside the Soviet Union. Notable writers include Varlam Shalamov, whose exquisitely artistic stories chronicled the horrors of the prison camps; Sinyavsky, whose complex novel *Goodnight!* appeared in Europe in 1984, long after he had been forced to leave the Soviet Union; and Venedikt Yerofeyev, whose grotesque latter-day picaresque *Moscow-Petushki* – published in a clandestine edition in 1968 – is a minor classic. Some of the best work published in the 1980s was in poetry, including the work of conceptualists such as Dmitry Prigov and the meta-metaphoric poetry of Aleksey Parshchikov, Olga Sedakova, Ilya Kutik, and others.

The effects on literature of the collapse of the Soviet Union were enormous. The period of *glasnost* under Gorbachev and the subsequent collapse of the USSR led first to a dramatic easing and then to the abolition of censorship. Citizenship was restored to emigre writers, and Solzhenitsyn returned to Russia. *Doctor Zhivago* and *We* were published in Russia, as were the works of Nabokov, Solzhenitsyn, Voynovich, and many others. The divisions between Soviet and emigre and between official and unofficial literature came to an end. Private foundations began awarding annual literary prizes, such as the Russian Booker Prize and the Little Booker Prize. The so-called Anti-Booker Prize – its name, a protest against the British origins of the Booker Prize, was selected to emphasize that it was a Russian award for Russian writers – was first presented in 1995 by the newspaper *Nezavisimaya Gazeta*.

In the 1990s Russians experienced the heady feeling that came with absorbing, at great speed, large parts of their literary tradition that had been suppressed, and with having free access to western literary movements. A Russian form of postmodernism, fascinated with a pastiche of citations, arose, along with various forms of radical experimentalism. During this period, readers and writers sought to understand the past, both literary and historical, and to comprehend the chaotic, threatening, and very different present.

7

MUSIC

The story of music in modern Russia is in certain recurrent aspects unique in the history of western music. These aspects can be summarized as: the geographical position of Russia, which means that the country's music is a product of both western and eastern root cultures and material; the absence of sophisticated home-grown music prior to the latter half of the nineteenth century, to be later sapped by the 1917 Revolution and a continuing pattern of emigration; the fact that the politics of the twentieth century swept away the upper middle classes and the aristocracy, and with them the pursuit of music as an amateur activity by composers of outstanding technical ability; the almost complete absence in Russia of the breaking down of traditional compositional methods and sounds that took place elsewhere during the twentieth century; the effects of the active state control of culture; the indirect political power of popular music culture; the phenomenon of a Russian artist's creativity and musical personality being weakened when the artist leaves Russia as an emigre; an innate Russian conservatism and links with tradition that predisposed twentieth-century music to continue to incorporate many characteristics of nineteenth-century music; the effect of Orthodox Church music; the unconscious rapport between composers and the people of Russia, and the composers' natural ability to speak to the heart of the masses; and Russian mysticism.

The Nineteenth Century

To understand music in modern Russia, one has first to start with the nineteenth century. There was little sophisticated secular music on a western model, especially home grown, prior to the blossoming of musical nationalism in the latter half of the nineteenth century and the extraordinary outburst of creativity at the turn of the century. Although in the eighteenth century the imperial court and some aristocratic houses imported Italian opera troupes and foreign *maestri di cappella* ("choirmasters"), the first Russian composer to gain international renown was Mikhail Glinka, a leisured aristocrat who mastered his craft in Milan and Berlin. His patriotic *A Life for the Tsar* (1836) and his Pushkin-inspired *Ruslan and Lyudmila* (1842) are the oldest Russian operas that remain in the standard repertoire.

Like Glinka, many of Russia's early composers came from the upper middle classes or the aristocracy and were essentially self-taught musical amateurs. Modest Mussorgsky (1838–1881), for example, worked in the civil service; Aleksandr Borodin (1833–1887), son of a Georgian prince, was as famous in his day for his work as a chemist as for his music; and Nikolay Rimsky-Korsakov (1844–1908) began his career in the navy. However, by the second half of the nineteenth

ALEKSANDR BORODIN (1833–87)

Russian composer

From 1862 Borodin took lessons from Mily Balakirev; fired by nationalist sentiment, the two men became the core of the group of Russian composers known as The Five. A professor of chemistry for much of his life, he left a small compositional output, which includes the orchestral suite *In the Steppes of Central Asia* (1880), two string quartets, and three symphonies, the second of which has remained highly popular. His opera *Prince Igor* – which contains the often-heard "Polovtsian Dances" – was left unfinished after 18 years of intermittent work.

century an active and institutionalized musical life was in place, thanks mainly to the efforts of the composer and piano virtuoso Anton Rubinstein, who, with royal patronage, founded in St Petersburg Russia's first regular professional orchestra (in 1859) and conservatory of music (in 1862). Both became models that were quickly imitated in other urban centres.

One of the first graduates of the St Petersburg Conservatory, Pyotr Ilyich Tchaikovsky (1840–93), steered an unlikely path between Russian nationalist tendencies and the cosmopolitan stance encouraged by his conservatory training. He was both a Russian nationalist and a westernizer of polished technical skill. Through his style and artistic creed he establishes an immediate rapport with the audience. In the words of the twentieth-century composer Igor Stravinsky, "Tchaikovsky drew unconsciously from the true, popular sources of our race," thus demonstrating the ability of Russian composers to identify with the spirit of the peoples of Russia.

PYOTR TCHAIKOVSKY (1840–93)

Russian composer

Sensitive and interested in music from his early childhood, Tchaikovsky turned to serious composition at the age of 14. In 1862 he began studying at the new St Petersburg Conservatory; from 1866 he taught at the Moscow Conservatory. His *Piano Concerto No. 1* (1875) was premiered in Boston and became immensely popular. He wrote his first ballet, *Swan Lake* (first performed 1877), on commission from the Bolshoi Ballet. In 1877 he received a commission from the wealthy Nadezhda von Meck (1831–94), who became his patron and long-time correspondent. The opera *Yevgeny Onegin* (1878) soon followed.

Though homosexual, Tchaikovsky married briefly; after three disastrous months of marriage, he attempted suicide. His composition was overshadowed by his personal crisis for years. His second ballet, *Sleeping Beauty* (1889), was followed by the opera *The Queen of Spades* (1890) and the great ballet *The Nutcracker* (1892). The *Pathétique Symphony* (1893) premiered four days before his death from cholera; claims that he was forced to commit suicide by noblemen outraged by his sexual liaisons are unfounded. He revolutionized the ballet genre by transforming it from a grand decorative gesture into a staged musical drama. His music has always had great popular appeal because of its tuneful, poignant melodies, impressive harmonies, and colourful, picturesque orchestration.

Mussorgsky – like the writer Aleksandr Pushkin – learned about Russian fairy tales from his nurse. Significantly, in 1866 Mussorgsky achieved artistic maturity with a series of remarkable songs about ordinary people such as "Darling Savishna", "Hopak", and "The Seminarist", which, along with his later songs, many to his own texts, describe scenes of Russian life with great vividness and insight, and realistically reproduce the inflections of the spoken Russian language. Another work dating from this time is the symphonic poem *Night on a Bare Mountain* (1867). In 1868 Mussorgsky reached the height of his conceptual powers in composition with the first song of his incomparable cycle *The Nursery* and a setting of the first few scenes of Nikolay Gogol's *The Marriage*. In 1869 he began his great work, the opera *Boris Godunov*, which was based on the drama of Pushkin.

Mussorgsky was counted among The Five, a group of composers who adopted a deliberately nationalist flavour; his colleagues were Borodin, Rimsky-Korsakov, Mily Balakirev, and César Cui. The name arose after Rimsky-Korsakov's performance of Slavonic music conducted by Balakirev in St Petersburg on May 24, 1867. In reviewing the concert, the critic Vladimir Stasov proudly proclaimed that henceforth Russia, too, had its own "mighty little heap" of native composers. The name caught on quickly and found its way into music history books. The Five were united in their aim to assert the musical independence of Russia from the West.

Rimsky-Korsakov held a number of influential posts: from 1874 to 1881 he was director of the Free Music School in St Petersburg; he served as conductor of concerts at the court chapel from 1883 to 1894; and he was chief conductor of the Russian symphony concerts between 1886 and 1900. In 1889 he led concerts of Russian music at the Paris World

Exposition, and in the spring of 1907 he conducted in Paris two historic Russian concerts in connection with Sergey Diaghilev's Ballets Russes. Rimsky-Korsakov can be described as nationalistic in several senses. First, he rendered an inestimable service to Russian music as the de facto editor and head of a unique publishing enterprise financed by the Russian industrialist M. P. Belyayev and dedicated exclusively to the publication of music by Russian composers. Second, with two exceptions, the subjects of his operas are taken from Russian or other Slavic fairy tales, literature, and history. These include *Snow Maiden* (1882), *Sadko*, *The Tsar's Bride* (1899), *The Tale of Tsar Saltan*, *The Legend of the Invisible City of Kitezh and the Maiden Fevroniya*, and *Le Coq d'or* (1909). And finally, in his superbly descriptive and masterful orchestration and sensuous melodies evoking mood, colour, and place, he demonstrates that Russia, in character, is essentially an oriental county.

The Early Twentieth Century

The early years of the last century saw the emergence of three major Russian composers: Aleksandr Scriabin (1871–1915), Sergey Rachmaninov (1873–1943), and Igor Stravinsky (1882–1971). The music of all three reveals some enduring features of nineteenth-century Russian music, as well as some of the themes that were to become prominent later in the twentieth century.

Scriabin, the supreme exponent of Russian mysticism, entered the Moscow Conservatory in 1888, where he studied the piano and composition; he later taught at the conservatory but from 1903 devoted himself entirely to composition and in

1904 settled in Switzerland. After 1900 he was much pre-occupied with mystical philosophy, and his Symphony No. 1, composed in that year, has a choral finale, to his own words, glorifying art as a form of religion. Ideas stemming from the theosophical movement, a blend of western occultism and eastern mysticism, similarly provided the basis of the orchestral *Poem of Ecstasy* (1908) and *Prometheus* (1911), which called for the projection of colours onto a screen during the performance. From 1906 to 1907 Scriabin toured the United States, where he gave concerts with V. I. Safonov and the conductor Modest Altschuler, and in 1908 he frequented theosophical circles in Brussels. In 1909 he returned to Russia. By then he was no longer thinking in terms of music alone; he was looking forward to an all-embracing "Mystery". This work was planned to open with a "liturgical act" in which music, poetry, dancing, colours, and scents were to unite to induce in the worshippers a "supreme, final ecstasy". He wrote the poem of the "Preliminary Action" of the "Mystery", but left only sketches for the music.

Scriabin's reputation stems from his grandiose symphonies and his sensitive, exquisitely polished piano music. His piano works include ten sonatas, an early concerto, and many preludes and other short pieces. As his thought became more and more mystical, egocentric, and ingrown, his harmonic style became ever less generally intelligible. Meaningful analysis of his work only began appearing in the 1960s, and yet his music had always attracted a devoted following among modernists.

Rachmaninov's music, although written mostly in the twentieth century, remains firmly entrenched in the nineteenth-century musical idiom. He was, in effect, the final expression of the tradition embodied by Tchaikovsky, a melodist of

Romantic dimensions still writing in an era of explosive change and experimentation. At the time of the Russian Revolution of 1905, Rachmaninov was a conductor at the Bolshoi Theatre. Although more of an observer than someone politically involved in the revolution, he also emigrated, with his family, in November 1906, to live in Dresden. There he wrote three of his major scores: the Symphony No. 2 in E Minor (1907), the symphonic poem *The Isle of the Dead* (1909), and the Piano Concerto No. 3 in D Minor (1909). In 1909 he made his first concert tour of the United States, highlighting his much-acclaimed pianistic debut in November of that year with the New York Symphony. In Philadelphia and Chicago he appeared with equal success in the role of conductor, interpreting his own symphonic compositions. Of these, the Symphony No. 2 is the most significant: it is a work of deep emotion and haunting thematic material. While touring, he was invited to become permanent conductor of the Boston Symphony, but he declined the offer and returned to Russia in February 1910.

The one notable composition of Rachmaninov's second period of residence in Moscow was his choral symphony *The Bells* (1913), based on Konstantin Balmont's Russian translation of the poem by Edgar Allan Poe. This work displays considerable ingenuity in the coupling of choral and orchestral resources to produce striking imitative and textural effects, a hallmark of many later Russian composers, stamped by the influence of the Orthodox Church's choral tradition.

After the Russian Revolution of 1917, Rachmaninov went into his second self-imposed exile, dividing his time between Switzerland and the United States. For the next 25 years he spent most of his time in an English-speaking country. But he missed Russia and the Russian people – the sounding board for his music, as he said. And this alienation had a devastating effect on his formerly prolific creative ability. He produced little of real originality but rewrote some of his earlier work. Indeed, he devoted himself almost entirely to giving concerts in the United States and Europe, a field in which he had few peers.

Stravinsky, a pupil of Rimsky-Korsakov, was catapulted to early fame through his association with Diaghilev, for whose Ballets Russes (see Chapter 9) he composed a trio of sensational works that had their premieres in Paris: *The Firebird* (1910), *Petrushka* (1911), and *The Rite of Spring* (1913). The first performance of *The Rite of Spring* at the Théâtre des Champs-Élysées on May 29, 1913, provoked one of the most famous first-night riots in the history of musical theatre. This highly original composition, with its shifting and audacious rhythms and its unresolved dissonances, was an early modernist landmark. From this point on, Stravinsky was known as "the composer of *The Rite of Spring*" and the destructive modernist par excellence. But while Stravinsky may have felt daringly avant-garde to his contemporaries, in effect these works of his for Diaghilev had not lost touch with mainstream Russian tradition.

Stravinsky's success with the Ballet Russes uprooted him from St Petersburg. He first took his family to France, then spent most of the war in Switzerland, but it was the Russian Revolution of October 1917 that finally extinguished any hope he may have had of returning to his native land. (Having returned to France in 1920, he took French citizenship in 1934; in 1940 he settled in California, and in 1945 he became a US citizen.)

Immediately after the First World War he continued to explore Russian folk idioms, notably in *The Wedding*, a ballet cantata based on the texts of Russian village wedding songs, and the "farmyard burlesque" *Renard* (1916); but his voluntary exile from Russia gradually prompted him to reconsider his aesthetic stance. The result was an important change in his music: he abandoned the Russian features of his early style and instead adopted a neoclassical idiom. His works of the next 30 years usually take some point of reference in past European music – a particular composer's work or the baroque or some other historical style – as a starting point for a highly personal and unorthodox treatment that nevertheless seems to depend for its full effect on the listener's experience of the historical model from which Stravinsky borrowed.

Having lost his property in Russia during the revolution, Stravinsky was compelled to earn his living as a performer, and many of the works he composed during the 1920s and 1930s were written for his own use as a concert pianist and conductor. His instrumental works of the early 1920s include the Octet for Wind Instruments (1923), Concerto for Piano and Wind Instruments (1924), Piano Sonata (1924), and the *Serenade* in A for piano (1925). These pieces combine a neoclassical approach to style with what seems a self-conscious severity of line and texture. Though the dry urbanity of this approach is softened in such later instrumental pieces as the Violin Concerto in D Major (1931), Concerto for Two Solo Pianos (1932–5), and the Concerto in E-flat (or *Dumbarton Oaks* concerto) for 16 wind instruments (1938), a certain cool detachment persists. Once Stravinsky left Russia and gained international recognition, he became a musical chameleon, indulging in the pluralism of styles so fashionable in the twentieth century outside Russia. It is not possible to decide how far Stravinsky led and created a number of musical fashions or how far he shrewdly anticipated fashions already in the making. But, again like several other Russian emigres, once having left Russia he seems to have largely lost his Russianness. This trait was reflected, but with even greater originality, in the latter half of the twentieth century by Alfred Schnittke (see below).

But, especially after his religious conversion in 1926, the mystical strain in Russian art can again be seen in Stravinsky's work. A religious theme can be detected in such major works as the operatic oratorio *Oedipus Rex* (1927), which uses a libretto in Latin, and the cantata *Symphony of Psalms* (1930), an overtly sacred work that is based on biblical texts. Religious feeling is also evident in the ballets *Apollon musagète* (1928) and *Persephone* (1934), and the Russian element in Stravinsky's music occasionally re-emerged during this period: the ballet *The Fairy's Kiss* (1928) is based on music by Tchaikovsky, and the *Symphony of Psalms* has some of the antique austerity of Russian Orthodox chant, despite its Latin text.

The Mid-Twentieth Century: Tradition, Innovation, and Politics

The traditional aspect of Russian music was consciously fostered and promoted by the Soviet regime, beginning from the political clampdown on culture in the late 1920s and coming to a head during the following decade in Joseph Stalin's insistence on so-called socialist realism in musical style and content – that music should be understandable by and appeal directly to the so-called masses, that it should be upbeat and cheering in its effect, and that it should celebrate the wonders of modern Russia. This meant in practice that composers were afraid, except in closet composition, to pursue the new avenues opened up elsewhere in Europe and America, or to allow themselves to be part of the revolution in established musical methodology; but, at the same time, it made them pursue and use existing traditional elements, elements already in their blood.

The effects of political control were both good and bad. The demise of the aristocracy presented the socialist regime with the challenge of creating a new audience. This the politicians turned to their favour, and the development of orchestras, conservatories, local schools of music, ballet companies, and other aspects of the performing arts – as in sport – offered an outlet for and an encouragement of the creative spirit and energies that might otherwise have sought other outlets; they created a sense of pride, and at the same time offered a sort of bread and circuses syndrome, an alternative world for the governed to enter into as an escape from their surrounding realities.

Once the socialist state had been structured and established, it is significant that, unlike so many western governments, the country's leaders realized the importance of the arts as a method of channelling the creativity of the governed classes, of creating social cohesion, and as a tool of cultural imperialism. One positive feature of state control was that performers were encouraged to follow the strictest disciplinary regimes and were offered the highest quality of technical teaching in the conservatories. Once established, the best artists could be assured of a high level of material security provided by the state. Among the great twentieth-century performers to emerge from this training were David Oistrakh, the world-renowned Soviet violin virtuoso acclaimed for his exceptional technique and tone production; Mstislav Rostropovich, conductor, pianist, and one of the greatest cellists of the twentieth century; Vladimir Horowitz, Russian-born American virtuoso pianist in the Romantic tradition, celebrated for his flawless technique and an almost orchestral quality of tone; violinist Gidon Kremer; pianists Svyatoslav Richter and Emil Gilels; and singer Galina Vishnevskaya.

On the other hand, the individuality of artistic creation was sapped by the developing political agenda. Composers in particular were not free to express themselves or their response to life around them, and in the earlier part of the century, not a few emigrated, while there was still a chance to get out. Even later, some performers made a break to the West, both in search of wider opportunities and acknowledging their responsibility as iconic figures to protest against the political regime. Among these was Rostropovich – who announced his decision not to return to Russia from a tour overseas in 1975 and was deprived of citizenship in 1978, a ruling reversed in 1990 – and Dmitry Shostakovich's son, Maxim. From the mid-1980s, when Mikhail Gorbachev's reform policies eased restrictions on Soviet artists, many of Russia's emigres, such as Rostropovich and Horowitz, made triumphant returns.

Sergey Prokofiev, Shostakovich, and Aram Khachaturian each reacted in differing ways to socialist strictures, but all three composers chose to remain in the Soviet Union.

The life and work of Prokofiev (1891–1953) nicely illustrate some of the themes already touched on – the stimulus and freedom of exile abroad combined with an almost mystical longing for the home country; the balance of traditional Russian and cosmopolitan musical elements; and an intimate relationship with the politics of his day.

Prokofiev initially welcomed the 1917 Revolution as a harbinger of social and national renewal, and his output in that year was prolific: he composed two sonatas, the Violin

Concerto No. 1 in D Major, the *Classical Symphony*, and the choral work *Seven, They Are Seven*; he began the magnificent Piano Concerto No. 3 in C Major; and he planned a new opera, *The Love for Three Oranges*. Stranded in the Caucasus by the civil war, he eventually decided to leave Russia and spent the next decade touring Japan, the United States, and western Europe, performing and writing. While living abroad Prokofiev was a modernist like Stravinsky, avidly seeking musical innovation.

But although Prokofiev enjoyed material well-being, success with the public, and contact with outstanding figures of western culture, in 1932 he returned to Russia for good. As the 1930s developed he gradually adapted to the new conditions and became one of the leading figures of Soviet culture, adopting a more conservative, accessible idiom in conformity with Soviet expectations. The outbreak of the Second World War sharpened Prokofiev's national and patriotic feelings. Regardless of the difficulties of the war years, he composed with remarkable assiduity, even when the evacuation of Moscow in 1941 made it necessary for him to move from one place to another until he was able to return in 1944. The crowning works of his Soviet period were the ballet *Romeo and Juliet* (1935–6), the cantata *Aleksandr Nevsky* (1939; adapted from the music that he had written for Sergey Eisenstein's film of the same name), and the operatic interpretation (1942) of Tolstoy's classic novel *War and Peace*. The realistic and epical traits of his art became more clearly defined at this time, and the synthesis of traditional tonal and melodic means with the stylistic innovations of twentieth-century music was more fully realized.

But Prokofiev's relationship with the authorities was not always easy, despite his organizational work for the

Composers' Union: in 1948, along with other Soviet composers, he was censured by the Central Committee of the Soviet
Communist Party for "formalism". After his death in 1953,
however, his popularity rose once again, and in 1957 he was
posthumously awarded the Soviet Union's highest honour, the
Lenin Prize, for his Symphony No. 7.

Dmitry Shostakovich (1906–1975) is renowned for his 15
symphonies, numerous chamber works, and concerti, many
of them written under the pressures of government-imposed
standards of Soviet art. Some uphold the Soviet view of the
composer as a sincere communist; others view him as a closet
dissident. As in literature and the other arts, the cultural
climate in the mid-1920s in the Soviet Union was remarkably
free, and so Shostakovich was able to write compositions
such as Symphony No. 1, of which the stylistic roots and
influences were numerous. He continued to openly experiment with avant-garde trends until the late 1920s, when
Joseph Stalin fastened an iron hand on Soviet culture. In
music a direct and popular style was demanded. Avant-garde
music and jazz were officially banned in 1932, and for a
while even the stylistically unproblematic Tchaikovsky was
out of favour, owing to his quasi-official status in tsarist
Russia. Shostakovich did not experience immediate official
displeasure, but when it came it was devastating. It has been
said that Stalin's anger at what he heard when he attended a
performance of *Lady Macbeth of the Mtsensk District* in
1936 precipitated the official condemnation of the opera and
of its creator. The opera was not performed again until the
cultural thaw in the 1960s.

Shostakovich was bitterly attacked in the official press, and
both the opera and the still unperformed Symphony No. 4
(1935–6) were withdrawn. The composer's next major work

was his Symphony No. 5 (1937), which was described in the press as "a Soviet artist's reply to just criticism". A trivial, dutifully "optimistic" work might have been expected: what emerged was compounded largely of serious, even sombre and elegiac music, presented with a compelling directness that scored an immediate success with both the public and the authorities.

With his Symphony No. 5 Shostakovich forged the style that he used in his subsequent compositions. Whereas the earlier symphony had been a sprawling work, founded upon a free proliferation of melodic ideas, the first movement of Symphony No. 5 was marked by melodic concentration and classical form. This single-mindedness is reflected elsewhere in Shostakovich's work in his liking for the monolithic baroque structures of the fugue and chaconne, each of which grows from, or is founded upon, the constant repetition of a single melodic idea.

While Shostakovich's works written during the mid-1940s contain some of his best music – especially the Symphony No. 8 (1943), the *Piano Trio* (1944), and the Violin Concerto No. 1 (1947–8) – the prevailing seriousness, even grimness, of these works led to his second fall from official grace. Like many other Russian artists, he suffered repression when, at the beginning of the Cold War, the Soviet authorities attempted to exert greater control over art. In Moscow in 1948, at a now notorious conference presided over by the Soviet theoretician Andrey Zhdanov, the leading figures of Soviet music, including Shostakovich, were attacked and disgraced. As a result, the quality of Soviet composition slumped in the next few years.

From the time of Stalin's death in 1953 Shostakovich was mostly left to pursue his creative career unhampered by official interference. The composer had visited the United States in 1949, and in 1958 he made an extended tour of western Europe, including Italy (where he had already been elected an honorary member of the Accademia Nazionale di Santa Cecilia, Rome) and Great Britain, where he received an honorary doctorate of music at the University of Oxford. In 1966 he was awarded the Royal Philharmonic Society's Gold Medal.

Aram Khachaturian (1903–1978) was a professor at both the Gnesin State Musical and Pedagogical Institute in Moscow and at the Moscow Conservatory. As a young composer, he was influenced by contemporary western music, though in his later works this influence was supplanted by a growing appreciation of folk traditions, not only those of his Armenian forebears, but also those of Georgia, Russia, Turkey, and Azerbaijan.

In 1948, along with Shostakovich and Prokofiev, Khachaturian was accused by the Central Committee of the Communist Party of bourgeois tendencies in his music. He admitted his guilt and was restored to prominence, writing a highly tuneful song in praise of Stalin. After Stalin's death in 1953, however, Khachaturian publicly condemned the Central Committee's accusation, which was formally rescinded in 1958. He was named People's Artist of the Soviet Union in 1954 and was awarded the Lenin Prize in 1959.

Khachaturian wrote music that appealed to the masses, music that glitters with all the traditional Russian expertise in orchestration, orientalism, rhythm, and tunefulness. He is best known for his Piano Concerto (1936) and his ballets *Gayane* (1942), which includes the popular, stirring "Sabre Dance", and *Spartacus* (1954).

The Late- and Post-Soviet Period

The best-known composers of the late- and post-Soviet period include Edison Denisov, Sofia Gubaidulina, and Alfred Schnittke. In the early 1990s Gubaidulina and Schnittke moved to Germany, where they joined other Russian emigres.

Of these, Schnittke (1934–1998) achieved the most popularity and fame in the West. Virtually unknown outside the Soviet bloc until the mid-1980s, Schnittke rather suddenly acquired a large western following through the efforts of a number of prominent Russian musicians, including Gennady Rozhdestvensky, Gidon Kremer, Yury Bashmet, and Mstislav Rostropovich. A postmodernist Russian composer, he created serious, dark-toned musical works characterized by abrupt juxtapositions of radically different, often contradictory, styles, an approach that came to be known as "polystylism". Like Shostakovich, Schnittke intermingled disjointed elements within a single work, but his combinations were far more jarring – an offhand Beethoven quotation, a distorted folk song, fragments of a medieval chant, and passages of ferociously dense, dissonant serialism might appear within the space of a few minutes.

In the Soviet period Schnittke was required to produce many works in easily digestible socialist realist style, particularly film scores, of which he wrote more than 60 between 1961 and 1984. His more demanding experimental works were viewed with official disfavour. Schnittke's works embraced a wide range of genres and include seven symphonies, numerous string concerti, a piano concerto, the oratorio *Nagasaki* (1958), six ballets, much choral and vocal music, and arrangements of works by Shostakovich, Alban Berg, and Scott Joplin. His best-known works include the *Concerto Grosso No. 1*

(1977) and the Violin Concerto No. 4 (1984), for which the violinist was instructed to mime the cadenza rather than actually play it.

Schnittke's work is ingenious in the extreme, but has something of the feeling of an objective commentary on twentieth-century disintegration of musical tradition. He emigrated to Germany after spending the most difficult years of his creative life in Russia. He alone of all the Russian composers mentioned in this chapter does not appear to illustrate any of the characteristic qualities of Russian music. But though in practice he can be said to be a Russian composer, his ancestry is Latvian and German.

Folk and Pop

In the nineteenth century the Orthodox Church forbade the presence of musical instruments, including organs, in churches and frowned on their use elsewhere. Yet traditional folk music continued to exist, and in the second half of the twentieth century the socialist regime encouraged the creation of traditional folk groups. These musicians used the many and varied instruments that one would expect to find in a crossroads culture. Folk instruments across the world are usually found to be specific examples of generic types. Russia is no exception. In addition to the ubiquitous balalaika and button accordion, among these instruments are the *lira* (hurdy-gurdy), *gudok* (bowed instrument), *gusli* (plucked instrument), *rozhok* (reed trumpet or horn), *kalyuka* (flute), *dudka* (flute), *kugikli* (pan-pipes), *domra* (lute), *volynka* (bagpipes), and various percussion instruments. Folk instrument manufacture flourishes in Russia today. Folk song always has been an integral part of

Russian daily life, and Russia's folk choirs, in a tradition dating back to the later nineteenth century, are justly famous. Folk music, both instrumental and vocal, was officially supported by the state from the time of the revolution as being valuably proletarian. In the 1960s it was used in an attempt to oppose the spread of western-style pop and rock, suppressed under Stalin.

Nevertheless, pop and rock music continued to exist. Particularly notable were two balladeers. The raspy-voiced actor and musician Vladimir Vysotsky, whose songs circulated on thousands of bootleg cassettes throughout the 1960s and 1970s, was perhaps the best-known performer in the Soviet Union until his death in 1980. Georgian Bulat Okudzhava had an almost equally loyal following. Jazz flourished openly with the sanction of the Soviet authorities, and evolved into one of the country's most popular musical forms. The Ganelin Trio, perhaps Russia's most famous jazz ensemble, toured western countries throughout the 1980s. The pop singer Alla Pugacheva also drew large audiences in the 1970s. As the rigidity of the regime relaxed in fits and starts in the 1960s and 1970s, such groups made a name for themselves outside Russia thanks to their appearances at festivals, including those organized by WOMAD (World of Music Arts and Dance).

From the end of the Stalin era up to the 1970s, rock musicians in Russia were content to reproduce not only the styles but the songs of British and American models; however, by the early 1980s there emerged a very strong culture of dissidence and counterculture, which expressed itself through western pop and rock. Russian rock found its native voice in the band Akvarium ("Aquarium"), led by charismatic songwriter and vocalist Boris Grebenshikov. The band's "concerts", played in living rooms and dormitories, were often broken up by the police, and, like Vysotsky, the band circulated its illegal music on bootleg cassettes, becoming the legendary catalyst of an underground counterculture and an inspiration to other notable bands, such as Kino.

After the fall of communism, the loss of Soviet funding and support undermined the creation of new music in Russia as well as in the former satellite states. Nevertheless, rock and pop music continued to flourish.

8

THE VISUAL ARTS AND FILM

The Visual Arts

Like music, the visual arts in Russia were slower to develop along European lines than was literature. With the exception of the portraitist Dmitry Levitsky, no great Russian painters emerged in the eighteenth and early nineteenth centuries. In the 1830s the Russian Academy of Arts (which had been founded in 1757) began sending Russian painters abroad for training. Among the most gifted of these were Aleksandr Ivanov and Karl Bryullov, both of whom were known for Romantic historical canvases. A truly national tradition of painting did not begin, however, until the 1870s with the appearance of the "Itinerants". Although their work is not well known outside Russia, the serene landscapes of Isaak Levitan, the expressive portraits of Ivan Kramskoy and Ilya Repin, and the socially oriented genre paintings of Vladimir Makovsky, Vasily Perov, and Repin arguably deserve an international reputation.

As with literature, there was a burst of creativity in the visual arts in the early twentieth century, with Russian painters playing a major role in the European art scene. Mikhail Vrubel (1856–1910) was the first powerful personality to emerge in the figurative arts in Russia since the Muscovite period. Above all he was a brilliant draughtsman; his work pointed the way to cubism and Futurism, and in this way prepared the merging of Russian art into the mainstream of the European movements before its flowering in suprematism and constructivism, when for the first time Russians emerged as leaders of the European avant-garde.

The early twentieth century was marked by a turning away from academic realism to primitivism, symbolism, and abstract painting. Mikhail Larionov and Natalya Goncharova looked for a new style that could combine the new aesthetic achievements of the West with inspiration from native Russian folk art. Their strip-like and often abstract formulations, to which they gave the name of Rayonism, date from 1911. Both Larionov and Goncharova were members of the Jack of Diamonds group of artists, who advocated the most advanced European avant-garde trends in their own painting and exhibited works by European artists such as Albert Gleizes and Ernst Ludwig Kirchner. Vasily Kandinsky (1866–1944) created his highly influential lyrical abstractions during this period, while Kasimir Malevich (1878–1935) began to explore the rigid, geometric abstraction of suprematism.

Suprematism, originated by Malevich in about 1913, was the first movement to advocate pure geometrical abstraction in painting. He constantly strove to produce pure, cerebral compositions, repudiating all sensuality and representation in art. Malevich explained that "the appropriate means of

NATALYA GONCHAROVA (1881–1962)

Russian painter, sculptor, and stage designer

The daughter of an aristocratic family, Goncharova studied painting and sculpture at the Academy of Fine Arts in Moscow. After an early preoccupation with sculpture, in 1904 she began seriously to paint, experimenting with the cubist and Futurist styles during the next few years. It was as a synthesis of these movements that Goncharova and Larionov (see below), whom she later married, conceived of Rayonism (founded c. 1910), which sought to portray in two dimensions the spatial qualities of reflected light. Both Goncharova and Larionov participated in the first Jack of Diamonds exhibition of avant-garde Russian art in Moscow in 1910. In 1912 Goncharova took part in Roger Fry's post-Impressionist exhibition in London and in the second exhibition of Der Blaue Reiter (The Blue Rider) in Munich.

Goncharova earned a high reputation in Moscow for her scenery and costume designs for the Kamerny Theatre. When she and Larionov moved to Paris in 1914 she became a designer for Sergey Diaghilev's Ballets Russes, her vibrant, Byzantine-inspired designs for the ballet *Le Coq d'or* being especially notable.

representation is always the one which gives fullest possible expression to feeling as such and which ignores the familiar appearance of objects". In his first suprematist works, which consisted of simple geometrical forms such as squares, circles, and crosses, he limited his palette to black, white, red, green, and blue. By 1916–17 he was presenting more complex shapes (fragments of circles, tiny triangles); extending his colour range to include brown, pink, and mauve; increasing the complexity

MIKHAIL FYODOROVICH LARIONOV
(1881–1964)

Russian-born French painter and stage designer

Larionov was a pioneer of pure abstraction in painting, most notably through his founding, with Goncharova, of the Rayonist movement. His early work was influenced by Impressionism and symbolism, but with the painting *Glass* (1909) he introduced a non-representational style conceived as a synthesis of cubism, Futurism, and Orphism. In the Rayonist manifesto of 1913 he asserted the principle of the reduction of form in figure and landscape compositions into rays of reflected light. Larionov also achieved renown as a designer for Diaghilev's Ballets Russes.

of spatial relationships; and introducing the illusion of the three-dimensional into his painting. His experiments culminated in the *White on White* paintings of 1917–18, in which colour was eliminated, and the faintly outlined square barely emerged from its background. Finally, at a one-man exhibition of his work in 1919, Malevich announced the end of the suprematist movement. His own artistic career was doomed when Soviet politicians imposed socialist realism. He died in poverty and oblivion.

Suprematism had a few adherents among lesser-known artists, such as Ivan Klyun, Ivan Puni, and Olga Rozanova. While not affiliated with the movement, Kandinsky showed the influence of suprematism in the geometrization of his forms after 1920. This geometrical style, together with other abstract trends in Russian art, was transmitted by way of Kandinsky and the Russian artist El Lissitzky to Germany, particularly to the Bauhaus school of architecture and applied art, in the early 1920s.

Other Russian artists of the early twentieth century subscribed to constructivism. Based on earlier experiments by Vladimir Tatlin (1885–1953), constructivism favoured strict geometric forms and crisp graphic design. The name of the movement derives from the *Realist Manifesto* jointly written by the expatriate Russian artists Antoine Pevsner and Naum Gabo; one of the directives of the manifesto was "to construct" art. Because of their admiration for machines and technology, functionalism, and modern industrial materials such as plastic, steel, and glass, members of the movement were also called artist-engineers. Many constructivists became actively involved in the task of creating living spaces and forms of daily life; they designed furniture, ceramics, and clothing, and they worked in graphic design and architecture.

One of the most prominent constructivists was Aleksandr Rodchenko (1891–1956), who favoured a completely abstract, highly geometric style using a ruler and compass. His earlier geometric paintings were made in response to the famous *White on White* painting of his rival, Malevich, but in 1919 Rodchenko began to make three-dimensional constructions out of wood, metal, and other materials, again using geometric shapes in dynamic compositions; some of these hanging sculptures were, in effect, mobiles. In the 1920s he abandoned painting altogether, since he wanted to forge closer ties between the arts and industry and to produce works that constructivists considered more appropriate in the daily lives of worker-consumers. He thus took up such art forms as photography; poster, book, and typographic design; furniture design; and stage and motion-picture set design. He held various government offices concerned with art-related projects, helped to establish art museums, and taught art.

The second major influence in the constructivist movement was El Lissitzky (1890–1941). In 1919 Lissitzky began to work on a series of abstract geometric paintings that he named *Proun*, an acronym for the Russian words translated as "Projects for the Affirmation of the New". In 1921 he became professor at the state art school in Moscow, but he left his country at the end of that year when the Soviet government turned against modern art. Based in Hannover between 1925 and 1928, Lissitzky co-founded a number of periodicals propagating the most progressive artistic tendencies of the 1920s. In the winter of 1928–9 he returned to Moscow, where he continued to be an innovative force. His experiments in spatial construction led him to devise new techniques in exhibiting, printing, photomontage, and architecture, which have had much influence in western Europe.

By the end of the 1920s the same pressures that confronted experimental writing were brought to bear on the visual arts. With the imposition of socialist realism, the great painters of the early 1920s found themselves increasingly isolated. Eventually, their works were removed from museums, and in many cases the artists themselves were almost completely forgotten and a good number went into exile. Countless pictures of Vladimir Lenin were produced – for example, Isaak Brodsky's *Lenin at the Smolny* (1930) – as were a seemingly unending string of rose-tinted socialist realist depictions of everyday life bearing titles such as *The Tractor Drivers' Supper* (1951). During this period, a number of Russia's leading twentieth-century artists, particularly Marc Chagall (1887–1985) and Kandinsky, produced major works outside the country.

Marc Chagall's poetic, whimsical paintings were based on his own personal mythology; his work defies classification within any one group or trend. Born in 1887 in Vitebsk (now in Belarus), Chagall in 1907 went to St Petersburg, where he studied intermittently for three years, at one point under the stage designer Léon Bakst. Characteristic works by Chagall from this period of early maturity are the nightmarish *The Dead Man* (1908), which depicts a roof violinist (a favourite motif), and *My Fiancée with Black Gloves* (1909), in which a portrait becomes an occasion for the artist to experiment with arranging black and white.

In 1910 Chagall left Russia for Paris, where over four years he came into contact with avant-garde poets and a number of young painters destined to become famous, including the expressionist Chaim Soutine, the abstract colourist Robert Delaunay, and the cubists Albert Gleizes, Jean Metzinger, Fernand Léger, and André Lhote. In such company he was encouraged to experiment and take risks, and he responded to the stimulus by rapidly developing the poetic and seemingly irrational tendencies he had begun to display in Russia. At the same time, he gave up the sombre palette he had employed at home. This period is often considered Chagall's best phase. Representative works are *Self-Portrait with Seven Fingers* (1912), *I and the Village* (1911), *Hommage à Apollinaire* (1911–12), *Calvary* (1912), *The Fiddler* (1912), and *Paris Through the Window* (1913). In these pictures Chagall was already essentially the artist he would continue to be for the next 60 years. His colours, although occasionally thin, were beginning to show the characteristic complexity and resonance he would eventually achieve. The often whimsical figurative elements, frequently upside down, are distributed on the canvas in an arbitrary fashion, producing an effect that

LEON BAKST (1866–1924)

Russian artist who revolutionized theatrical design both in scenery and in costume

Bakst attended the Imperial Academy of Arts at St Petersburg but was expelled after painting a too-realistic "Pieta". He returned to Russia after completing his studies in Paris and became a court painter. He was a co-founder with Sergey Diaghilev of the journal *Mir Iskusstva* ("World of Art") in 1899. Bakst began to design scenery in 1900, first at the Hermitage court theatre and then at the imperial theatres.

In 1906 Bakst went to Paris, where he began designing stage sets and costumes for Diaghilev's newly formed ballet company, the Ballets Russes. The first Diaghilev ballet for which he designed decor was *Cléopâtre* (1909), and he was chief set designer thereafter, working on the ballets *Scheherazade* and *Carnaval* (both 1910), *Le Spectre de la rose* and *Narcisse* (both 1911), *L'Après-midi d'un faune* and *Daphnis et Chloé* (both 1912), and *Les Papillons* (1914). Bakst achieved international fame with his sets and costumes, in which he combined bold designs and sumptuous colours with minutely refined details to convey an atmosphere of picturesque, exotic orientalism. In 1919 he settled permanently in Paris. His designs for a London production of Pyotr Ilyich Tchaikovsky's *Sleeping Beauty* in 1921 are regarded as his greatest work.

sometimes resembles a film montage and suggests the inner space of a reverie. The general atmosphere of these works can imply a Yiddish joke, a Russian fairy tale, or a vaudeville turn. Often the principal character is the romantically handsome,

curly-haired young painter himself. Memories of childhood
and of Vitebsk were major sources of imagery for Chagall
during this period.

Initially enthusiastic about the Russian Revolution of October 1917, Chagall returned briefly to his native Vitebsk,
where he launched ambitious projects for a local art academy
and museum; but after two and a half years, marked by
increasingly bitter aesthetic and political quarrels with the
faculty of the art academy, he gave up and moved to Moscow.
There he turned his attention for a while to the stage, producing sets and costumes. In 1922, however, he left Russia for
good. Until the outbreak of the Second World War he travelled
extensively, working in Brittany in 1924, in southern France in
1926, in Palestine in 1931 (as preparation for his Bible etch-
ings), and, between 1932 and 1937, in the Netherlands, Spain,
Poland, and Italy. His reputation as a modern master was
confirmed by a large retrospective exhibition in 1933 at the
Kunsthalle in Basel, Switzerland. The outbreak of war, and the
Nazi menace for European Jewry, forced Chagall to move yet
again, this time, in July 1941, with his family to the United
States. Adolf Hitler's rise to power had changed his painterly
visions, as reflected in the powerful *White Crucifixion* (1938),
in which Jewish and Christian symbols are conflated in a
depiction of German Jews terrorized by a Nazi mob; the
crucified Christ at the centre of the composition is wrapped
in a tallith, a Jewish prayer shawl.

Chagall was prolific for the last 30 years of his life, continuing to paint on canvas while also designing theatre sets – he
completed a number of projects for the Paris Opéra and the
New York Metropolitan Opera, including his highly regarded
set and costume designs for the 1967 production of Mozart's
The Magic Flute – and in the late 1950s mastering the difficult

art of stained glass. He designed a number of windows at international locations such as the Cathedral of Metz in France (1958–60), the synagogue of the Hadassah-Hebrew University Medical Center in Jerusalem (1960–1), the United Nations building in New York (1964), and the Art Institute of Chicago (1977). His stained-glass windows are often considered to be some of the strongest work of his late career; the medium's capacity for brilliant colour was perfectly suited to his magical imagery.

Chagall's repertory of images, including massive bouquets, melancholy clowns, flying lovers, fantastic animals, biblical prophets, and fiddlers on roofs, helped to make him one of the most popular major innovators of the twentieth-century School of Paris. He presented dreamlike subject matter in rich colours and in a fluent, painterly style that, while reflecting an awareness of artistic movements such as expressionism, cubism, and even abstraction, remained invariably personal. Although critics sometimes complained of facile sentiments, uneven quality, and an excessive repetition of motifs in the artist's large total output, there is agreement that at its best it reached a level of visual metaphor seldom attempted in modern art.

Perhaps the most influential of all Russian painters to work primarily outside Russia was Vasily Kandinsky. Having travelled widely in his youth, when he decided in his late twenties that, rather than take up a professorship in jurisprudence, he would become a painter, nothing seemed more natural to him than to pack his bags and take a train to Germany, a seedbed of artistic activity and learning.

It took many further years of study and familiarization with various artistic traditions and trends before the emergence of Kandinsky's strikingly personal style. His instincts had always been to abstraction in art, however: he later recalled that, as an adolescent, he had a strong conviction that each colour had a mysterious life of its own. Gradually, the many influences he had undergone coalesced. His impulse to eliminate subject matter altogether stemmed from his desire for a kind of painting in which colours, lines, and shapes, freed from the distracting business of depicting recognizable objects, might evolve into a visual "language" capable – as was, for him, the abstract "language" of music – of expressing general ideas and evoking deep emotions.

The vision was not, of course, entirely new, and in these years just before the First World War Kandinsky was by no means alone in his attack on figurative art. Between 1910 and 1914 the list of pioneer abstract artists included many fine painters, working under the umbrella of a variety of movements. But if Kandinsky does not quite deserve to be called, as he often is, the "founder" of non-figurative painting, he remains a pioneer of the first importance.

In his *Blue Mountain* (1908) the evolution toward non-representation was already clearly under way: the forms are schematic, the colours non-naturalistic, and the general effect that of a dream landscape. By 1910 his *Improvisation XIV* was already, as its somewhat musical title suggests, practically abstract; with the 1911 *Encircled*, he had definitely developed a kind of painting that, though not just decoration, has no discernible point of departure in the depiction of recognizable objects. After that came such major works as *With the Black Arch*, *Black Lines*, and *Autumn*: in such pictures, done between 1912 and 1914 in a slashing, splashing, dramatic style that anticipates the New York abstract expressionism of the 1950s, most art historians see the peak of the artist's achievement.

On the outbreak of the First World War Kandinsky returned to Russia, where, in 1917, he married a Moscow woman, Nina Andreyevskaya, and hoped to reintegrate himself into Russian life. His intention was encouraged by the new Soviet government, which at first showed itself anxious to win the favour and services of avant-garde artists. In 1918 he became a professor at the Moscow Academy of Fine Arts, and further official appointments followed. But by the early 1920s, when it became clear that the Soviet government was veering away from avant-garde art towards socialist realism, he and his wife left Moscow for Berlin.

Invited to teach at the Bauhaus school of architecture and applied art, Kandinsky evolved in the general direction of geometric abstraction, but with a dynamism and a taste for detail-crowded pictorial space that recall his earlier sweeping-gesture technique. That Kandinsky was keenly interested in theory during these years is evident from his publication in 1926 of his second important treatise, *Point and Line to Plane*. In his first treatise, *Concerning the Spiritual in Art* (1912), he had emphasized in particular the supposed expressiveness of colours, comparing yellow, for example, to the aggressive, allegedly earthly sound of a trumpet and comparing blue to the allegedly heavenly sound of the pipe organ. Now, in the same spirit, he analysed the supposed effects of the abstract elements of drawing, interpreting a horizontal line, for example, as cold and a vertical line as hot.

His personal trajectory continued to be directed in part by political developments. Although he had been a German citizen since 1928, when the Nazis forced the Bauhaus to close in 1933 he emigrated to Paris. During this final period his painting, which he began to prefer to call "concrete" rather than "abstract", became to some extent a synthesis of the

organic manner of the pre-First World War Munich period
and the geometric manner of the Bauhaus period. The visual
language that he had been aiming at since at least 1910 turned
into collections of signs that look like almost-decipherable
messages written in pictographs and hieroglyphs; many of the
signs resemble aquatic larvae, and now and then there is a
figurative hand or a lunar human face. Typical works are
Violet Dominant, *Dominant Curve*, *Fifteen*, *Moderation* and
Tempered Élan. The production of such works was accompanied by the writing of essays in which the artist stressed the
alleged failure of modern scientific positivism and the need to
perceive what he termed "the symbolic character of physical
substances". Kandinsky died in 1944. His influence on
twentieth-century art, often filtered through the work of more
accessible painters, was profound.

The visual arts took longer to recover from the Stalinist
years than did literature. It was not until the 1960s and 1970s
that a new group of artists, all of whom worked "underground", appeared. Major artists included Ernst Neizvestny,
Ilya Kabakov, Mikhail Shemyakin, and Erik Bulatov. They
employed techniques as varied as primitivism, hyperrealism,
grotesque, and abstraction, but they shared a common distaste
for the canons of socialist realism.

Beginning in the mid-1980s, and thanks to the liberalization
policies of Mikhail Gorbachev, artistic experimentation began
a resurgence within Russia, and many Russian painters enjoyed successful exhibitions both at home and abroad. In the
late 1980s the greatest works of Russian art of the early
twentieth century were again made available to the public.
But by this time a large number of Russian artists had
emigrated, and many became well known on the world art
scene. Particularly notable was the team of Vitaly Komar and

Alex Melamid, who became internationally recognized in the 1990s for a project in which they systematically – and ironically – documented what people throughout the world said they valued most in a painting. The early years of the twenty-first century saw the extensive re-emergence of contemporary Russian artists on the world art market scene, often fetching very high prices for figurative art, perhaps in part thanks to the emergence of an industrial and commercial nouveau riche in Russia.

Film

A glance at the development of Russia's film industry draws into focus some of the recurring issues in Russian culture, such as the relationship between art and politics, the advantages and disadvantages of state-sponsored artistic activity, and the native Russian vs. imported western debate.

Before the October 1917 Revolution, Russia for all practical purposes had no native film industry. In the industrialized nations of the West, motion pictures had first been accepted as a form of cheap recreation and leisure for the working class, but in pre-revolutionary Russia the working class was composed largely of former serfs too poor to support a native industry, and so the small movie business that did develop was dominated by foreign interests and foreign films. The first native Russian company was not founded until 1908, and by the time of the revolution there were perhaps 20 more; but even these were small, importing all their technical equipment and film stock from Germany and France.

From Russia's entry into the First World War in August 1914, its film industry came under government control. Since foreign films could no longer be imported, the tsarist government established the Skobelev Committee to stimulate domestic production and produce propaganda in support of the regime; when the tsar fell in March 1917 the Provisional Government reorganized it to produce anti-tsarist propaganda. When the Bolsheviks inherited the committee eight months later, they transformed it into the Cinema Committee of the People's Commissariat of Education.

The potential of film to communicate quickly and effectively was quickly seized upon by Vladimir Ilyich Lenin, the first political leader of the twentieth century to recognize the importance of film as propaganda and control. More specifically, Lenin saw the potential of film to unite the huge, disparate nation over which the Bolsheviks, then a minority party of some 200,000 members, had assumed leadership. He declared: "The cinema is for us the most important of the arts." His government gave top priority to the rapid development of the Soviet film industry, which was nationalized in August 1919 and put under the direct authority of Lenin's wife, Nadezhda Krupskaya.

With little to build upon (most of the pre-revolutionary producers had fled to Europe, taking their equipment and film stock with them), one of the first acts of the Cinema Committee was to found a professional film school in Moscow to train directors, technicians, and actors for the cinema. The All-Union State Institute of Cinematography was the first such school in the world and is still among the most respected. Initially it trained people in the production of *agitki*, existing newsreels re-edited for the purpose of agitation and propaganda (agitprop). The *agitki* were transported on specially equipped agit-trains and agit-steamers to the provinces, where they were exhibited to generate support for the revolution.

During the Russian Civil War (1918–20) nearly all Soviet films were *agitki* of some sort, and most of the great directors of the Soviet silent cinema were trained in that form.

An outstanding teacher at the school was Lev Kuleshov, who formulated the groundbreaking editing process called montage, which he conceived of as an expressive process whereby dissimilar images could be linked together to create non-literal or symbolic meaning. As a teacher and theorist Kuleshov deeply influenced an entire generation of Soviet directors.

Two of Kuleshov's most brilliant students were Sergey Eisenstein and Vsevolod Illarionovich Pudovkin. Eisenstein, one of the great pioneering geniuses of the modern cinema, approached his art from an intellectual angle, formulating a modernist theory of editing based on the psychology of perception and Marxist dialectic. His first theoretical manifesto, "The Montage of Attractions", was published in the radical journal *Lef*: the article advocated assaulting an audience with calculated emotional shocks for the purpose of agitation.

In 1924 Eisenstein produced his first film, *Strike*, a semi-documentary representation of the brutal suppression of a strike by tsarist factory owners and police. This was the first revolutionary mass-film of the new Soviet state. Conceived as an extended montage of shock stimuli, the film concludes with the now famous sequence in which the massacre of the strikers and their families is intercut with shots of cattle being slaughtered in an abattoir. The film was an immediate success, and Eisenstein was next commissioned to direct a film celebrating the twentieth anniversary of the failed 1905 Revolution against tsarism. Originally intended to provide a panorama of the entire event, the project eventually came to focus on a single representative episode – the mutiny of the battleship

Potemkin and the massacre of the citizens of the port of Odessa by tsarist troops. *Battleship Potemkin* (1925) emerged as one of the most important and influential films ever made, especially in Eisenstein's use of montage. Although agitational to the core, *Battleship Potemkin* is a work of extraordinary pictorial beauty and great elegance of form. With the addition of a stirring revolutionary score by the German Marxist composer Edmund Meisel, the appeal of *Battleship Potemkin* became nearly irresistible, and, when exported in early 1926, it made Eisenstein world-famous.

Although more state commissions followed in the late 1920s and early 1930s, increasingly Eisenstein's work drew critical disapproval. Stalin himself despised Eisenstein because he was an intellectual and a Jew: only the director's international stature prevented him from being publicly purged. Instead, Stalin used the Soviet state-subsidy apparatus to foil Eisenstein's projects and attack his principles at every turn, a situation that resulted in the director's failure to complete another film until *Alexander Nevsky* was commissioned in 1938. With a score by Sergey Prokofiev, the film became a classic. Eisenstein's later films included the operatically stylized *Ivan the Terrible, Parts I and II* (1944–6), a veiled critique of Stalin's autocracy.

Pudovkin developed a new theory of montage, but one based on cognitive linkage rather than dialectical collision. He maintained that "the film is not shot, but built, built up from the separate strips of celluloid that are its raw material". His films are more personal than Eisenstein's: the epic drama that is the focus of Eisenstein's films exists in Pudovkin's films merely to provide a backdrop for the interplay of human emotions. Pudovkin's major work is *Mother* (1926), a tale of strike-breaking and terrorism in which a woman loses first her husband and then her son to the opposing sides of the 1905 Revolution. The film was internationally acclaimed for the innovative intensity of its montage, as well as for its emotion and lyricism. Pudovkin's later films included *The End of St Petersburg* (1927) and *The Heir to Genghis Khan* (or *Storm over Asia*; 1928). Although Pudovkin was never persecuted as severely by the Stalinists as Eisenstein, he, too, was publicly charged with formalism for his experimental sound film *A Simple Case* (1932), which he was forced to release without its sound track. Pudovkin made several more sound films but remains best-known for his silent work.

Two other seminal figures of the Soviet silent era were Aleksandr Dovzhenko and Dziga Vertov, whose *kino-glaz* ("film-eye") theory – that the camera, like the human eye, is best used to explore real life – had a huge impact on the development of documentary film-making and cinema realism in the 1920s. But with the restraints imposed on Soviet filmmakers by Stalin's insistence on socialist realism from 1929 onwards, it became impossible for the great film-makers of the post-revolutionary era to produce creative or innovative work.

Soviet cinema went into rapid decline after the Second World War: film production fell from 19 features in 1945 to 5 in 1952. Although Stalin died the following year, the situation did not improve until the late 1950s, when such films as Mikhail Kalatozov's *The Cranes Are Flying* (1957) and Grigory Chukhrai's *Ballad of a Soldier* (1959) emerged to take prizes at international film festivals. Some impressive literary adaptations were produced during the 1960s (Grigory Kozintsev's *Hamlet*, 1964; Sergey Bondarchuk's *War and Peace*, 1965–7), but the most important phenomenon of the decade was the graduation of a whole new generation of Soviet directors from the All-Union State Institute of Cinematography, many of them from the non-Russian republics. By far the most brilliant of the new directors were Sergey Paradzhanov and Andrey Tarkovsky, who both were later persecuted for the unconventionality of their work. Paradzhanov's greatest film was *Shadows of Forgotten Ancestors* (1964), a hallucinatory retelling of a Ukrainian folk legend of ravishing formal beauty. Tarkovsky created a body of work whose seriousness and symbolic resonance had a major impact on world cinema – *Andrey Rublyov* (1966), *Solaris* (1971), *Mirror* (1974), *Stalker* (1979), *Nostalgia* (1983) – even though it was frequently tampered with by Soviet censors. During the 1970s the policy of socialist realism was again put into practice, so that only two types of films could safely be made – literary adaptations and *bytovye*, or films of everyday life, such as Vladimir Menshov's *Moscow Does Not Believe in Tears* (1980).

Although under the *glasnost* policy introduced by Mikhail Gorbachev Russian film-makers were free from the diktat of the communist authorities, the industry suffered from drastically reduced state subsidies. The state-controlled film-distribution system also collapsed, and this led to the dominance of western films in Russia's theatres. Private investment did not quickly take the place of subsidies, and many in Russia complained that the industry often produced elitist films primarily for foreign film festivals while the public was fed a steady diet of second-rate movies.

Nonetheless, Russian cinema continued to receive international recognition. Two films – Menshov's *Moscow Does Not Believe in Tears* and Nikita Mikhalkov's *Burnt by the Sun* – received the Academy Awards for best foreign-language film, in 1980 and 1994, respectively. The work of Andrey Konchalovsky, who has plied his craft in Russia as well as in Europe and the United States with features such as *Runaway Train*

(1985) and *House of Fools* (2002), is also highly regarded. In the late 1990s Aleksandr Sokurov emerged as a director of exceptional talents, gaining international acclaim for *Mother and Son* (1997) and *Russian Ark* (2002), the first feature film ever to be shot in a single take.

9

THEATRE AND BALLET

Theatre

Russian drama in the nineteenth century got off to a slow start because of strict government censorship, particularly after 1825. This atmosphere was conducive to the flowering of Romanticism, especially as manifest in patriotic spectacles. Melodrama, Shakespeare, and musical plays were the backbone of Russian repertory until the 1830s. The best-known plays of the new realistic school were those of Aleksandr Ostrovsky, Nikolay Gogol, and Ivan Turgenev. Until 1883 the imperial theatres, under strict government controls, had a monopoly on productions in Russia's two major cities, Moscow and St Petersburg. It was not until the monopolies were rescinded that public theatre was able to expand, although the state troupes, such as the Bolshoi in Moscow, continued to offer the most professional productions.

Theatrical life in Russia was dominated in the first decades of the twentieth century by the directors Konstantin

Stanislavsky and Vsevolod Meyerhold. Just as Russian writers regarded literature as an art of social significance, so Stanislavsky believed that theatre was a powerful influence on people and that actors should serve as the people's educators. These convictions led in 1898 to the foundation, with Vladimir Nemirovich-Danchenko, of a people's theatre, the Moscow Art Theatre (later called the Moscow Academic Art Theatre), which became the arena for his reforms. Nemirovich-Danchenko undertook responsibility for literary and administrative matters, while Stanislavsky was responsible for staging and production.

Disappointed with the initial performances, Stanislavsky reflected that it should be felt there were living characters on stage, the mere external behaviour of the actors being insufficient to create a character's unique inner world. Fighting against the artificial and highly stylized theatrical conventions of the late nineteenth century, Stanislavsky sought instead the reproduction of authentic emotions at every performance. To seek knowledge about human behaviour, he turned to science and began experimenting in developing the first elements of what became known as the Stanislavsky method, his most lasting contribution to the theatre. He turned sharply from the purely external approach to the purely psychological. A play was discussed around the table for months. He became strict and uncompromising in educating actors. He insisted on the integrity and authenticity of performance on stage, repeating for hours during rehearsal his dreaded criticism, "I do not believe you."

A turning point in Russian theatre came with Stanislavsky and Nemirovich-Danchenko's restaging in 1898 of Anton Chekhov's *The Seagull*. This new production was a triumph, heralding the birth of the Moscow Art Theatre as a new force in world theatre. In staging the play, Stanislavsky and Nemirovich-Danchenko had discovered a new manner of performing which emphasized the ensemble. Stanislavsky felt that, though actors had to have a common training and be capable of an intense inner identification with the characters that they played, they should still remain independent of the role in order to subordinate it to the needs of the play as a whole. The new production of *The Seagull* was also pivotal for Chekhov. After the failure of the original production in St Petersburg in 1896 Chekhov had resolved never to write another play, but, following the acclaim he received for Stanislavsky's production, Chekhov went on to write, specially for the Moscow Art Theatre, *The Three Sisters* (1901) and *The Cherry Orchard* (1903), plays which are still performed across the world today.

Commanding respect from followers and adversaries alike, Stanislavsky became a dominant influence on Russian intellectuals of the time. In 1912 he formed the First Studio, where his innovations were adopted by many young actors. In 1918 he undertook the guidance of the Bolshoi Opera Studio, which was later named after him. There in 1922 he staged Pyotr Ilyich Tchaikovsky's *Yevgeny Onegin*, which was acclaimed as a major reform in opera direction. From 1922 to 1924 the Moscow Art Theatre toured Europe and the United States with Stanislavsky as its administrator, director, and leading actor.

The Stanislavsky method, or system, developed over 40 years. He tried various experiments, focusing much of the time on what he considered the most important attribute of an actor's work – bringing an actor's own past emotions into play in a role. But he was frequently disappointed and dissatisfied with the results of his experiments. He continued nonetheless his search for "conscious means to the subconscious" – that is, the search for the actor's emotions. In 1935 he was taken by the modern scientific conception of the interaction of brain and body, and started developing a final technique that he called the "method of physical actions". It taught emotional creativity; it encouraged actors to feel physically and psychologically the emotions of the characters that they portrayed at any given moment. The method also aimed at influencing the playwright's construction of plays.

Meyerhold was initially one of Stanislavsky's actors, but he soon broke with his master's insistence on realism and began to formulate his own avant-garde theories of symbolic, or "conditional", theatre. In 1906 he became chief producer at the theatre of Vera Komissarzhevskaya, a distinguished actress of the time, and staged a number of symbolist plays that employed his radical ideas of non-representational theatre. Meyerhold directed his actors to behave in puppet-like, mechanistic ways, thus introducing into Russia a style of acting that became known as biomechanics.

Meyerhold's unorthodox approach to the theatre led him to break with Komissarzhevskaya in 1908. Thereafter, drawing upon the conventions of *commedia dell'arte* and oriental theatre, he went on to stage productions in St Petersburg and elsewhere, putting his talent and energy into creating a new theatre for the new state. Throughout the 1920s and into the 1930s, he staged brilliant, inventive productions, both of contemporary drama and of the classics; his greatest artistic success as a director began with Fernand Crommelynck's *The Magnificent Cuckold* (1920) and ended with his controversial production in 1935 of Aleksandr Pushkin's story "The Queen of Spades".

Although Meyerhold had welcomed the 1917 Revolution, his fiercely individualistic temperament and artistic eccentricity brought reproach and condemnation from Soviet critics.

In the 1930s he was accused of mysticism and neglect of socialist realism. Refusing to submit to the constraints of artistic uniformity and defending the artist's right to experiment, in 1939 he was arrested and imprisoned. Weeks later, his actress wife, Zinaida Raikh, was found brutally murdered in their apartment. Nothing more was heard of him in the West until 1958, when his death in 1942 was announced in the *Great Soviet Encyclopedia*; in a later edition the date was changed to 1940.

After Joseph Stalin's death in 1953, the heavy restrictions on Soviet theatre began to relax, signalling a slow, cautious, and intermittent return to experimentation. The scale of the Soviet theatre was gigantic: companies played in more than 50 languages; there were vast numbers of theatres, many with huge and superbly equipped stages; companies of 100 actors or more were not unusual, and they maintained extensive repertoires. Yet the security derived from enormous state subsidies, combined with the vast output of work, tended to give rise to mediocre standards.

So large was the Soviet theatregoing public that the professional theatre could not satisfy the demand for dramatic entertainment, and every encouragement was given to the amateur movement. Most professional theatrical companies accepted responsibility for at least one amateur group, the members of the company giving much time to advising and training it. Amateur companies of outstanding merit were given the title "people's theatre".

In the 1960s the Soviet theatre gradually began to free itself from ideology, placing more emphasis on entertainment value. By the late 1970s one or two of the experimental companies could once more take their place alongside the best in Europe. The Rustaveli Company from Georgia was acclaimed during its visits to Britain in 1979 and 1980. Yury Lyubimov, director of the prestigious Taganka Theatre in Moscow, successfully reproduced his adaptation of Fyodor Dostoyevsky's novel *Crime and Punishment* in London in 1983 with British actors. In search of even more artistic freedom, he defected to the West the following year.

Theatre companies were afforded creative independence in the late 1980s. Until then, state policy had dictated that at least 50 per cent of a theatre's repertoire had to consist of contemporary Soviet plays, and at least 25 per cent of Russian classics and plays from the various Soviet states. This period was marked by the establishment of several experimental theatrical groups, as well as by an increase in commercial backing for productions. Works by foreign playwrights that had previously been banned began to be performed, and the government monopoly on theatre effectively came to an end. Labour unions were formed within the industry, and the National Union of Theatrical Leaders was established as an umbrella organization for all unions. After the collapse of the Soviet Union in 1991, the former Soviet republics sought to establish individual identities in theatre.

Puppet theatre has been another extremely successful area of theatrical performance in modern Russia. The central figure in this genre in the twentieth century was Sergey Obraztsov, a puppet master who effectively established puppetry as an art form in the Soviet Union. In 1931 Obraztsov was chosen by the Soviet government as the first director of the State Central Puppet Theatre, Moscow. His performances displayed marked technical excellence and stylistic discipline. In dozens of tours outside the Soviet Union, notably the 1953 tour of Great Britain and the 1963 tour of the United States, his shows enchanted audiences with classic figures, such as the dancing couple whose tango movements require the skill of seven puppeteers, and the female gypsy who sings bass.

A number of rod-puppet theatres were founded as a result of Obraztsov's tours. The Obraztsov Puppet Theatre (formerly the State Central Puppet Theatre) continues in the twenty-first century to give delightful performances for audiences of all ages. The same can be said for the spectacular presentations of the Moscow State Circus, which has performed throughout the world to great acclaim. Using since 1971 a larger building and renamed the Great Moscow State Circus, it excelled even in the darkest of the Cold War years.

Ballet

Classical ballet remains in the twenty-first century one of the primary expressions of Russian culture. Ballet was first introduced into Russia in the early eighteenth century, developed to maturity in the following century, and, unlike many other art forms, continued to flourish under Soviet rule. Some of the world's greatest performers, choreographers, theatre designers, and composers of ballet scores have been Russian, and many are still household names, having acquired international reputations through defection, emigration, or, in the case of the Ballets Russes, as part of a travelling troupe.

The country's first dedicated ballet school was formed in 1734. Throughout the nineteenth century dancers and choreographers, even those of non-Russian origin, worked for the Russian Imperial Theatres and were effectively government employees. The French-born dancer and choreographer Marius Petipa worked for more than 60 years at

St Petersburg's Mariinsky Theatre, and had a profound influence on modern classical Russian ballet. He directed many of the greatest artists in Russian ballet and developed ballets that retain an important position in Russian dance repertoire, including Tchaikovsky's ballets *Swan Lake* and *The Sleeping Beauty*. As in music and the visual arts, it was only towards the middle of the nineteenth century, however, that Russians infused the predominantly western European (particularly French and Italian) dance styles with Russia's own folk traditions.

The Ballets Russes

While from an international perspective Russian dancers had been considered supreme since the 1820s, the Russian ballet was spectacularly brought to the attention of the West by Sergey Diaghilev, who in 1909 founded the Ballets Russes. The opening season took place at the Théâtre du Châtelet in Paris, with dancers Anna Pavlova, Vaslav Nijinsky, and Michel Fokine. The performances set all Paris ablaze, and over the next 20 years the Ballets Russes, though never performing in Russia itself, boasted some of the best dancers from the imperial theatres in St Petersburg and Moscow, and became the foremost ballet company in the West. Diaghilev toured with his ballet uninterruptedly from 1909 to 1929, throughout Europe, in the United States, and in South America. During his later seasons he introduced the works of forward-looking composers and painters from France, Italy, Great Britain, and the United States. Among the composers represented in his repertory were Richard Strauss, Claude Debussy, Maurice Ravel, and Sergey Prokofiev.

ANNA PAVLOVA (1881–1931)

Russian ballet dancer

Pavlova studied at the Imperial Ballet School from 1891 and joined the Mariinsky Theatre company in 1899, and became prima ballerina in 1906. In 1913 she left Russia to tour with her own company, which showcased her outstanding performances in classical ballets such as *Giselle*; the most famous numbers were a succession of short solos such as "The Dying Swan", choreographed for her by Michel Fokine. Her tours took ballet to audiences in many countries for the first time and did much to popularize ballet worldwide.

Diaghilev had a flair for bringing the right people together and a determination to create a novel form of spectacle based on a synthesis of the arts – dance, music, libretto, costume, and stage design – a "total work of art" in which no one element dominated the others. The company premiered some of the most significant ballets of the early twentieth century and popularized a distinctly Russian style, characterized by sensuousness, drama, exoticism, and primitive dynamism.

Diaghilev's art reached its height in the three ballet masterpieces of the young Russian composer Igor Stravinsky: *The Firebird* (1910), *Petrushka* (1911), and *The Rite of Spring* (1913). In *Petrushka,* perhaps the greatest of the Diaghilev ballets, Stravinsky, at Diaghilev's insistence, transformed a conventionally conceived piano concerto (on which he had been working) into a mimed ballet, bringing into real life the fantasy dramas of puppets at a showman's fair. The incident is indicative of the extraordinary psychological influence Diaghilev was able to exert over his collaborators. In *The Rite of*

Spring Stravinsky produced one of the most explosive orchestral scores of the twentieth century, and the production created an uproar in the Paris theatre at its first performance. The scandalous dissonances and rhythmic brutality of the music provoked among the fashionable audience such protestations that the dancers were unable to hear the orchestra in the nearby pit. They carried on, nevertheless, encouraged by the choreographer Nijinsky, who stood on a chair in the wings, shouting out and miming the rhythm.

One of the many enduring features of the Ballet Russes was its innovative approach to ballet as theatre. Performances were characterized by their bold use of colour – Natalya Goncharova's design for *Le Coq d'or* in 1914 was unprecedented in its use of vivid colours, chiefly shades of red, yellow, and orange, with other colours for discordant emphasis – and innovations in stage design. Léon Bakst, whose designs for *Cléopâtre* (1909) were his first commission for Diaghilev, produced stage sets and costumes with brilliant palettes and well-coordinated decors. In later seasons Diaghilev engaged as designers Pablo Picasso, Georges Rouault, Henri Matisse, and André Derain.

Of course Diaghilev worked closely with and depended on an exceptionally talented array of dancers and choreographers. Tamara Karsavina had been prima ballerina at the Mariinsky Theatre. Her repertoire included *Giselle* and Odette/Odile in *Swan Lake*, but she is best known as the leading ballerina of the Ballets Russes from its beginning in 1909 until 1922. Between 1909 and 1914 (paired with Nijinsky until 1913) she created most of the famous roles in Fokine's neoromantic repertoire. Fokine was the first choreographer to put Diaghilev's ideas into practice. He worked with Stravinsky and Ravel, and his major scenic artists were Alexandre Benois and Bakst, whose contributions to theatrical design had influences beyond the sphere of ballet. *Firebird* and *Petrushka* are among his most famous creations.

Nijinsky succeeded Fokine as the company's choreographer. A classic dancer, Nijinsky was an anti-classic choreographer, specializing in turned-in body movements and in unusual footwork. In 1912 he choreographed *Afternoon of a Faun* to music written by Debussy – it is the only Nijinsky ballet still performed. Léonide Massine assumed the role of choreographer after Nijinsky. He quickly became noted for his wit and the precisely characterizing gestures of his dancers. His musical collaborators included Stravinsky, Manuel de Falla, Ottorino Respighi, and Erik Satie, and his designers included leading painters such as Derain and Picasso.

Following Diaghilev's death, Massine created a furore in the 1930s with his ballets based on symphonies by Tchaikovsky and Johannes Brahms. It was considered inappropriate to use symphonic music for dance, and the incorporation of the style and movements of modern dance into the plotless ballets added to the controversy. Another of Diaghilev's choreographers was Nijinsky's sister, Bronislawa Nijinska (1891–1972), who became famous for her massive ensemble groupings. Diaghilev's last choreographic discovery was the Russian-trained George Balanchine (1904–83). Balanchine's 1928 ballet *Apollon musagète* was the first of many collaborations with Stravinsky, and led the way to the final enthronement of neoclassicism as the dominant choreographic style of the following decades.

The artistic effects of Diaghilev's Ballets Russes were far-reaching. Ballet performance had changed irrevocably, and many of those who had worked with him continued and developed further his ideals. Pavlova formed her own company, travelling to Europe, the Americas, Australia, and Asia.

A troupe assembled by Ida Rubinstein had Nijinska as a choreographer, and Stravinsky and Ravel as composers. A number of ballet teachers left Russia of their own accord to teach in and direct schools in Paris, London, and Berlin. Another Diaghilev dancer, Dame Marie Rambert (1888–1982), founded the Ballet Rambert in London, and, in New York, Balanchine set up the School of American Ballet in 1934. From it he drew the dancers for the several companies that led ultimately to the founding of the New York City Ballet in 1948. Russian-born ballet librettist Boris Kochno became a major influence on post-Second World War French ballet.

Other Ballet in the Soviet Period

Ballet enjoyed great success in the Soviet period, not because of any innovations but because the great troupes of the Bolshoi Theatre in Moscow and the Kirov (Mariinsky) Theatre in Leningrad (St Petersburg) were able to preserve the traditions of classical dance that had been perfected prior to 1917 in tsarist Russia. The Soviet Union's choreography schools produced one internationally famous star after another. Among the greatest talents were Maya Plisetskaya, Rudolf Nureyev (who defected in 1961), and Mikhail Baryshnikov (who defected in 1974).

The Post-Soviet Period

Theatrical life in post-Soviet Russia has continued to thrive. The Moscow and St Petersburg theatres have maintained their leading position, but they have been joined by hundreds of other theatres throughout the country. Liberated from state

RUDOLF NUREYEV (1938–93)

Russian ballet dancer

Born in Irkutsk, Nureyev studied ballet in Leningrad (1955–8), where he joined the Kirov Ballet as a soloist. He defected during the company's tour to Paris in 1961. Thereafter he danced as a guest artist with many companies, especially the Royal Ballet, where he regularly partnered Margot Fonteyn. His performances, combining an intensely romantic sensibility with stunning muscularity and technique, made him an international star. He choreographed new versions of *Romeo and Juliet, Manfred*, and *The Nutcracker*. From 1983 to 1989 he was artistic director of the Paris Opera Ballet.

censorship, the theatres have experimented with bold and innovative techniques and subject matter. The repertoire of the theatres has experienced a shift away from political topics and towards classical and psychological themes. The Moscow Academic Art Theatre remains prestigious. The Bolshoi is another of the most renowned theatres, but since the late 1990s its dominance has been challenged by the Novaya (New) Opera Theatre in Moscow. Among other successful theatres in Moscow are the Maly (Little) Theatre for drama, the Luna Theatre, Arbat Opera, Moscow City Opera, and the Helikon Opera.

The Bolshoi Theatre, founded in 1825, was so successful a venue for the performing arts that in 1924 a smaller auditorium was added to the theatre complex, and in 1961 the Kremlin Palace of Congresses, with a capacity of about 6,000, was acquired as a third performing space for bigger productions. The company was kept intact during the Russian Revolution of 1917, both world wars, and the dissolution of the Soviet Union in 1990–1. Since the mid-1950s the Bolshoi's opera and ballet troupes have travelled extensively; in the twenty-first century they continue to attract audiences worldwide.

PART 4

RUSSIA TODAY

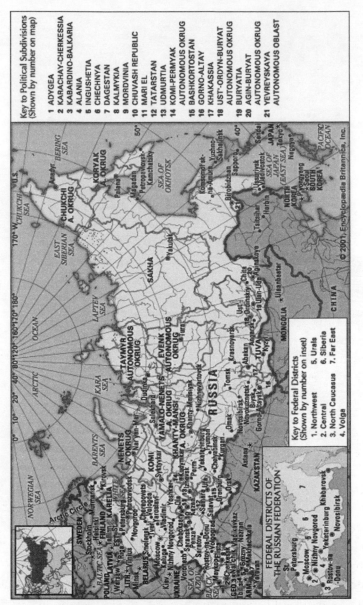

Key to Political Subdivisions
(Shown by number on map)

1 ADYGEA
2 KARACHAY-CHERKESSIA
3 KABARDINO-BALKARIA
4 ALANIA
5 INGUSHETIA
6 CHECHNYA
7 DAGESTAN
8 KALMYKIA
9 MORDVINIA
10 CHUVASH REPUBLIC
11 MARI EL
12 TATARSTAN
13 UDMURTIA
14 KOMI-PERMYAK
   AUTONOMOUS OKRUG
15 BASHKORTOSTAN
16 GORNO-ALTAY
17 KHAKASSIA
18 UST'-ORDYN-BURYAT
   AUTONOMOUS OKRUG
19 BURYATIA
20 AGIN-BURYAT
   AUTONOMOUS OKRUG
21 YEVREYSKAYA
   AUTONOMOUS OBLAST

Key to Federal Districts
(Shown by number on inset)

1. Northwest   5. Urals
2. Central   6. Siberia
3. North Caucasus 7. Far East
4. Volga

FEDERAL DISTRICTS OF
THE RUSSIAN FEDERATION

© 2001, Encyclopaedia Britannica, Inc.

Present-day Russia

10

GOVERNANCE AND THE ECONOMY

Governance

During the Soviet era the Russian Soviet Federated Socialist Republic (the RSFSR) was subject to a series of Soviet constitutions, the last in 1977, under which it nominally was a sovereign socialist state within (after 1936) a federal structure. Until the late 1980s, however, the government was dominated at all levels by the Communist Party of the Soviet Union (CPSU), whose head was the country's de facto leader. Indeed, in each of the elections that were held there was a single slate of candidates, most of whom were in effect chosen by the Communist Party.

From the late 1980s until 1991, fundamental changes took place in the political system and government structures of the Soviet Union that altered both the nature of the Soviet federal state and the status and powers of the individual republics. In 1988 the Soviet Congress of People's Deputies was created, and a Congress of People's Deputies was established in each of the Soviet republics. For the first time, elections to these bodies presented voters with a choice of candidates, including non-communists, though the Communist Party continued to dominate the system.

Thereafter, the pace of change accelerated. In June 1990 the Russian Congress proclaimed that Russian laws took precedence over Soviet laws, and the following year Boris Yeltsin became the republic's first democratically elected president. An abortive coup in August 1991 by hardliners opposed to the reforms begun under Soviet leader Mikhail Gorbachev in the late 1980s led to the collapse of most Soviet government organizations, the abolition of the Communist Party's leading role in government, and the dissolution of the Communist Party itself. Republic after republic declared its "sovereignty", and in December, when the Soviet Union was formally dissolved, Russia was established as an independent country.

Constitutional Framework

The structure of the new Russian government differed significantly from that of the former Soviet republic. It was characterized by a balance between the executive and legislative branches that led them to compete for supremacy, primarily over issues of constitutional authority and the pace and direction of democratic and economic reform. Conflicts came to a head in September 1993 when President Yeltsin dissolved the Russian parliament (the Congress of People's Deputies and the Supreme Soviet); some deputies and their allies rebelled and were suppressed only through military intervention.

On December 12, 1993, three-fifths of Russian voters ratified a new constitution proposed by Yeltsin, and representatives were elected to a new legislature. Under the new constitution the president, who is elected in a national vote and can serve a maximum of two consecutive terms, is vested with significant powers. As Russia's head of state, the president is empowered to appoint the chairman of the government (prime minister), key judges, and cabinet members. The president is also commander-in-chief of the armed forces, and can declare martial law or a state of emergency. When the legislature fails to pass the president's legislative initiatives, he may issue decrees that have the force of law.

Under the new constitution the Federal Assembly became the country's legislature. It consists of the Federation Council (an upper house in which each of Russia's administrative divisions has two representatives) and the State Duma (a 450-member lower house). The president's nominee for chairman of the government is subject to approval by the Duma, but if it persists in rejecting a nominee the president may dissolve it and call new elections. All legislation must first pass the State Duma before being considered by the Federation Council. A presidential veto of a bill can be overridden by the legislature with a two-thirds majority. With a two-thirds majority (and approval by the Russian Constitutional Court), the legislature may remove the president from office for treason or other serious criminal offences. The Federation Council must approve all presidential appointments to the country's highest judicial bodies (Supreme Court, Constitutional Court, and Supreme Arbitration Court).

The constitution provides for welfare protection, access to social security, pensions, free health care, and affordable housing. The constitution also guarantees local self-governance, though national law takes precedence over regional and local laws. The constitution also enumerates many areas that either are administered jointly by the regions and the central government or are the exclusive preserve of the central government. In the decade after the constitution's enactment, the government implemented several measures to reduce the power and influence of regional governments and governors; for example, in 2000 President Vladimir Putin created seven federal districts above the regional level to increase the central government's power over the regions.

Regional and Local Government

Under the Russian constitution the central government retains significant authority, but regional and local governments exercise authority over municipal property and policing, and they can impose regional taxes. Owing to a lack of assertiveness by the central government, Russia's regional and local governments exerted considerable power in the initial years after the passage of the 1993 constitution. However, the power of the country's administrative divisions was diluted in 2000 when seven federal districts (Central, Far East, North-West, Siberia, Southern, Urals, and Volga), each with its own presidential envoy, were established by the central government. The envoys were given the power to implement federal law and to coordinate communication between the president and the regional governors. Legally, the envoys in federal districts had solely the power of communicating the executive guidance of the federal president. In practice, however, the guidance has served more as directives, as the president was able to use the envoys to enforce presidential authority over the regional governments.

Legislation has further affirmed the power of the federal government over the regions. Legislation enacted in 2004 permitted the president to appoint the regional governors, who earlier were elected. In the first decade of the twenty-first century, the country began to undergo administrative change aimed at subordinating smaller regions to neighbouring members of the federation.

In practice the powers of local governments vary considerably. Some local authorities, particularly in urban centres, exercise significant power and are responsible for taxation and the licensing of businesses. Moscow and St Petersburg have particularly strong local governments; both possess a tax base and a structure that dwarf the country's other regions. Local councils in smaller communities are commonly rubber-stamp agencies, accountable to the city administrator, who is appointed by the regional governor. In the mid-1990s municipal government was restructured: city councils (dumas), city mayors, and city administrators replaced former city soviets.

Justice

Russia's highest judicial body is the Supreme Court, which supervises the activities of all other judicial bodies and serves as the final court of appeal. In 1991 a Constitutional Court was established to review Russian laws and treaties and to rule on the constitutionality of laws. The Constitutional Court is presided over by 19 judges, who are nominated by the president and approved by the Federation Council. Appointed to life terms, judges for both the Supreme Court and the Constitutional Court must be at least 25 years of age and hold a law degree. The Russian legal system has attempted to overcome the repression practised during the Soviet era by requiring public trials and guaranteeing a defence for the accused. The Supreme Arbitration Court of the Russian Federation rules on commercial disputes.

Political Process

Soviet-era politics was authoritarian and predictable. The CPSU dominated the political process, and elections were merely ritualistic, with voters not allowed a choice between freely competing political parties. Political reform in the 1980s and 1990s brought greater freedom, but it also spawned a multitude of political parties, which disagreed fundamentally over the pace and direction of reforms. Although reform-oriented parties won victories in the early 1990s, institutions such as the army and the intelligence services continued to exert considerable influence, and many bureaucrats were highly resistant to change. Some political parties that were popular at the time of Russia's independence were moribund by the beginning of the twenty-first century, and some coalitions were formed solely around the appeal of charismatic leaders. In contrast to 1995, when 43 political parties competed, only 26 contested the 1999 election. Legislation enacted under the Vladimir Putin regime further reduced the number of political parties by mandating that they have at least 10,000 members, and registered offices in at least half of Russia's regions, to be eligible to compete in national elections. In the 2007 legislative elections, only four parties gained enough votes to be represented in the State Duma.

All citizens become eligible to vote when they reach the age of 18 years. Presidential elections are contested in two rounds;

if no candidate receives a majority in the first round, there is a run-off between the top two candidates. For elections to the State Duma, voters cast separate ballots for a party and for a representative from a single-member district. Half the seats in the State Duma are allocated on the basis of the party vote (with all parties winning at least 5 per cent of the national vote guaranteed representation on a proportional basis), and half through the single-member-district contests. Each regional governor and the head of each regional assembly appoints one member to serve on the Federation Council.

Several of the political parties that formed in the 1990s had a notable impact. Despite the dissolution of the CPSU and the general demise of communism, the Communist Party of the Russian Federation emerged as a major political force. Indeed, in both 1996 and 2000 the Communist Party's leader finished second in the presidential balloting, and in 2000 its contingent in the State Duma was the largest (though the party was a distant second in 2003). The ultra-nationalist and xenophobic Liberal Democratic Party (LDP) capitalized on popular disenchantment and fear in the early 1990s. Led by Vladimir Zhirinovsky, who finished third in the presidential election of 1991, the LDP won more than one-fifth of the vote and 64 seats in the State Duma elections in 1993. By the end of the decade, however, support for the party had dropped dramatically; its support rebounded slightly in 2003, when it won nearly one-eighth of the vote. Throughout the 1990s Yeltsin's government was viewed unfavourably by a large proportion of the Russian public. To secure legislative support for his policies, Yeltsin encouraged the formation of the Our Home Is Russia Party in 1995 and the Unity Party in 1999; both parties finished behind the Communist Party in parliamentary elections. The most liberal parties found themselves unable to secure a firm base outside the intelligentsia. One of the most intriguing parties that formed in the 1990s was the Women of Russia Party, which captured 8 per cent of the vote in the 1993 State Duma election, though its level of support had dropped by about three-fourths by the end of the decade. In 2001 a number of parties merged to form the pro-Putin United Russia Party; beginning in 2003, this bloc held the largest number of seats in the State Duma.

In the Soviet era women played a prominent role in politics. The Soviet Congress of People's Deputies required that women constitute at least one-third of the total membership. Quotas subsequently were removed after the dissolution of the Soviet Union, and representation for women had declined dramatically by the mid-1990s to roughly 10 per cent in the State Duma and 5 per cent in the Federation Council.

In 2005 a People's Chamber was established to serve as an advisory board for Russia's civil society. A Soviet-style amalgam of officials (President Putin supervised the confirmation of the initial members), it provided additional support for the presidency.

Security

The Russian armed forces consist of an army, navy, air force, and strategic rocket force, all under the command of the president. About half the troops are conscripts: military service, lasting 18 months for the army or 24 months for the navy, is compulsory for men over age 18, although draft evasion is widespread. In addition to an extensive reserve force, Russia maintains defence facilities in several former Soviet republics and contributes a small proportion of its

COMMONWEALTH OF INDEPENDENT STATES

Free association of sovereign states formerly part of the Soviet Union

The Commonwealth of Independent States (CIS) was formed in 1991. It comprises Russia and 11 other former Soviet republics: Ukraine, Belarus, Kazakhstan, Kyrgyzstan, Tajikistan, Turkmenistan, Uzbekistan, Armenia, Azerbaijan, Georgia (which has, however, announced its intention to withdraw from the CIS in 2009), and Moldova. Its administrative centre is in Minsk, Belarus. The Commonwealth's functions are to coordinate its members' policies regarding their economies, foreign relations, defence, immigration policies, environmental protection, and law enforcement.

troops to the joint forces of the Commonwealth of Independent States. Russia's military capacity has declined since the break-up of the Soviet Union. Nonetheless, it still has one of the world's largest armed forces establishments, which includes a vast nuclear arsenal.

During the Cold War the Soviet Union established the Warsaw Pact (1955), a treaty that was designed to counter the United States-led North Atlantic Treaty Organization. The Warsaw Treaty Organization was dissolved in 1991, after which Russia maintained an uneasy military relationship with the United States and NATO, particularly during the fighting in the Balkans in the 1990s. Nevertheless, by the end of the 1990s Russia and NATO had signed a cooperation agreement, and in 2002 the NATO–Russia Council was established. In

1991 Russia assumed the Soviet Union's permanent seat on the United Nations Security Council.

Foreign and domestic intelligence operations are managed, respectively, by the Foreign Intelligence Service and the Federal Security Service, agencies that emerged in the 1990s after the reorganization in 1991 of the Soviet KGB (Committee for State Security). High officials are protected by the Presidential Security Service, which was established in 1993. A Federal Border Service, which combats trans-border crimes (particularly drug trafficking and smuggling), and several other intelligence agencies were also established in the 1990s. Local police forces have been overwhelmed by the organized crime that flourished in Russia after the fall of communism. Well-trained private security forces have become increasingly common.

The Economy

By virtue of its great size and abundant natural resources, the Russian republic played a leading role in the economy of the Soviet Union. In the first decades of the Soviet regime, these resources made possible great economic advances, including the rapid development of mining, metallurgy, and heavy engineering; the expansion of the railway network; and a massive increase in the energy supply. In the 1960s a second phase of Soviet industrial development began to exert a particularly strong effect on the Russian republic. In addition to further growth in established industries – especially in the production of oil, gas, and electricity and in the chemical industries – there was a marked diversification in industrial output, including a limited expansion in consumer goods. In the years before the dissolution of the Soviet Union, however, the economy of Russia and of the entire country was in a state of decline, and official statistics masked industrial inefficiencies.

After the collapse of the Soviet Union in 1991, the Russian government implemented radical reforms designed to transform the economy from one that was centrally planned and controlled to one based on capitalist principles. Privately owned industrial and commercial ventures were permitted, and state-owned enterprises privatized. To encourage privatization, the government issued vouchers to Russian citizens that enabled them to purchase shares in privatized firms, though in practice these vouchers frequently were sold for cash and were accumulated by entrepreneurs. A commodity- and stock-exchange system also was established.

The privatization process was slow, however, and many firms – particularly in the heavy industries – remained under state ownership. In 2001 the government legalized the sale of land, though only for urban housing and industrial real estate, which together accounted for only a small fraction of Russia's total area. At the beginning of the twenty-first century, similar legislation was under discussion for rural and agricultural areas. Though full private ownership of land is provided for in the 1993 constitution, the practice has not yet been implemented. The conversion to market-based agriculture was slow, as many clung to the old, familiar collective system.

The reforms beginning in the 1990s caused considerable hardships for the average Russian citizen; in the decade after the dissolution of the Soviet Union, the Russian economy contracted by more than two-fifths. The removal of price controls caused a huge escalation in inflation and prices; the value of the ruble, the country's currency, plummeted; and real incomes fell dramatically. Conditions had begun to improve by the mid-1990s, but in 1998 a severe financial crisis forced the government to sharply devalue the ruble. Numerous banks became insolvent, and millions of citizens lost their life savings. In response, the licensing of private banks became more rigorous, and the government cracked down on rampant tax evasion. Taxes on medium and small enterprises were moderated, and the government created incentives to reinvest profits in the domestic economy. By the early twenty-first century, the Russian economy was showing signs of recovery and stable growth. Steady earnings from oil exports permitted investments in factories, and the devalued currency made Russian goods more competitive on the international market.

In the post-Soviet years, foreign direct investment was encouraged, but it was constrained by state intervention in industry, by corruption, and by an unpredictable legal system. Violence by organized crime syndicates deterred western investment, and, although the activity of such groups was curtailed in the early twenty-first century, it still presented severe obstacles to both western and Russian businesses. Investment by non-Russian companies was also discouraged by the Russian government assuming ownership of various key industries, including oil and gas, aviation, and motor car manufacturing.

In addition to the difficulties the country encountered in its effort to restructure the economy, Russia had suffered serious long-term environmental degradation during the Soviet period, the full extent of which became apparent only in the 1990s. Its most visible aspects – such as the Chernobyl accident at a nuclear power plant in Ukraine in 1986, widespread industrial pollution, and the drastic reduction in the volume of the Aral Sea as a result of inflow diversions – were symptomatic of decades of wasteful resource exploitation. These environmental concerns placed another burden on Russia's already over-whelmed economic structure.

Agriculture, Forestry, and Fishing

The Russian environment is so harsh that agricultural land constitutes less than one-sixth of the country's territory, and less than one-tenth of the total land area is arable. Overall, agriculture contributes little more than 5 per cent to Russia's GDP, though the sector employs about one-eighth of the total labour force.

The main product of Russian farming has always been grain (mostly wheat, though barley, rye, and oats are also widely grown), which occupies considerably more than half of the crop-land. The rest of the crop-land is devoted to fodder crops and industrial crops such as sunflowers, sugar beets, and flax.

Given that Russia is such a vast country, with wide regional differences in terms of relief, soil, and climate, its agricultural patterns also have pronounced regional variations. In European Russia the further south one goes the more land is devoted to crops – virtually none are grown in the north region, whereas about two-thirds of cultivable land is devoted to crops in the central "black earth" region. In west and east Siberia and the far east, crops are largely confined to the southern fringe. Even in west Siberia, where the cultivated zone is at its widest, crops occupy less than one-tenth of the region's territory, and much less in east Siberia and the far east. Cereals occupy more than two-thirds of the crop-land in most regions, but less than half in the damper north-west and central regions, where fodder crops and livestock are more important. The intensity of farming and the yields achieved are generally much higher in the European section than in Siberia. The same is also the case for livestock farming.

In general, the old collective farms and state farms have continued to function in post-Soviet Russia. Privatized farms have experienced significant obstacles, because many in the agricultural sector treated them as pariahs, and the land that many were allocated was unproductive or inaccessible. Thus, the bulk of the grain continues to be produced by very large agricultural enterprises, particularly those in the Northern Caucasus and in the Volga regions.

Russia contains the world's largest forest reserves. More than two-fifths of the country is forested, and the country has more than one-fifth of the world's total forests – an area nearly as large as the continental United States. However, Russian forests grow very slowly because of the cold, and the country has lost about one-third of its original forest area. Although further deforestation is discouraged, logging continues to endanger the last intact forest landscapes of northern European Russia, and the problem is expanding to areas east of the Urals. The forestry industry in Russia employs some one million people. The lumbering, pulp, paper, and woodworking industries are particularly import-ant, contributing to Russia's export income. The wood is predominantly softwood.

The fishing industry plays a significant role in the Russian economy. With access to the substantial resources of both the Atlantic and Pacific oceans, marine fishing is particularly well developed, and Russia's fleet of factory ships can process huge catches at remote locations. The chief European ocean-fishing ports are Kaliningrad and St Petersburg on the Baltic Sea, and Murmansk and Arkhangelsk in the far north. Russia's chief Pacific port is Vladivostok, but there are several others, particularly in Sakhalin and Kamchatka provinces. Smaller-scale fishing takes place in the Sea of Azov and the Black and

Caspian seas (the Caspian sturgeon is the source of the world's finest caviar), but reduced river flows and pollution from agricultural run-off, industrial waste, and sewage dumping have thinned fish populations. There are important inland fisheries on lakes and rivers, including a good deal of fish farming.

The Russian fishing industry rivals the size of the world's other leading producers (Japan, the United States, and China), and produces about one-third of all canned fish and some one-fourth of the world's total fresh and frozen fish. The privatization of fishing in the 1990s shifted the industry's focus from production for domestic consumption to exports. Especially important catches are pollack, herring, cod, and salmon. Russia's earnings from the export of fish are steadily larger than from grain export. Salmon, crabmeat, caviar, beluga, sterlet, and herring are among the important seafoods generating export income.

Resources and Power

Russia has enormous energy resources and significant deposits of many different minerals. Its coal reserves are particularly extensive. The biggest fields lie in remote and untapped areas of east Siberia and the far east; the bulk of current output comes from more southerly fields along the Trans-Siberian Railway. About three-fourths of Russia's coal is produced in Siberia, some two-fifths from the Kuznetsk Basin alone and the remainder from the Kansk-Achinsk, Cheremkhovo, and South Yakut basins and numerous smaller sources. The production of hard (anthracite) coal in European Russia takes place mainly in the eastern Donets Basin and, in the Arctic, in the Pechora Basin around Vorkuta.

Privatization of the coal industry began in the 1990s, and by the early twenty-first century some three-fifths of overall coal production was coming from privatized mines. However, the removal of state subsidies also forced the closure of many unprofitable mines. Mines in regions with access to substantial reserves of oil and natural gas largely survived.

Russia is among the world's leading producers of oil, extracting about one-fifth of the global total. It also is responsible for more than one-fourth of the world's total natural gas output. The great bulk of these oil and natural gas reserves comes from the huge fields that underlie the northern part of the west Siberia region, though another significant source is the Volga-Ural zone; the North Caucasus region, once the Soviet Union's leading producer, is now of little importance. Extensive pipeline systems link production sites with all regions of the country, with the neighbouring former Soviet republics, and with many European countries.

Electricity is generated by around 600 large thermal power plants and more than 100 hydroelectric stations, as well as several nuclear power plants. Most electricity production is fuelled by oil and gas. Nuclear power production expanded rapidly before development was checked by the Chernobyl accident in 1986. Much of Siberia's electricity output is transmitted to the European region of Russia along high-voltage lines.

Russia produces about one-sixth of the world's iron ore, mainly from the Kursk Magnetic Anomaly (central black earth region), the Kola Peninsula, the Urals, and Siberia. Although there is steel production in every economic region, the largest steel-producing plants are located mainly in the Urals, the central black earth region, and the Kuznetsk Basin. Non-ferrous metals are available in great variety from many districts, but by far the most important are those of the Ural region, which is Russia's main centre of non-ferrous metallurgy. Russia is also a major producer of cobalt, chrome, copper, gold, lead, manganese, nickel, platinum, tungsten, vanadium, and zinc. The country produces much of its aluminium from plants powered by the Siberian hydroelectric stations, but bauxite deposits are relatively meagre.

Chemicals

Because of the complex history of the development of the chemical industries and the great variety of raw materials involved, chemical manufacture is widely dispersed. As oil and gas input increased in the second half of the twentieth century, new chemical plants were built, particularly in regions served by pipelines, which helped to reduce dependence on traditional resources. Chemical industries requiring large quantities of electric power, such as those based on cellulose, are particularly important in Siberia, where both timber and electricity are plentiful. Overall, Russia's chemical industry lags in scale and diversity compared with those of the United States, Canada, China, and the countries of the European Union.

Heavy and Light Industry

Russia's machine-building industry provides most of the country's needs, from steam boilers and turbines to consumer durables and automation components. Durable consumer goods are produced primarily in areas with a tradition of skilled industry, notably in and around Moscow and St Petersburg. Russia's factories also produce armaments, which are sold to many countries and contribute significantly to Russia's export income. Textile industries are heavily concentrated in European Russia, which produces a large share of the country's clothing and footwear.

Transport and Telecommunications

Russia's vast size and the great distances that often separate sources of raw materials and foodstuffs from consumers place a heavy burden on the transport system. One result has been the continuing dominance of the railways, which account for about nine-tenths of the country's freight turnover (three-fifths if pipelines are included) and half of all passenger movement. Nevertheless, the rail network is a very open one, and its density varies regionally: that of European Russia is nearly seven times as dense as that found in the Asian portion of the country. Indeed, east of the Urals the term "network" is a misnomer, since the system consists of only a few major trunk routes (e.g., the Trans-Siberian Railway and Baikal–Amur Main Line) with feeder branches to sites of economic importance. The railways are owned and run by a joint-stock company controlled by the state. Much of the country's rolling stock is obsolete.

Apart from highways linking the major cities of European Russia, the road system is underdeveloped and carries only a tiny fraction of all freight. The private motor car became a symbol of middle-class status in the post-Soviet years, but the percentage of people owning vehicles is still quite small. Inland waterways carry a much larger volume than roads. Although the greatest volume is carried on the Volga system, river transport is most vital in areas devoid of railways. In addition to its vital role in foreign trade, maritime transport has some importance in linking the various regions of Russia, particularly those that face the Arctic seaboard. Traffic on the Arctic Ocean route is seasonal.

Air transport plays an increasingly important role. Russian airlines carry only a minute fraction of all freight, chiefly high-value items to and from the remote parts of Siberia, where aircraft are sometimes the only means of transport. Airlines are responsible for nearly one-fifth of all passenger movement. Aeroflot (renamed Aeroflot-Russian Airlines in June 2000), formerly the state airline of the Soviet Union, is the country's largest air carrier; the Russian government retains majority ownership. Most major cities have services to international or domestic locations.

The Russian telecommunications sector is inferior to those of other industrialized countries. For example, in the early 1990s only about one-third of the country's households had a telephone. But the country's infrastructure in this respect has been greatly improved, largely through foreign investment. In 1997 the State Committee on Communications and Informatics was set up to regulate telecommunications policies, oversee the liberalization of the sector, and encourage competition; by the beginning of the twenty-first century, there were more than 1,000 telecommunications companies. Nevertheless, several large companies, such as Svyazinvest and Rostelekom, control much of the industry. Internet use in Russia grew very slowly in the 1990s, particularly outside the major urban areas, but it has since grown fairly steadily.

Finance

Russia's monetary unit is the ruble, which is now freely convertible, a radical departure from the practice of artificial exchange rates and rigid restrictions that existed during the Soviet era. The Russian Central Bank (RCB), which took over the functions of the Soviet-era Gosbank, is exclusively responsible for regulating the country's monetary system. The bank's primary function is to protect and stabilize the ruble, which it attempts to do through its control of foreign exchange. The constitution adopted in 1993 gives the RCB greater independence from the central government than the Gosbank had enjoyed, but its head is appointed by the president and subject to approval by the State Duma, the lower house of the Russian legislature. In 1995 the RCB was granted the authority to oversee all banking transactions, set exchange-rate policies, license banks, and service the country's debt. To maintain its hard-currency reserves, the RCB relies on the obligation of all exporters to convert half their hard-currency earnings into rubles. The RCB supervises and inspects the country's commercial banks.

During much of the 1990s Russia's financial system was in a state of chaos, largely because many of the thousands of banks that formed after the fall of communism became insolvent, particularly during the economic crisis of the late 1990s. Even with consolidation of the banking industry, at the beginning of the early twenty-first century there were more than 1,000 Russian commercial banks, many of which were state-owned or offered few financing opportunities for small- and medium-size businesses. Dozens of foreign banks also operate in the country.

The state-owned Russian commercial banks, such as Vneshtorgbank and Sberbank, shadow the RCB both in the pursuit of stability and in operations philosophy. The banking sector is frequently accused of cronyism, benefiting only an elite, particularly former communist apparatchiks. Before the banking crisis in the late 1990s, private commercial banks mushroomed, but most of them acted as outsourcing financial agents for enterprises inherited from the Soviet era. By the beginning of the twenty-first century two major clusters of banks had survived. One cluster, which included the National Reserve Bank, Gazprombank, Promstroybank, and the International Moscow Bank, served the oil and gas industry; the second cluster, consisting of the Bank of Moscow, Mosbusinessbank, Guta Bank, Most Bank, Unikombank, the International Financial Corporation, Sobinbank, MDM Bank, Toribank, Promradtekhbank, and dozens of smaller banks, focused on servicing the government of Moscow.

Trade

During the communist era the Russian republic traded extensively with the other Soviet republics, from which it "imported" a variety of commodities that it was unable to produce in sufficient quantities itself, such as cotton, grain, and minerals. In return, Russia "exported" oil and gas to republics with a weak energy base, such as Belorussia (now Belarus) and the Baltic states, and sent its skilled-engineering products and consumer goods to most of its partners.

By the late 1990s trade between the former union republics no longer continued in any systematic manner, above all because agreement could not be reached on the prices to be charged for goods exchanged at artificially low rates during the Soviet period. Still, Russia generally has a positive trade balance with the former republics of the Soviet Union.

International trade during the Soviet era was rather limited until the 1960s, and most of it was governed by bilateral and multilateral arrangements with the other members of the Council for Mutual Economic Assistance (Comecon), the Soviet-led trade organization of communist East European countries. As Soviet economic expansion slowed during the 1970s and 1980s, it became apparent that further growth required large quantities of high-tech equipment from the West. To finance these imports, Russia came to rely heavily on oil and gas exports as a source of its hard-currency needs. With Comecon's collapse and the dissolution of the Soviet Union itself, individual republics began to develop their own trading relations with the outside world. Russia, with its large resources of oil, gas, and minerals, seemed well placed to continue the type of trading relations with the West already developed by the former Soviet Union. In 1994 Russia signed an agreement that strengthened economic ties with the European Union, and it soon joined economic discussions with the Group of Seven (G-7), which represented the most advanced economies of the world; in 1997 it was admitted to membership of the Group of Eight (G-8). However, Russia's integration into the world economy was not complete, as it did not fully participate in that organization's economic and financial discussions, and its application to join the World Trade Organization was delayed.

Foreign trade is tremendously important to the Russian economy. The country has generally enjoyed a healthy trade surplus since the dissolution of the Soviet Union. Primary exports include oil, metals, machinery, chemicals, and forestry products. Principal imports include machinery and foods. Among Russia's leading trade partners are Germany, the United States, Belarus, Ukraine, and Kazakhstan.

Services

During the Soviet era the service sector suffered from drastic inadequacies. The state-owned services, which made little effort to respond to consumer demand, were characterized by inefficient bureaucratization. In the post-Soviet era private-sector services grew dramatically, and many of the shortages that characterized the previous era were eliminated. By the beginning of the twenty-first century, services accounted for more than half of GDP. Still, complaints remained regarding the provision of services by the public sector, particularly the police, schools, and hospitals. Owing to budget shortfalls, many of the public-sector services are poorly financed and have been unable to retain skilled employees.

Travel and tourism account for several million jobs in Russia. Some 20 million foreign visitors travel to Russia each year, though many of these visitors are seasonal workers from former Soviet republics. Freed from the restrictions of Soviet times, Russians have increasingly travelled abroad.

Labour and Taxation

Before the dissolution of the Soviet Union, an overarching All-Union Central Council of Trade Unions nominally represented the interests of workers, though it was controlled by the governing Communist Party. In the mid-1980s there was increasing labour unrest, particularly from miners, and greater rights were granted to workers. Since the collapse of communism, labour relations have been in constant flux, and several labour codes have been adopted. Trade union reform in 2001 effectively produced the Federation of Independent Trade Unions of the Russian Federation, which represents some 50 million workers organized into various branches, and exercises a monopoly on most union activity. Alternative trade unions were unable to operate unless they represented at least half of the employees at a company.

The primary and secondary sectors continue to provide employment for a large proportion of the workforce, with one-eighth of workers employed in agriculture and one-fifth in mining and manufacturing. Still, the service sector (including banking, insurance, and other financial services) has grown appreciably and now employs about three-fifths of all Russian workers.

Tax laws have undergone dramatic reform since the dissolution of the Soviet Union. As a result of high tax rates, the large number of unreported incomes (particularly related to organized-crime syndicates), and general fraud, the government failed to collect a significant proportion of the revenue to which it was legally entitled. In the early twenty-first century, to combat fraud and encourage investment, the government simplified the tax system and reduced the overall tax burden, particularly on businesses. Corporate taxes were reduced by about one-third, a flat tax was imposed on incomes, and the value-added tax on the sale of goods was reduced. A single natural-resource extraction tax also replaced three existing resource taxes. The value-added tax is a large source of government revenue.

Despite Russia's abundant natural resources and relative strength in human capital, the country faces an uncertain economic future. In order to overcome the more negative factors – such as a low level of innovation, the persistence of strong vested interests, inadequate managerial skills, under-developed technological capabilities, the restricted demand for new products and processes, little long-term bank lending, a lack of venture capital, and modest foreign direct investment in manufacturing – the promotion of effective economic development strategies remains a government priority in the face of competition from other dynamic emerging economies, in particular China and India.

11

EVERYDAY LIFE IN MODERN RUSSIA

Over the course of the twentieth century Russia witnessed sea changes in all areas of life, in government, in forms of social organization, and in freedoms of all sorts. It was a century that saw Russia move definitively from an essentially peasant economy to become an industrial superpower. These changes inevitably have left their mark, and for many meant that economic hardship has dictated the tone of everyday life. Of course there have been other, more imperceptible transformations, and constants, too.

One of the most significant factors that have generated widespread changes in Russia's lifestyles and social customs has been the growth of a Russian middle class. This began in the Leonid Brezhnev era (1964–82) and saw another period of expansion in the *glasnost* era of the late 1980s. Definitions of this class, and estimates of its extent, differ widely, but it is generally agreed that today it constitutes about one-fourth of Russian society, and is largely concentrated in and around Moscow, St Petersburg, and other urban areas. In the later twentieth century increased salaries meant that ownership of consumer goods, such as refrigerators and cars, became a realistic expectation for some, and, more recently, travel abroad has become popular, and the purchase of imported luxury goods has increased. Many wealthy individuals have bought private land and built second homes, often of two or three stories. Underlying these new developments are changes in values: as distinct from Soviet practice, the new values include self-reliance and viewing work as a source of joy and pride; the middle class also tends to avoid political extremes, to participate in charitable organizations, and to patronize theatres and restaurants.

The collapse of the Soviet Union in 1991 ushered in further dramatic change. The effects have been visible in a wide spectrum of activities, from health care and education to the construction boom and a revival of religious practice and enjoyment of folk and religious festivals.

Food, Drink, and Festivals

One of the constants in Russian everyday life, as in all countries, has been food and drink. Russia's staple foodstuffs reflect the natural environment of steppe and forest, with a predominance of grain products – especially wheat, rye, oats, and millet – and an abundance of berries and mushrooms from the country's vast forested areas. Russia also has huge resources of fish – including caviar – while since the 1990s a wide array of imported packaged products are now found in Russian cities, thus adding to the country's natural richness and diversity of food products.

One of Russia's most celebrated dishes – at least internationally – is borsch, a soup made with beets. The Ukrainian (and arguably the original) version is often eaten with a sour cream garnish and with *pirozhki*, turnovers filled with beef and onions, and can be eaten hot or cold. A dish celebrated across the world, borsch can be prepared in a great variety of ways, some clear and light, others thick and substantial. Sometimes it is even made with kvass, a mild beer fermented from grain or bread.

Another popular dish, both in Russia and across the world, is caviar, the processed, salted roe of certain species of fish, notably sturgeon. Like borsch, this too was once considered a humble foodstuff: for many years caviar in Russia was consumed as a staple of the poor – it was not until the eighteenth century that it became the preserve of the aristocracy. And while it retains its connotations of luxury and wealth abroad, in Russia today caviar continues to feature at weddings, holiday feasts, and other festive occasions. Indeed, many Russians believe in the magical health benefits of caviar, seeing it as a kind of general panacea.

The main source of Russian caviar is the Caspian Sea. An idea of the scale of production can be seen in the export figures: in 1919, after the Bolsheviks had nationalized production, though exports amounted to only one-tenth of the annual harvest, Russia was able to export widely across the world and to supply the United States with the bulk of its needs, following the overfishing of its own natural reserves. During the Soviet era, despite Russia continuing to be a major exporter, caviar was readily available to the country's citizens. But in the 1960s it disappeared from the shelves, becoming a delicacy reserved for the political elite. With the opening of a market economy in the 1990s, caviar became more expensive still, though readily available at a price. According to consumption figures, this does not seem to have had a significant effect: Russians today consume 1,000 tonnes of caviar a year, a massive 92 per cent of it poached, according to figures provided by the World Wildlife Fund; Russia's agriculture ministry puts the figure even higher, at 1,200 tonnes, most of it acquired illegally.

This has brought another factor into play: the environment. Sturgeon numbers went into decline in the 1960s, and then in the 1990s the economic crisis following the collapse of the Soviet Union led to a sharp increase in poaching in the Volga delta, an activity to which the authorities largely turned a blind eye. The poachers, who paid little heed to the age and size of the fish they caught, caused a further sturgeon decline. Following warnings issued by ecologists that Russian caviar could disappear altogether as the Caspian Sea's sturgeon population reaches dangerously low levels and even risks extinction, since August 1, 2007, the harvest and sale of black caviar have been banned in Russia.

If caviar is a symbol of Russia in restaurants and shops across the world, so too is vodka, Russia's national drink. Vodka originated during the fourteenth century; the name is a diminutive of the Russian *voda* ("water"). It is an inexpensive drink to produce, since it can be made from a mash of the cheapest and most readily available raw materials suitable for fermentation. Potatoes were traditionally employed, but have largely been supplanted in Russia and in other vodka-producing countries by cereal grains. A distilled liquor, clear in colour and without definite aroma or taste, it ranges in alcoholic content from about 40 to 55 per cent.

In Russia, vodka accompanies many family meals, especially on special occasions. Vodka is traditionally consumed straight, unmixed and chilled, in small glasses, and is accompanied by a fatty salt herring, a sour cucumber, a pickled mushroom, or a piece of rye bread with butter. It is considered bad manners and a sign of weak character to become visibly intoxicated from vodka.

The basic vodkas have no additional flavouring, but they are sometimes infused with cranberries, lemon peel, pepper, or herbs. *Zubrovka*, yellowish in colour, highly aromatic, and with a somewhat bitter undertone, is produced by steeping several stalks of *zubrovka*, or buffalo grass, in vodka.

Vodka is not the only popular drink in Russia, of course. Normally, Russians prefer to finish their daily meals with a cup of tea or coffee (the latter more common in the larger cities). Alternatively, kvass remains popular, a traditional drink that can be made at home from stale black bread. On a hot summer's day, chilled kvass is used to make *okroshka*, a traditional cold soup laced with cucumbers, boiled eggs, sausages, and salamis.

As in many countries, Russia's culinary traditions are closely woven into the fabric of its religious and folk festivals. Some of these date from pagan times. During *Maslyanitsa* – the oldest Russian folk holiday, marking the end of winter – pancakes (symbolizing the sun) are served with caviar, various fish, nuts, honey pies, and other garnishes and side dishes. The meal is accompanied by tea in the ever-present samovar (tea kettle) and is often washed down with vodka. At Easter baked goods can be found in abundance and include round-shaped sweet bread and Easter cake. Traditionally, *pashka*, a mixture of sweetened curds, butter, and raisins, is served with the cake. Hard-boiled eggs painted in bright colours also are staples of the Easter holiday. During *Troitsa* (Pentecost), homes are adorned with fresh green branches, and girls often make garlands of birch branches and flowers to put into water for fortune-telling. In

August there is a cluster of three *Spas* holidays that celebrate honey and the sowing of the apple and nut crops, respectively.

Russia also has several official holidays, including the Russian Orthodox Christmas (January 7), Victory Day in the Second World War (May 9), Independence Day (June 12), and Constitution Day (December 12). Women's Day (March 8), formerly known as International Women's Day and celebrated elsewhere in the world by its original name, was established by the Soviet authorities to highlight the advances women made under communist rule. During the holiday women usually receive gifts such as flowers and chocolates.

Sport

Sport played a major role in the Soviet state in the post-the Second World War period. The achievements of Soviet athletes in the international arena, particularly in the Olympic Games (the Soviets first participated in the 1952 Summer and the 1956 Winter Olympics), were a source of great national pride. Although Soviet athletes were declared amateurs, they were well supported by the State Committee for Sport. Soviet national teams were especially successful in ice hockey – winning numerous world championships and Olympic gold medals – volleyball, and, later, basketball. Soviet gymnasts and track-and-field athletes (male and female), weight lifters, wrestlers, and boxers were consistently among the best in the world. Even since the collapse of the Soviet empire, Russian athletes have continued to dominate international competition in these areas.

As in most of the world, football (soccer) enjoys wide popularity in Russia. At the centre of the country's proud tradition is

LEV YASHIN (1929–90)

Russian footballer

Lev Yashin was considered by many to be the greatest goalkeeper in the history of soccer. He played his first football game for Moscow Dynamo in 1953 and remained with the club until his retirement in 1971. During that time Dynamo won five league titles and three cups. He also enjoyed considerable success with the Soviet national team, helping the team win the gold medal at the 1956 Olympics in Melbourne, Australia, and claim the first-ever European Championship in 1960. At the World Cup Yashin was the keeper for Soviet runs to the quarterfinals in 1958 and 1962, as well as for the team's fourth-place finish in 1966.

Throughout his career Yashin collected nicknames such as "black panther", "black spider", and "black octopus" because of his black uniform and his innovative style of play. He was one of the first keepers to dominate the entire penalty area, and on the goal line he was capable of acrobatic saves. In his career he recorded 207 shutouts and 150 penalty saves. In 1963 he was named European Footballer of the Year, the only time a keeper has won the award.

legendary goalkeeper Lev Yashin, whose spectacular play in the 1956 Olympics helped Russia capture the gold medal. Today there are three professional divisions for men, and the sport is also growing in popularity among women.

Ice hockey was introduced to Russia only during the Soviet era, yet the national team soon dominated international competitions. The Soviet squad claimed more than twenty world championships between 1954 and 1991. The success of the national team can be attributed to both the Soviet player-development system and the leadership of coach Anatoly Tarasov, who created the innovative team passing style characteristic of Soviet hockey. Goalkeeper Vladislav Tretyak (the first Soviet player inducted into the Hockey Hall of Fame in Toronto) and defender Vyacheslav Fetisov – who was among the first players allowed by the Soviet authorities to play in the North American National Hockey League (NHL) – were two of the finest players in those great Soviet teams. Although Russia's top professional league is quite popular, many of the best Russian players now ply their trade in the NHL.

The first Russian world chess champion was Alexander Alekhine, who left Russia after the 1917 Revolution. Undaunted by Alekhine's departure, the Soviet Union was able to produce top-ranked players by funding chess schools to find and train talented children. The best of these students were then supported by the state – they were the first chess professionals – at a time when no one in the West could make a living wage from chess alone. From 1948 Soviet and Russian grand masters, including Mikhail Botvinnik, Vasily Smyslov, Boris Spassky, Anatoly Karpov, Garry Kasparov, and Vladimir Kramnik, held the title of world champion almost continuously. During the same period, three Russian women reigned as women's world champion: Lyudmila Rudenko, Olga Rubtsova, and Elizaveta Bykova.

On the amateur level, the lack of facilities and equipment has prevented many average Russian citizens from participating in sporting activities, but jogging, football, and fishing are popular pastimes, and no doubt the sporting scene will change as the twenty-first century progresses.

GARRY KASPAROV (b. 1963)

Russian chess master and politician

Kasparov was born in Baku, Azerbaijan, and began playing chess at the age of six. He became an international grandmaster following his victory in the 1980 World Junior (under 20) Championship. In 1984–5 Kasparov met world champion Anatoly Karpov in a match that was aborted after five months of play; in late 1985 Kasparov won a 24-game return match 13–11. The International Chess Federation (FIDE) stripped him of his title in 1993 in a conflict over the venue for a championship match, but the rest of the chess world still accepted him as champion. In 1996 Kasparov defeated IBM's custom-built chess computer Deep Blue in a match that attracted worldwide attention. In a 1997 rematch an upgraded Deep Blue prevailed. In 2000 Kasparov lost a 16-game championship match to Vladimir Kramnik of Russia.

Kasparov retired from competitive chess in 2005, though not from involvement in chess. In particular, he produced an acclaimed series of books, *Kasparov on My Great Predecessors* (2003–6), covering many of the game's great players. He also kept in the public eye with his decision in 2005 to start a political organization, the United Civil Front, to oppose Russian President Vladimir Putin. In 2006 Kasparov was one of the prime movers behind a broad coalition of political parties that formed the Other Russia, a group held together by only one goal: ousting Putin from power. In 2007, following several protest marches organized by the coalition in which Kasparov and other participants were arrested, the Other Russia chose Kasparov as its candidate for the 2008 presidential election but was unable to nominate him by the deadline.

Religion

The rebirth of religion is another dimension of the change in lifestyles of the new Russia. Religious institutions have filled the vacuum created by the downfall of communist ideology, and religious festivities are now once again a regular feature of popular culture. Moreover, for believers and non-believers alike, the Russian Orthodox Church – for nearly a thousand years the country's dominant religious institution – has been a major influence throughout the country's history, not only in relation to religious belief and practice, but in creating and maintaining cultural and national identity. Today Russian Orthodoxy is still the country's largest religious denomination, constituting about half of all total congregations, and is also the largest independent Eastern Orthodox Church in the world; its membership is estimated at more than 85 million people. Yet despite the revival of religious practices since the late 1980s, the non-religious still constitute an overwhelming majority of the population.

Christianity was introduced into the East Slavic state of Kievan Rus by Greek missionaries from Byzantium in the ninth century, but it was the baptism of Vladimir, Prince of Kiev, in 988 that propelled Russia from paganism to Christianity. This led to the adoption of the Cyrillic alphabet and to centuries of alignment with Byzantine culture and traditions.

Under Vladimir's successors, and until 1448, the Russian church was headed by the metropolitans of Kiev and formed a metropolitanate of the Byzantine patriarchate; thereafter the Russian bishops elected their own patriarch without recourse to Constantinople, and the Russian church was thenceforth independent.

Just as in the arts, the fate of the religious institutions ebbed and flowed according to changing political climate. In the twentieth century, and particularly under Soviet rule, periods of persecution and repression were followed by brief interludes of revival and expansion. Although the constitution of the Soviet Union nominally guaranteed religious freedom, religious activities were greatly constrained, and membership of religious organizations was considered incompatible with membership of the Communist Party. When the Soviets first came to power they soon declared the separation of church and state, and nationalized all church-held lands. These administrative measures were followed by brutal state-sanctioned persecutions that included the wholesale destruction of churches, and the arrest and execution of many clerics. The Russian Orthodox Church was further weakened in 1922, when the Renovated Church, a reform movement supported by the Soviet government, brought division among clergy and faithful.

In 1943, benefiting from the sudden reversal of Joseph Stalin's policies toward religion, Russian Orthodoxy underwent a resurrection: a new patriarch was elected, theological schools were opened, and thousands of churches began to function. Between 1945 and 1959 the official organization of the church was greatly expanded, although individual members of the clergy were occasionally arrested and exiled. The number of open churches reached 25,000. But a new and widespread persecution of the church was subsequently instituted under the leadership of Nikita Khrushchev and Leonid Brezhnev. Then, beginning in the late 1980s, under Mikhail Gorbachev, the new political and social freedoms resulted in many church buildings being returned to the church, to be restored by local parishioners. The collapse of the Soviet Union in 1991 made religious freedom a reality, and revealed that large sections of the population had continued to practise a variety of faiths. Indeed, Russian nationalists who emerged from the 1990s identified the Russian Orthodox Church as a major element of Russian culture. Tsar Nicholas II, the Russian emperor who had been murdered by the Bolsheviks after the October Revolution of 1917, and members of his family were canonized by the church in 2000.

Other Christian denominations are much smaller and include the Old Believers, who separated from the Russian Orthodox Church in the seventeenth century, and Baptist and Evangelical groups. Catholics, both Western rite (Roman) and Eastern rite (Uniate), and Lutherans were numerous in the former Soviet Union but lived mainly outside present-day Russia, where there are few adherents. Muslims constitute Russia's second-largest religious group. In 1997 legislation was enacted that constrained denominations outside five "traditional" religions – Russian Orthodoxy, several other Christian denominations, Islam, Judaism, and Buddhism – restricting the activities for at least fifteen years of groups not registered in the country. For example, groups not meeting this requirement at the time the law was implemented (such as Roman Catholics and Mormons) were unable to operate educational institutions or disseminate religious literature.

Although there is some degree of correlation between language and religion, the two do not correspond entirely. Slavs are overwhelmingly Orthodox Christian. Turkic speakers are predominantly Muslim, although several Turkic groups in Russia are not. For example, Christianity predominates among the Chuvash, Buddhism prevails among large numbers of Altai, Khakass, and Tuvans, and many Turkic speakers east of the Yenisey have retained their shamanistic beliefs (though some have converted to Christianity). Buddhism is common among the Mongolian-speaking Buryat and Kalmyk.

Jews long suffered discrimination in Russia, including purges in the nineteenth century, repression under the regime of Joseph Stalin, and Nazi atrocities on Russian soil during the Second World War. Beginning with Gorbachev's reformist policies in the 1980s, Jewish emigration to Israel and elsewhere was permitted on an increasing scale, and the number of Jews living in Russia (and all parts of the former Soviet Union) has decreased. Prior to the break-up of the Soviet Union, about one-third of its Jewish population lived in Russia (though many did not practise Judaism), and now about one-tenth of all Jews in Russia reside in Moscow. In the 1930s the Soviet government established Yevreyskaya in the far east as a Jewish autonomous province, though by the end of the twentieth century only about 5 per cent of the province's population was Jewish.

Social Issues

Some of Russia's most pressing social problems have been inherited from the Soviet and earlier past. Others are more recent developments, fostered by the speed of change and economic collapse that followed the demise of the Soviet Union in 1991.

Public health is among the most serious social concerns. During much of the Soviet period, when social welfare programmes were funded by the central government, advances in health care and material well-being led to a decline in mortality, the control or eradication of the more dangerous infectious diseases, and an increase in the average lifespan. From the 1990s a major portion of the public welfare budget continued to be directed into free medical service, training, pensions, and scholarships with the aim of improving the material and social conditions of workers in Russia, but employer-based social insurance and pension funds, to which workers contributed, were also introduced.

Nevertheless, after 1991 public health deteriorated dramatically. The death rate reached its highest level of the twentieth century (excluding wartime) in the 1990s. Life expectancy fell dramatically (though it began to rise again by the end of the decade), and infectious diseases that had been under control spread again. In addition, the country suffered high rates of cancer, tuberculosis, and heart disease. Various social, ecological, and economic factors underlay these developments, including funding and medicine shortages, adequately paid and trained medical personnel (for example, many medical schools lack sufficient supplies and instructors), poor intensive and emergency care, the limited development of specialized services such as maternity and hospice care, contaminated food and drinking water, duress caused by economic dislocation, poor nutrition, contact with toxic substances in the workplace, and high rates of alcohol and tobacco consumption. Air pollution in heavily industrialized areas has led to relatively high rates of lung cancer in these regions, and high incidences of stomach cancer have occurred in regions where consumption of carbohydrates is high and intake of fruits, vegetables, milk, and animal proteins is low.

Alcoholism has long been a severe public health problem in Russia. At the beginning of the twenty-first century it was estimated that some one-third of men and one-sixth of women were addicted to alcohol. The problem is particularly acute in rural areas and among the Evenk, Sakha, Koryak, and Nenets peoples in Russia's northern regions. Widespread alcoholism has its origins in the Soviet-era "vodka-based economy", which countered shortages in the supply of food and consumer goods with the production of vodka, a non-perishable product that was easily transportable. The government has sponsored media campaigns to promote healthy living and imposed strict tax regulations aimed at reducing the profitability of vodka producers; in addition, group-therapy sessions have spread. There have also been proposals to prohibit the sale of hard liquors in the regions with the highest rates of alcoholism.

Housing

Prior to the dissolution of the Soviet Union, nearly all the housing stock of urban areas was owned by the state. Indeed, private property was prohibited in urban areas, and in rural areas the size of private homes was strictly limited. High-rise apartment buildings with a very unpretentious architecture made up the bulk of the stock. Local authorities had charge of renting arrangements, and in "company towns" the manage-ment of state enterprises was given this responsibility. Rental payments were kept extremely low and, in most cases, were not enough to pay maintenance costs. Deterioration of hous-ing was rapid and vandalism widespread. In addition, many apartments were shared by tenants, with joint-access kitchens and bathrooms, and the space of the average apartment in

Russia was about one-third to one-half the size of those found in western Europe.

The housing sector underwent vigorous privatization in the 1990s, and there was a decline in state-supported construction. Many renters were offered free title to their units, though many older Russians decided to forgo the necessary paperwork and continued to rent. Nevertheless, by the mid-1990s more than half of Russia's housing was privately owned, with the remainder administered by municipal authorities. Conditions improved considerably in owner-occupied housing, as the owners in apartment buildings were able to ensure the enforcement of maintenance rules, but public housing, owing to a lack of funds from local authorities, continued to deteriorate.

In the 1990s many of the housing shortages characteristic of the Soviet period disappeared, and the floor space of homes per person steadily increased, largely as the result of a construction boom for private homes. For example, the construction of private housing tripled in urban areas and nearly doubled in the rural areas. However, there were sharp declines in the construction of public housing, particularly in rural areas.

Education

Education in the Soviet Union was highly centralized, with the state owning and operating nearly every school. The curriculum was rigid, and the system aimed to indoctrinate students in the communist system. As with many aspects of the Soviet system, schools were often forced to operate in crowded facilities and with limited resources. With democratization there was widespread support for educational reforms. In 1992 the federal government passed legislation enabling regions where non-Russians predominated to exercise some degree of autonomy in education, but diplomas can still be conferred only in the Russian, Bashkir, and Tatar languages, and the federal government has responsibility for designing and distributing textbooks, licensing teachers, and setting the requirements for instruction in the Russian language, sciences, and mathematics. School finance and the humanities, history, and social science curricula are entrusted to regional authorities.

Pre-school education in Russia is very well developed; some four-fifths of children aged three to six attend crèches or kindergartens. Schooling is compulsory for nine years. It starts from the age of seven (in some areas from six) and leads to a basic general education certificate. An additional two or three years of schooling are required for the secondary-level certificate, and some seven-eighths of Russian students continue their education past this level. Non-Russian schoolchildren are taught in their own language, but Russian is a compulsory subject at the secondary level.

Admission to an institute of higher education is selective and highly competitive. First-degree courses usually take five years. Higher education is conducted almost entirely in Russian, although there are a few institutions, mainly in the minority republics, where the local language is also used.

Russia's oldest university is Moscow State University, which was founded in 1755. Throughout the nineteenth century and into the twentieth, Russian universities in Moscow, St Petersburg, and Kazan produced world-class scholars, notably the mathematician Nikolay Lobachevsky and the chemist Dmitry Mendeleyev. Although universities suffered severely during the purges of the Stalinist regime, a number have continued to provide high-quality education, particularly in the sciences. In addition to Moscow State University, the most important institutions include St Petersburg State University (founded 1819) and Novosibirsk State University (1959).

Since the demise of the Soviet Union, the quantity and diversity of universities and institutes have undergone unprecedented expansion. In 1991 the country had some 500 institutions of higher education, all of which were controlled by the state. By the beginning of the twenty-first century, the number of state schools had increased by nearly one-fifth, though many suffered from inadequate state funding, dated equipment, and overcrowding. The state schools were joined by more than 300 private colleges and universities, which were all established after 1994. Licensed by the state, these schools have generally enjoyed better funding than the state schools; however, they have been very costly and have served mainly Russia's new middle class.

PART 5

PLACES

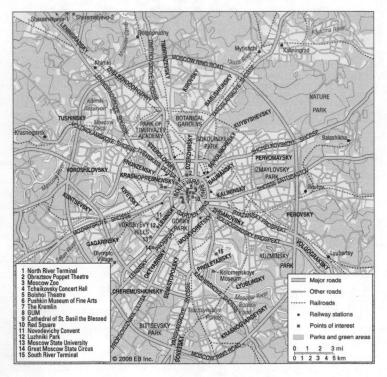

1 North River Terminal
2 Obraztsov Puppet Theatre
3 Moscow Zoo
4 Tchaikovsky Concert Hall
5 Bolshoi Theatre
6 Pushkin Museum of Fine Arts
7 The Kremlin
8 GUM
9 Cathedral of St. Basil the Blessed
10 Red Square
11 Novodevichy Convent
12 Luzhniki Park
13 Moscow State University
14 Great Moscow State Circus
15 South River Terminal

Major roads
Other roads
Railroads
Railway stations
Points of interest
Parks and green areas

0   1   2   3 mi
0 1 2 3 4 5 km

© 2008 EB Inc.

Moscow

12

THE MAJOR SITES TO VISIT

Moscow

The capital of the Russian Federation, Moscow today is not only the country's industrial, cultural, scientific, and educational capital and political centre, but the most populous city in Russia, with over 10 million inhabitants. For more than 600 years the city has also been the spiritual centre of the Russian Orthodox Church.

Moscow is an upbeat, vibrant, and sometimes wearisome city. Much of Moscow was reconstructed after it was occupied by the French under Napoleon I in 1812 and almost entirely destroyed by fire. Since then, Moscow has frequently been refurbished and modernized, and continues to experience rapid social change. Russia's Soviet past collides with its capitalist present everywhere in the country, but nowhere is this contrast more visible than in Moscow. Vladimir Ilyich Lenin's Mausoleum remains intact, as do many dreary five-storey apartment buildings from the era of Nikita

Khrushchev's rule (the mid-1950s to the mid-1960s); yet glitzy cars and western-style supermarkets, casinos, and nightclubs are equally visible. Many Orthodox churches, as well as some synagogues and mosques, have been restored, Moscow's novel theatres have reclaimed leadership in the dramatic arts, and traditional markets have been revived and expanded. These markets, which under the Soviets were known as kolkhoz (collective-farm) markets and sold mainly crafts and produce, are now more sophisticated retail establishments.

Unlike St Petersburg, Moscow is viewed as a traditional Russian city and has a well-defined city centre, marked by the Kremlin. Other characteristics of Moscow are its physical layout in radial spokes and rings that have been extended over time, its hodgepodge of architectural styles, and its historical buildings that were mainly built by Russian architects. Moscow's buildings were predominantly wooden until the 1920s, when brick and stone came into use.

Climate

Moscow's climate is dominated by westerly winds from the Atlantic. Winters are long, yet significantly milder than in similar climatic regions of North America. Snow is common, beginning usually about mid-November and lasting generally until mid-March, but the city is well equipped to keep the streets clear. The average January temperature is 14 F (–10 C), though there can be considerable variation; temperatures have dropped to near –45 F (–43 C). Spring is relatively brief, and the temperature rises rapidly during late April. Summers are warm, and July, the warmest month, has an average temperature in the mid-60s F (about 18 C). Rainy days are not uncommon, but the summer rainfall often comes in brief, heavy downpours and thunderstorms. Autumn, like spring, is short, with rapidly falling temperatures.

Until the late 1950s there was increasing air pollution in Moscow. Smog was common, often with heavy concentrations of sulphur dioxide. A major campaign to control noxious emissions was launched, assisted greatly by a changeover from coal to natural gas as the principal fuel. Some factories that had contributed to pollution were moved out of the city. Slight improvement in Moscow's air had been marked, but since the 1980s the growing number of motor vehicles and the increase in the number of power generators have once again bolstered the concentrations of such exhaust pollutants as carbon monoxide and sulphur dioxide.

History

Moscow has played a vital role in Russian history. It was the capital of Muscovy (the Grand Principality of Moscow) in the late thirteenth century – hence, the people of Moscow are known as Muscovites. Gradually the princes of Moscow extended their rule over the other surrounding Russian princedoms, and the town became the leader in the long struggle against Mongol hegemony. By the second half of the fifteenth century, especially after the annexation of Novgorod in 1478, Moscow had become the undisputed centre of a unified Russian state.

When in 1712 Peter I (the Great) transferred the capital to his new city of St Petersburg on the Gulf of Finland, Moscow was quick to recover and retained its major role in the cultural life of Russia. The eighteenth century saw the foundation of Moscow University – the first in Russia – and a medical and surgical college. Industry flourished, too, and by the time of

Napoleon's invasion in 1812 the population had grown to 275,000.

The Napoleonic invasion has become legendary: after a bitter fifteen-hour battle on August 26 (September 7, New Style) at Borodino on the approaches to Moscow, the Russian commander-in-chief, General M. I. Kutuzov, evacuated both troops and civilians from the city, which was occupied by the French a week later. A fire broke out and spread rapidly, eventually destroying more than two-thirds of all the buildings. Looting was rife. The lack of supplies and shelter and the continual harassment by Russian skirmishing forces made it impossible for Napoleon to winter in Moscow, however, and on October 7 (October 19, New Style) the French troops began their catastrophic retreat.

In 1813 a Commission for the Construction of the City of Moscow was established. It launched a great programme of rebuilding, which included a partial replanning of the city centre. Among many buildings constructed or reconstructed at this time were the Great Kremlin and Armoury palaces, the university, the Manezh (riding school), and the Bolshoi Theatre. Industry also expanded rapidly in this century, and the Moscow stock exchange was established. The emancipation of the serfs in 1861 and the beginning of the railway era with the opening of the line to St Petersburg in 1851 greatly increased labour mobility, and large numbers of peasants from the villages began moving to the city. Between 1897 and 1915 Moscow yet again doubled in size, to a population of nearly 2 million.

Moscow resumed its status as capital city in March 1918 when Lenin and the Soviet government moved to Moscow. In the civil war period (1918–20), Moscow, like other Soviet cities, suffered greatly, with grave food shortages, loss of

population, and reduction of industry. But in the years following the final establishment of Soviet power and peace, recovery
was swift, and the city functioned as one of the main spring-
boards for industrialization elsewhere in the Soviet Union.
During the Second World War, the Germans in late 1941
reached the outskirts of Moscow, less than 25 miles (40 km)
from the Kremlin. Many factories were evacuated, together
with much of the government and most residents. From
October 20 the city was declared to be in a state of siege.
Its remaining inhabitants built and manned anti-tank defences
while the city was bombarded from the air. A desperate
counter-attack on December 6 threw the German forces back
from the outskirts and saved Moscow. Recovery was quick
after the war, with further growth of the city's economy. Two
major events have marked the city's progress: in 1947, two
years after the war's end, Moscow celebrated its 800th anniversary, and in 1980 it hosted the Summer Olympic Games.

In the post-war period, migration to Moscow caused a
housing shortage that reached grave proportions in the
1950s. Under Nikita Khrushchev a major construction programme was initiated. Much of the old housing, often single-
storied and made of wood, was cleared, and extensive new
tracts of large apartment buildings sprang up around the
historic core of the city. Considerable urban renewal took
place in the central areas, and high-rise buildings now dominate the skyline.

As the capital of post-Soviet Russia, Moscow was at the
centre of the country's historic transformation. In the decade
following the Soviet collapse, many historical buildings, especially churches, underwent a sweeping renovation on a scale
without precedent in the city's history. Moscow is a city whose
splendour continues to bedazzle.

The Sights

A map of Moscow presents a pattern of concentric rings that circle the rough triangle of the Kremlin and its rectangular extension, the Kitay-gorod, with outwardly radiating spokes connecting the rings; the whole pattern is modified by the twisting, north-west- to south-east-trending Moskva (Moscow) River. These rings and radials mark the historical stages of the city's growth: successive epochs of development are traced by the Boulevard Ring and the Garden Ring (both following the line of former fortifications), the Moscow Little Ring Railway (built in part along the line of the former Kamer-Kollezhsky customs barrier), and the Moscow Ring Road.

As throughout its history, the Kremlin remains the heart of the city. It is the symbol of both Russian and (for a time) Soviet power and authority, and since 1991 it has served as the official residence of the president of the Russian Federation. The Kremlin's crenellated red brick walls and its 20 towers (19 with spires) were built at the end of the fifteenth century, when a host of Italian builders arrived in Moscow at the invitation of Ivan III (the Great). One of the most important towers, the Saviour (Spasskaya) Tower, leading to Red Square, was built in 1491 by Pietro Solario, who designed most of the main towers; its belfry was added in 1624–5. The chimes of its clock are broadcast by radio as a time signal to the whole country. Also on the Red Square front is the St Nicholas (Nikolskaya) Tower, built originally in 1491 and rebuilt in 1806. The two other principal gate towers – the Trinity (Troitskaya) Tower, with a bridge and outer barbican (the Kutafya Tower), and the Borovitskaya Tower – rise from the western wall.

RED SQUARE

Large public square in central Moscow

Red Square lies north of the Moskva River, adjacent to the Kremlin, and covers some 18 acres (7.3 hectares). Dating from the late fifteenth century, it has long been a busy market area as well as a focal point in Russian history as the scene of executions, demonstrations, riots, and parades. Located around it are the State Historical Museum (1875–81), the nine-towered Cathedral of St Basil the Blessed (1554–60), the former state department store GUM, and the tomb of Lenin. The square and Kremlin were designated a UNESCO World Heritage site in 1990.

Within the Kremlin walls is one of the most striking and beautiful architectural ensembles in the world: a combination of churches and palaces, which are open to the public and are among the city's most popular tourist attractions, and the highest offices of the state, which are surrounded by strict security. Around the centrally located Cathedral Square are grouped three magnificent cathedrals, superb examples of Russian church architecture at its height in the late fifteenth and early sixteenth centuries. These and the other churches in the Kremlin ceased functioning as places of worship after the Russian Revolution of 1917, but from 1990 services recommenced in most Kremlin churches. The Cathedral of the Assumption is the oldest, built of white stone in 1475–9 in the Italianate-Byzantine style. Its pure, simple, and beautifully proportioned lines and elegant arches are crowned by five golden domes. The Orthodox metropolitans and patriarchs of the fourteenth to eighteenth centuries are buried there. Across the square is the Cathedral of the Annunciation, built in 1484–9 by craftsmen from Pskov (though burned in 1547, it was rebuilt in 1562–4). Its cluster of chapels is topped by golden roofs and domes. Inside are a number of early fifteenth-century icons attributed to Theophanes the Greek and to Andrey Rublyov, considered by many to be the greatest of all Russian icon painters. The third cathedral, dedicated to St Michael the Archangel, was rebuilt in 1505–8: in it are buried the princes of Moscow and the tsars of Russia (except Boris Godunov) up to the founding of St Petersburg.

Just off the square stands the splendid, soaring white bell tower of Ivan III; built in the sixteenth century and damaged in 1812, it was restored a few years later. At its foot is the enormous Tsar Bell, cast in 1733–5 but never rung. Nearby is the Tsar Cannon, cast in 1586. Beside the gun are located the mid-seventeenth-century Cathedral of the Twelve Apostles and the adjoining Patriarchal Palace.

On the west of Cathedral Square is a group of palaces of various periods. The Palace of Facets – so called from the exterior finish of faceted, white stone squares – was built in 1487–91. Behind it is the Terem Palace of 1635–6, which incorporates several older churches, including that of the Resurrection of Lazarus, dating from 1393. Both became part of the Great Kremlin Palace, built as a royal residence in 1838–49 and formerly used for sessions of the Supreme Soviet of the USSR; its long, yellow-washed facade dominates the river front. It is connected to the Armoury Palace, built in 1844–51 and now housing the Armoury Museum, with a large collection of treasures of the tsars. Along the north-east wall of the Kremlin are the Arsenal (1702–36), the former Senate building (1776–88), and the School for Red Commanders (1932–4). The only other Soviet-period building within the

Kremlin is the Palace of Congresses (1960–1), with a vast auditorium used for political gatherings and as a theatre.

The Kitay-gorod is a historic quarter of Moscow and a major tourist site. Within the Kitay-gorod, along the east wall of the Kremlin, lies Red Square, the ceremonial centre of the capital and the scene of holiday parades. The austere Lenin Mausoleum blends into the wall, which itself contains the graves of most of the Soviet leadership. At the southern end of Red Square is the Church of the Intercession, better known as the Cathedral of St Basil the Blessed. Built in 1554–60 to commemorate the defeat of the Tatars of Kazan and Astrakhan by Ivan IV (the Terrible), it is a unique and magnificent architectural display, each of its ten domes differing in design and colour. Along Red Square facing the Kremlin is the late nineteenth-century former State Department Store – usually called by its Russian acronym, GUM (*Glavny Universalny Magazin*) – now a privatized shopping mall, with its long aisles, iron bridges linking the upper floors, and vast skylights. The slightly earlier State Historical Museum (1875–83) closes off the northern end of the square. In 1990 the Kremlin and Red Square areas were designated a UNESCO World Heritage site.

Many old churches survive in the Kitay-gorod. Of particular note is the Church of the Trinity of Nikitniki (1628–34), built for the merchant Grigory Nikitnikov. Other notable churches in this quarter are the fifteenth-century Church of St Anne of the Conception and the Epiphany Cathedral (1693–6). The Kitay-gorod was for centuries the commercial centre of Moscow, and its narrow, crowded streets still contain former banks, the stock-exchange building, and warehouses. Many of the old buildings near the river, however, were demolished in the 1960s to make room for the massive Rossiya Hotel (completed in 1967; torn down in 2006); nevertheless, a row of buildings, including the sixteenth-century house of the Romanov boyars, the Old English Embassy, and the seventeenth-century Monastery of the Sign, remains.

Moscow is also home to the country's national library, the Russian State Library, formerly the V. I. Lenin Library. It is notable for its extensive collection of early printed books and a collection of manuscripts that includes ancient Slavonic codices. Originally founded in 1862 as the library of the Rumyantsev Museum, it was reorganized after the Russian Revolution of 1917 under the leadership of Lenin, who had studied libraries in Russia and western Europe. Its initial collection incorporated the contents of confiscated private libraries and the Rumyantsev Museum collection. One of the largest libraries in the world, the Russian State Library contains more than 38 million printed books, periodicals, and serials and is the national book depository of Russia.

Cultural Life

Moscow has dozens of theatres. One of the most renowned is the Bolshoi Theatre, which was founded in 1825, though its present splendid building facing Theatre (formerly Sverdlov) Square dates from 1856. Also on Theatre Square is the Maly (Little) Theatre for drama. Another prestigious theatre, the Moscow Academic Art Theatre, founded as the Moscow Academic Theatre in 1898 by the actor, director, and producer Konstantin Stanislavsky and the playwright-producer Vladimir Nemirovich-Danchenko, was especially noted in its early days for its performances of the plays of Anton Chekhov. In the late 1980s the Moscow Academic Art Theatre split into two companies, one of which is named after Chekhov and the other after Maksim Gorky. Also of worldwide fame are the Obraztsov Puppet Theatre (formerly the State Central Puppet Theatre) and the Great Moscow State Circus, which in 1971 acquired new quarters on the Vorobyovy Hills. The repertory companies of the theatrical groups tour frequently both in Russia and abroad. There are several concert halls, notably the Tchaikovsky Concert Hall and the two halls of the conservatory. Moscow's orchestras have won international repute, as have a number of Moscow-based folk dance and choral ensembles.

The museums and art galleries in the capital include several of international rank. Foremost among these are the Pushkin Museum of Fine Arts, with a fine international collection, and the Tretyakov Gallery. The latter, which began in 1856 as the private collection of a connoisseur, Pavel Tretyakov, is noteworthy for its superb collection of icons, including several by Andrey Rublyov. Other notable museums are the Armoury Museum in the Kremlin and the State Historical Museum on Red Square. The Central Museum of the Great Patriotic War (the Second World War) is part of the sprawling memorial site at Poklonnaya Hill that opened in 1995.

Beginning in the late 1980s with the Soviet policy of *glasnost* and continuing with the Russian successor government in the early 1990s, religious repression gave way to policies endorsing religious freedom, and houses of worship in Moscow underwent massive and pervasive renovation and returned to use. The Russian Orthodox Church reopened its network of museums for the first time since the early 1900s, and pedestrian routes created around Moscow's greatest sites are intended to increase tourism.

The Luzhniki Park complex is the leading Moscow facility for sports and was one of the main arenas for the 1980

Olympic Games. The Luzhniki Stadium is flanked by a smaller arena, a swimming pool, and the indoor Sports Palace. There are many stadiums and swimming pools in the area, including some heated open-air pools that are in use year-round. In addition, there are a large number of football fields, gymnasiums, and volleyball and basketball courts; most of these are attached to individual places of work or to sports clubs. Moscow has several first-division football teams that now have corporate sponsors but whose origins date from the 1920s, when they were affiliated with powerful institutions of communist society: Dynamo (tied to the KGB), CSKA (the army's team), Lokomotiv (representing railway workers), and the defiantly independent Spartak (once only loosely linked to a food producers' cooperative but now controlled by LUKOIL, a Russian oil giant).

Outside the Garden Ring, Moscow is well endowed with parks and open spaces. Gorky Central Park of Culture along the right bank of the Moscow River is the closest to the centre and, with its amusement park, is very popular. On the east side Izmaylovsky Park is a large green area, covering nearly 3,000 acres (1,200 hectares). To the north-east is the more formal Sokolniki Park, which leads to an extensive tract of forest called Losiny Ostrov ("Moose Island"). North of the city centre are the Botanical Gardens of the Academy of Sciences, one of several such gardens in the city, and the grounds of the Moscow K. A. Timiryazev Agricultural Academy. Bittsevsky Park, also of considerable size, has been established adjacent to the Ring Road south of the city centre. Moscow Zoo, one of the world's leading zoos, is a popular attraction west of the city centre. The Khimki Reservoir, just north-west of Moscow, is used for boating and aquatic sports, but even more popular are the other reservoirs to the north, just outside Greater Moscow.

The surrounding forest-park zone provides extensive space for recreation.

St Petersburg

St Petersburg is the second largest city of Russia and one of the world's major cities. It has played a vital role in Russian history since its founding in 1703 – for two centuries (1712–1918) it was the capital of the Russian empire. The city is remembered as the scene of the February and October Revolutions of 1917 and for its fierce defence while besieged during the Second World War. Architecturally, it ranks as one of the most splendid and congenial cities of Europe. Its historic district was designated a UNESCO World Heritage site in 1990.

An important port, St Petersburg is situated in the extreme north-west of Russia, about 400 miles north-west of Moscow and only about 7 south of the Arctic Circle. Greater St Petersburg – the city itself with its satellite towns – forms a horseshoe shape around the head of the Gulf of Finland and includes the island of Kotlin in the gulf. Its population is about 4.5 million.

St Petersburg is rich in cultural, historical, and architectural landmarks. Founded by Peter I as Russia's "window on Europe", it bears the unofficial status of Russia's cultural capital and most European city, a distinction that it strives to retain in its perennial competition with Moscow. The city has three distinctive characteristics – first, its harmonious mix of western European and Russian architecture; second, its lack of an unequivocal city centre; and third, its many waterways. The short but full-flowing tributaries and canals of the Neva

River that stretch to the Baltic coast are inseparable from St Petersburg's panorama, and the bridges and natural canals of the river have earned the city the nickname "the Venice of the North". Because of St Petersburg's northerly location, the city enjoys the "white nights" from June 11 to July 2, when daylight extends to nearly nineteen hours – another of St Petersburg's most acclaimed characteristics, duly celebrated with a variety of festivals organized by the Mariinsky and Hermitage theatres and the Rimsky-Korsakov St Petersburg State Conservatory.

Climate

The mitigating effect of the Atlantic Ocean provides St Petersburg with a milder climate than might be expected for its far northern site. Nevertheless, winters are rather cold, with a mean January temperature of about 21 F (–6 C), a few degrees warmer than that for Moscow. Winter temperatures can drop below –40 F (–40 C), however. Snow cover lasts on average about 132 days. The Neva begins to freeze normally in about mid-November, and the ice is solid by the start of December; break-up begins in mid-April and is usually completed by the end of the month. Summers, the wettest period, are moderately warm, with an average temperature of 65 F (18 C) in July.

The city's low and originally marshy site has left it vulnerable to flooding, especially in the autumn, when strong cyclonic winds drive gulf waters upstream, and also at the time of the spring thaw. Exceptionally severe inundations occurred in 1777, 1824, and 1924. To control the destructive floodwaters, the city built in the 1980s a dyke, 18 miles (29 km) long, across the Gulf of Finland. A number of canals have also been cut to assist drainage.

History

The area of the current city of St Petersburg was settled as early as the eighth century, but it was not until 1703 that Peter I laid the foundation stones for the Peter-Paul Fortress on Zayachy Island. This date is taken as the founding date of St Petersburg. In the spring of the following year, Peter established the fortress of Kronshlot (later Kronshtadt), on Kotlin Island in the Gulf of Finland, to protect the approaches to the delta. At the same time, he founded the Admiralty shipyard on the riverbank opposite the Peter-Paul Fortress.

Although the first dwellings were single-storied and made of wood, it was not long before stone buildings were erected. The city was planned as an imposing capital, on a regular street pattern, with spacious squares and broad avenues radiating out from the Admiralty. Architects, craftsmen, and artisans were brought from all over Russia and from many foreign countries to construct and embellish the new town.

The city's political and cultural importance swiftly rose in 1712 when it was established as the capital of Russia, in preference to Moscow. Forced immigration of the noble and merchant classes led to the building of private palaces and government buildings: among the earliest were the Exchange (now the Naval Museum), the Naval Customs House (now the Pushkin House, or Institute of Russian Literature), and marine hospital. In addition to the construction of a harbour – which led as early as 1726 to St Petersburg handling 90 per cent of Russia's foreign trade – work began on the Vyshnevolotsky Canal in the Valdai Hills, the first link in a chain that by 1709 gave the capital a direct water route to central Russia and all of the Volga River basin.

Within its grand architectural setting and as the permanent residence of the imperial court, cultural life developed and flourished. The University of St Petersburg was founded in 1724. In 1773 the Institute of Mines was established. Many of the most celebrated names in Russia in the spheres of learning, science, and the arts are associated with the city: Mikhail V. Lomonosov, Dmitry Mendeleyev, Ivan Pavlov, Aleksandr Pushkin, Leo Tolstoy, and Fyodor Dostoyevsky, among others. Dostoyevsky's *Crime and Punishment* was set in the city, and the buildings described in the novel are a focus of tourism. As early as 1738 the first ballet school in Russia was opened in St Petersburg; in the nineteenth century, under Marius Petipa, the Russian ballet rose to worldwide renown and produced such dancers as Vaslav Nijinsky, Tamara Karsavina, and Anna Pavlova. In 1862 the first conservatory of music in Russia opened its doors, and there the premieres of works by Pyotr Ilyich Tchaikovsky, Nikolay Rimsky-Korsakov, Sergey Rachmaninov, and other composers were performed.

The outbreak of the First World War in 1914 brought an upsurge of patriotic fervour centred on the tsar. The Germanic form of the city's name was changed to its Russian version, Petrograd. But with the fall of the imperial Romanov dynasty during the subsequent 1917 Revolution, the city's destiny was inevitably at stake, and Moscow became capital again the following year. In 1924, following Lenin's death, Petrograd was renamed Leningrad, as St Petersburg was known until 1991. Much of the initial burden of developing the national economy fell on Leningrad and its established industrial plant and workforce, which by 1939 was responsible for 11 per cent of all Soviet industrial output. Then, in the Second World War, came destruction. The city was one of the initial targets of the German invasion in 1941; by September of that year, German troops were on the outskirts of the city and had cut off communication with the rest of the Soviet Union, while Finnish troops advanced from the north. Many of the inhabitants and nearly three-fourths of the industrial plant were evacuated eastward ahead of the German advance. The remainder of the population and the garrison then began to endure what has become known as the 900-day siege; the German blockade in fact lasted 872 days, from September 8, 1941, to January 27, 1944. Leningrad put up a desperate and courageous resistance in the face of many assaults, constant artillery and air bombardment, and appalling suffering from shortages of supplies. An estimated 660,000 people died, a very high proportion from scurvy and starvation. In particular, the exceptionally bitter winter of 1941–2, when temperatures fell to –40 F (–40 C), was one of extreme hardship and loss of life. Not until the 1960s did the city regain its pre-war size of 3 million inhabitants; by the 1980s the population had passed the 4 million mark.

It was only in the 1970s that the need to preserve the city's unique cultural heritage was fully recognized. City planners then pioneered new forms of industrial administration, drawing on the city's strength as a scientific and technical centre. The collapse of the Soviet Union in 1991 brought further changes, some of which were positive – new cafés and restaurants were opened, bridges and landmarks were illuminated, and cultural venues were constructed. On the other hand, homeless people and beggars, never a feature of the city in late Soviet decades, became fairly widespread, and the crime rate increased significantly.

The Sights

In lieu of a distinctive city centre on the standard Russian medieval model (epitomized by Moscow), St Petersburg's main thoroughfare, Nevsky Prospekt (avenue), particularly the stretch running from the Admiralty to the Moscow Railway Terminal, is considered the city's centre. Central St Petersburg is divided into four sections by the Neva River and its distributaries. The Admiralty Side lies along the left (south) bank of the Neva itself, at this point called the Bolshaya (Great) Neva. Between the Bolshaya Neva and the river's other main arm, the Malaya (Little) Neva, is Vasilyevsky Island, one of the first areas of the city to be developed. The Malaya Neva and the river's extreme right (north) distributary, the Bolshaya Nevka, enclose a group of islands known as the Petrograd Side, while east of the Bolshaya Nevka and north of the Neva proper lies the Vyborg Side.

As the city grew, it displayed a remarkable richness of architecture and harmony of style. Initially the style was one of simple but elegant restraint, represented in the cathedral of the Peter-Paul Fortress and in the Summer Palace. In the mid-eighteenth century an indelible stamp was put on the city's appearance by the architects Bartolomeo F. Rastrelli, Savva I. Chevakinsky, and Vasily P. Stasov, working in the Russian baroque style, which combined clear-cut, even austere lines with richness of decoration and use of colour. To this period belong the Winter Palace, the Smolny Convent, and the Vorontsov palace, among others; outside the city were built the summer palaces of Peterhof (now Petrodvorets) and of Tsarskoye Selo (now Pushkin). After a transitional period dominated by the architecture of Jean-Baptiste M. Vallin de la Mothe and Aleksandr Kokorinov, toward the end of the eighteenth century a pure neoclassical style emerged under the architects Giacomo Quarenghi, Carlo Rossi, Andrey Voronikhin, and others. The Kazan and St Isaac's cathedrals, the Smolny Institute, the new Admiralty, the Senate, and the

Mikhaylovsky Palace (now the State Russian Museum) are representative of the splendid buildings of this period.

The Admiralty Side formed the nucleus of Peter's original city, and while it has been reconstructed over the years, it has retained much of the original layout and encompasses some of the city's principal sights: the elegant spire of the Admiralty itself, topped by a weather vane in the form of a ship; the Winter Palace and Hermitage; the famous equestrian statue of Peter, known as the *Bronze Horseman*, created in 1782 by Étienne Falconet; St Isaac's Cathedral, one of the largest domed buildings in the world, visible all over St Petersburg; the Nevsky Prospekt thoroughfare, with its grand Stroganov, Shuvalov, and Anichkov palaces and grand churches; the Summer Garden and Summer Palace; and, intersecting with its radial avenues, the natural channels and canals that so distinguish the city.

The Winter Palace rises like a huge and massive rectangle between Palace Square and the river. The former principal residence of the tsars, the present structure, a baroque master-piece, was built between 1754 and 1762 by Bartolomeo F. Rastrelli. Both the exterior and the interior of the palace were designed in dazzlingly luxurious style. In 1837 the building was destroyed by fire, and only the adjoining Hermitage survived; the Winter Palace was recreated in 1839 almost exactly according to Rastrelli's plans. The striking appearance of the palace is highlighted by white columns against a green background, with golden stucco mouldings; 176 sculptured figures line the roof. The whole complex, now called the Hermitage, or State Hermitage Museum, is a treasury of mostly western European painting and sculpture, an art col-lection of worldwide significance that originated in 1764 as the private holdings of Tsarina Catherine II. The Hermitage was opened to the public in 1852, and following the October Revolution of 1917 the imperial collections became public property. The Summer Garden, founded on an island in 1704, has parks and gardens that by the end of the eighteenth century contained more than 250 statues and busts, mostly the work of Venetian masters. In the north-eastern portion of the garden stands the Summer Palace, Peter's first building project in the city, erected in 1710–14 in early Russian baroque style and designed by Domenico Trezzini. The Neva embankment is fronted by a fence (1784), the iron grille of which is reputed to be among the world's finest examples of wrought ironwork. So light and delicate is its design that the grillwork almost seems to be suspended in air.

Other city landmarks include the squat, horizontal Peter-Paul Fortress and, soaring above it, the slender, arrow-like spire of the Cathedral of St Peter and St Paul. The cathedral was built in 1712–33 by Trezzini, and the tsars and tsarinas of Russia from the time of Peter (except for Peter II and Nicholas II) are buried here. Trezzini also designed St Peter's (Petrovsky) Gate (1718) as the eastern entrance to the fortress. Just to the east of the Peter-Paul Fortress, where the Bolshaya Nevka begins, the cruiser *Aurora* is permanently moored as a museum and training vessel for the Naval College. It was the *Aurora* that in 1917 fired the blank shot that served as the signal to storm the Winter Palace during the October Revolution. Also associated with the 1917 Revolution is one of the most famous features of the Vyborg Side, the Finland Railway Station, which faces the Admiralty Side across the Neva. In April 1917 Lenin returned to Russia via this station and made here his initial pronouncement of a new course that would bring the Bolsheviks to power.

Further Afield

The most famous of the communities around St Petersburg is Petrodvorets (called Peterhof before 1944 and still popularly called by this name), whose unique garden-park setting, stretching in terraces rising above the Gulf of Finland, contains representative works from two centuries of Russian architectural and park styles. The Great Palace, the former residence of Peter I, stands at the edge of the second terrace, its bright yellow walls contrasting with white stucco decorations and the gilt domes of its lateral wings. Built in the baroque style (1714–28), it was reconstructed and expanded by Rastrelli from the mid-1740s to the mid-1750s. On the north the building commands a view of the Grand Cascade, a grandiose structure including a grotto, 64 fountains, and two cascading staircases which lead to an enormous semicircular basin containing a giant statue of Samson wrestling with a lion. This statue, symbolizing the military glory of Russia, is a copy of the original statue, which was carried off by the Nazis during the Second World War. In fact, much of the town's treasure was plundered, and this magnificent vista becomes all the more remarkable when it is remembered that much of it is a post-Second World War restoration.

Another remarkable site is the town of Pushkin (called Tsarskoye Selo before 1917, Detskoye Selo in 1918–37), which arose in the early eighteenth century as one of the tsarist residences. The Catherine Palace (1717–23; enlarged by Aleksey V. Kvasov and Chevakinsky, 1743–8; rebuilt by Rastrelli, 1752–7) is notable for its dimensions, the beauty and majesty of its form, and the wealth of its sculptural decoration. The golden suite of splendid halls (including the Amber Room) exemplifies Russian baroque at its peak. The community is also the site of the Chinese Village (1782–96) in Alexander

Park and the gallery (1780–90) named after its architect, Charles Cameron, the terraces of which contain more than 50 busts of figures from ancient Greek and Roman history. The Lycée, a school for the offspring of the nobility, had the great Pushkin as a student, and a famous statue of the poet stands near the town's Egyptian Gates. The town suffered severe damage during the German onslaught, but has been restored.

Culture

In addition to its rich architectural heritage, St Petersburg boasts numerous outstanding cultural institutions, which remain one of its enduring attractions. It has many large and grand, as well as small but reputable, theatres and auditoriums. The Mariinsky Theatre (called the Kirov State Academic Theatre of Opera and Ballet during the Soviet period) has long enjoyed an international reputation, and its resident company is frequently on tour abroad. Other important venues are the Maly, Tovstonogov, Pushkin, and Musical Comedy theatres. The largest of several concert halls is the October Great Concert Hall, which seats some 4,000 people. The city's musical tradition has been enhanced by the Rimsky-Korsakov Conservatory.

Notable museums include the Hermitage (see above) and the State Russian Museum, both of international prominence. The latter museum traces the history of Russian art from the tenth century to the present.

There are a large number of libraries in the city, headed by the Saltykov-Shchedrin Public Library on Nevsky Prospekt, established in 1795; of all the libraries in Russia, it is second only to Moscow's Russian State Library. Another important specialized collection is the Institute of Russian Literature (Pushkin House) on Vasilyevsky Island.

St Petersburg has abundant recreational facilities and green spaces for such a large city. Among the notable stadiums in the area is Kirov Stadium. Other opportunities for outdoor recreation are provided by the Kirov Park of Culture and Rest, the zoo, the botanical gardens, and numerous other smaller parks and gardens.

Novgorod

Novgorod, in north-western Russia, long flourished as one of the greatest trading centres of eastern Europe, with links by river routes to the Baltic, Byzantium, Central Asia, and all parts of European Russia. Trade with the Hanseatic League was considerable, since Novgorod was the limit of Hanseatic trade into Russia. Prosperity was based upon furs obtained in the forests of northern Russia, much of which came under Novgorod's control.

During the twelfth century, Novgorod was engaged in prolonged struggles with the princes of Suzdal and gained victories in 1169 and 1216. Although the town avoided destruction in the great Tatar invasion of 1238–40, Tatar suzerainty was acknowledged. Under Alexander Nevsky, Prince of Vladimir, Novgorod's defenders repulsed attacks by the Swedes on the Neva River in 1240 and by the Teutonic Knights on the ice of Lake Peipus in 1242. During the fourteenth and fifteenth centuries, Novgorod was involved in a long, bitter struggle for supremacy with Moscow, and frequently sought help from Lithuania. Although the city survived Muscovite onslaughts in 1332 and again in 1386 by

Dmitry Donskoy, it was defeated by Vasily II in 1456. It continued to oppose Moscow and again sought Lithuanian assistance, but in 1471 Ivan III defeated Novgorod and annexed much of its northern territories, finally forcing the city to recognize Moscow's sovereignty in 1478. Opposition by its citizens to Moscow continued until Ivan IV in 1570 massacred many of them and deported the survivors. In 1611 Novgorod was captured by the Swedes, who held it for eight years. From Peter the Great's reign (1682–1725) the city declined in importance, although it was made a provincial seat in 1727.

During the Second World War, Novgorod suffered heavy damage, but the many historic buildings were subsequently restored. These include the kremlin (fortress) on the left bank of the Volkhov (the Sofiyskaya Storona). It was first built of wood in 1044, and its first stone walls date from the fourteenth century. Within the kremlin the St Sofia Cathedral, built in 1045–50 on the site of an earlier wooden church, is one of the finest examples of early Russian architecture, with magnificent bronze doors from the twelfth century. The Granite Palace (1433), the bell tower (1443), and the St Sergey Chapel date from the fifteenth century. The Chapel of St Andrew Stratilata was built in the seventeenth century. On the other side of the Volkhov (the Torgovaya Storona) stands the Cathedral of St Nicholas, dating from 1113. In and around Novgorod are many other surviving churches, including the twelfth-century cathedrals of the Nativity of Our Lady and of St George, the fourteenth-century churches of the Transfiguration and of St Theodore Stratilata, and the seventeenth-century Znamensky Cathedral.

Modern Novgorod is important as a tourist centre and as a major producer of chemical fertilizers. It also has metal and woodworking industries. Its population stands at more than 200,000.

Murmansk

Murmansk is a small city by modern standards – with a population of only about 350,000 – but is the largest city in the world north of the Arctic Circle. Its name, appropriately, is said to derive from the local Sami word *murman*, meaning "the edge of the earth".

Nor does the town have a long history. It was founded in 1915 as Romanov-na-Murmane, after Russia's then imperial royal dynasty. It functioned during the First World War as a supply port and in 1918 as a base for the British, French, and American expeditionary forces against the Bolsheviks. In the Second World War Murmansk served as the main port for Anglo-American convoys carrying war supplies to the Soviet Union through the Arctic Ocean. Its military and naval functions continue to this day.

One of the town's major assets is its ice-free harbour, which makes it Russia's only port with unrestricted access to the Atlantic and world sea routes. From December to May it replaces icebound St Petersburg as the major port of the north-west. This is why today the town is an important fishing port – its fish-processing plant is one of the largest in Europe – and most of its industry related to the sea and seafaring: fishing, fish processing, and shipbuilding. It is also home to a research institute of marine fisheries and oceanography.

Following the collapse of the Soviet Union in 1991, Murmansk's economy suffered, as major industries were unprofitable under market economy conditions, and most fishing vessels were contracted out to Norwegian and other foreign companies. As a result, many people left the city, and in the 1990s the city's population dropped by more than one-fourth, though by the early twenty-first century the city had made a successful transition to a market economy.

Today tourism is on an upward trend in Murmansk and the surrounding area, though the climate tends to restrict visitors to the summer months, when, thanks to the Arctic location, almost continuous daylight can be enjoyed (the reverse of course is true in winter). With the region's mountains, lakes, and abundant rivers, sport and ecological tourism are the main sectors, offering fishing, hunting, mountaineering, skiing, walking, and mushroom- and berry-gathering. People are also drawn to the region to explore its mineralogical deposits, and excursions are available to view the amethyst deposits of the Tersky Coast, among many others.

Volgograd

Volgograd, the administrative centre of the Volgograd region in south-western Russia, lies on the Volga River. It was founded as the fortress of Tsaritsyn in 1589 to protect newly acquired Russian territory along the river.

Like several other cities in the early twentieth century, Tsaritsyn had its name changed for political reasons: during the Russian Civil War (1918–20) Joseph Stalin organized the city's defence in a major battle against the White armies, and in 1925 the city was renamed in his honour. In the Second World War the infamous battle of Stalingrad proved to be a turning point in the war.

The city was totally rebuilt after the war, and new apartment buildings and factories spread far out along the river. The University of Volgograd was opened in 1980, and the modern city has a population of just under 1 million. Its current name was adopted in 1961, after the denunciation of Stalin.

THE BATTLE OF STALINGRAD, 1942–3

From the summer of 1942 to February 2, 1943, the German army made an unsuccessful assault on the city, marking the farthest extent of the German advance into the Soviet Union. As a major industrial centre, Stalingrad was an important prize in itself, and control of the city would have cut Soviet transport links with southern Russia via the Volga River. The German campaign against Stalingrad also served to anchor the northern flank of the larger German drive into the oilfields of the Caucasus.

Under some of the harshest conditions of the entire war, the German 6th Army under Friedrich Paulus continued its attack until, faced with the stiff resistance of the Soviet 62nd Army under General Vasily I. Chuikov, the onset of the notorious Russian winter, the increasing difficulty of renewing supplies, and the incessant street fighting, it was eventually forced (against Hitler's express command) to surrender. But the losses were immense, on all sides: the Soviets recovered 250,000 German and Romanian corpses in and around Stalingrad, and total Axis losses (Germans, Romanians, Italians, and Hungarians) are believed to have been 800,000 dead. Official Russian military historians estimate that 1,100,000 Soviet soldiers lost their lives in the campaign to defend the city.

The modern city has numerous sites of historical and architectural interest, including the Volgograd Fine Arts Museum and the State Panoramic Museum. The former, founded in 1960, shows primarily work by Russian artists, though it also houses collections of European art from the seventeenth to the nineteenth centuries. The State Panoramic Museum offers a panorama of the battle of Stalingrad, dioramas, and numerous exhibits relating to the battle, including the tunic of Marshal Zhukov – who oversaw the defence of Stalingrad and planned and directed the successful Russian counteroffensive – and the sword of honour presented by King George VI of Britain to the citizens of Stalingrad in 1943. There are also artefacts relating to other areas of the city's military history.

Siberia

Irrevocably linked since the twentieth century with the Soviet *Gulag*, the name Siberia conjures up grim images of exile, labour camps, and suffering; but today, though the population remains sparse compared with the pattern in the rest of Russia, the land's rich mineral resources – notably its deposits of coal, petroleum, natural gas, diamonds, iron ore, and gold – are a source of wealth and labour, as are the manufacture of steel, aluminium, and machinery, and agriculture is practised in the more southerly regions, where wheat, rye, oats, and even sunflowers are grown.

The name "Siberia" may be derived from the Tatar term for "sleeping land", perhaps an allusion to its unmitigatedly harsh climate. Russian occupation began in 1581 with a Cossack expedition that overthrew the small khanate of Sibir. During the late sixteenth and seventeenth centuries, Russian trappers and fur traders and Cossack explorers penetrated throughout Siberia to the Bering Sea. With the decline of the fur trade in the eighteenth century, the mining of silver and other metals became the main economic activity in Siberia. Though a trickle of runaway serfs and the forced exile of a number of criminals and political prisoners added to the population of the region over the years, larger-scale settlement did not begin until the building of the Trans-Siberian Railway (1891–1905).

Growth continued in the Joseph Stalin era. From the first Soviet Five-Year Plan (1928–32), industrial expansion was considerable, with coal-mining and iron-and-steel complexes begun in the Kuznetsk Coal Basin and along the line of the Trans-Siberian Railway, partly through the use of forced labour. Forced-labour camps spread throughout Siberia during the 1930s, the most important being the camp complexes in the extreme north-east and along the lower Yenisey River, whose inmates were used mostly in mining operations. During the Second World War, owing to the evacuation of many factories from the western portions of the Soviet Union, Siberia (together with the Urals) became the industrial backbone of the Soviet war effort for a few years. Agriculture, by contrast, suffered greatly from collectivization in 1930–3 and was neglected until the Virgin Lands Campaign of 1954–6, when south-western Siberia (including northern Kazakhstan) was the principal area to be opened to cultivation.

The late 1950s and 1960s saw major industrial development take place, notably the opening up of large oil and natural gas fields in western Siberia and the construction of giant hydroelectric stations at locations along the Angara, Yenisey, and Ob rivers. A network of oil and gas pipelines was built between the new fields and the Urals, and new industries were also established, such as aluminium refining and cellulose pulp making. The construction of the BAM (Baikal–Amur Main

Line) railway between Ust-Kut, on the Lena River, and Komsomolsk-na-Amure, on the Amur, covering a distance of 2,000 miles (3,200 km), was completed in 1980.

The Trans-Siberian Railway

The Trans-Siberian Railway is the longest single rail system in Russia, stretching from Moscow eastwards for 5,778 miles (9,198 km) to Vladivostok, or on to the port station of Nakhodka beyond Vladivostok, a total distance of 5,867 miles (9,441 km). Today a major tourist attraction, the Trans-Siberian played a significant role in the economic, military, and imperial history of the Russian empire and the Soviet Union.

Historically, the completion of the railway marked the turning point in the history of Siberia, opening up vast areas to exploitation, settlement, and industrialization. Construction began in 1891, with the Russians initially securing Chinese permission to build a line directly across Manchuria (the Chinese Eastern Railway) from the Transbaikal region to Vladivostok. However, with the outbreak of the Russo-Japanese War of 1904–5, Russia feared Japan's possible takeover of Manchuria, and so proceeded to build a longer and more difficult alternative route, the Amur Railway, through to Vladivostok; this line was completed in 1916. The original Trans-Siberian Railway thus had two completion dates: in 1904 all the sections from Moscow to Vladivostok were linked and completed, running through Manchuria; in 1916 there was finally a Trans-Siberian Railway wholly within Russian territory.

There are four primary routes that may be taken. The main Trans-Siberian line runs from Moscow. Before reaching

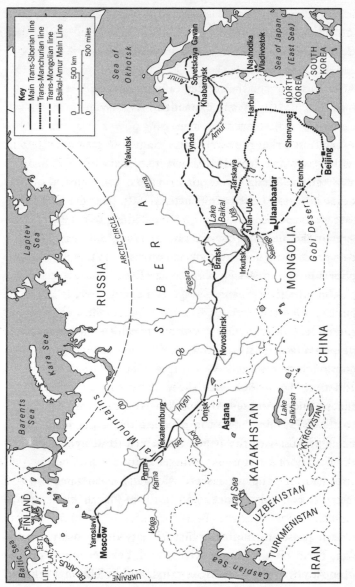

The Trans-Siberian Railway

RUSSO-JAPANESE WAR (1904–5)

Conflict between Russia and Japan over territorial expansion in East Asia

After Russia leased the strategically important Port Arthur (now Lushun, China) and expanded into Manchuria (north-eastern China), it faced the increasing power of Japan. When Russia reneged on its agreement with Japan to withdraw troops from Manchuria, the Japanese fleet attacked the Russia naval squadron at Port Arthur and began a siege of the city in February 1904. Japanese land forces cut the Russian army off from coming to aid Port Arthur and pushed it back to Mukden (now Shenyang). The reinforced Russian army took the offensive in October, but poor military leadership blunted its effectiveness.

After the long Japanese siege of Port Arthur, in January 1905 the corrupt Russian commander surrendered the garrison without consulting his officers, despite adequate stores and ammunition for its continued defence. Heavy fighting around Mukden ended in March 1905 with the withdrawal of Russian troops under Aleksey Kuropatkin. The decisive naval battle of Tsushima gave the Japanese the upper hand and brought Russia to the peace table. With the signing of the Treaty of Portsmouth, Russia abandoned its expansionist policy in eastern Asia, and Japan gained effective control of Korea and much of Manchuria.

Siberia it passes through the historic city of Yaroslavl on the Volga, Perm on the Kama River, and Yekaterinburg on the eastern slopes of the Ural Mountains, and in Siberia it takes in the industrial cities of Irkutsk and Khabarovsk before terminating in Vladivostok at the extreme south-eastern tip of Russia. The Trans-Manchurian line runs alongside the Trans-Siberian as far as Tarskaya, east of Lake Baikal, and then diverts south-east into China, progressing down to Beijing, the Chinese capital. The Trans-Mongolian and Trans-Siberian lines run side by side as far as Ulan-Ude, at the confluence of the Selenga and Uda rivers, but the Trans-Mongolian line then continues south to Ulaanbaatar in Mongolia, and eventually terminates in Beijing. The fourth and most recent addition to the railway, the Baikal–Amur Main Line – completed as an alternative to the primary Trans-Siberian line – diverges from the main route several hundred miles west of Lake Baikal, passing the lake at its northernmost shore. Its eastern terminus is at Sovetskaya Gavan, on the Pacific.

Travellers who take the full rail trip on the passenger train *Rossiya* from Moscow to Nakhodka (including a compulsory overnight stay in Khabarovsk) will spend about eight days on board. There are nearly 1,000 stations – one every 6 miles (10 km) – along the main route. Numerous fascinating Russian cities and towns can be seen and visited along the route.

Yaroslavl

The city of Yaroslavl lies on the right bank of the Volga River, 175 miles (282 km) north-east of Moscow. Believed to have been founded in 1010 by Prince Yaroslav the Wise, it served as the capital of an independent principality from 1218 until 1471, when it came under the rule of Moscow. Yaroslavl was sacked by the Tatars in 1238 and by Ivan I Kalita in 1332, and was captured by Novgorod in 1371, but on each occasion its recovery was swift. The opening of trade with the West during the sixteenth century brought prosperity to the town, which occupies a fortunate position at the intersection of the great Volga River and Moscow–Arkhangelsk trade routes. The Yaroslavl Great Manufactory, one of the earliest and largest textile mills in Russia, was established in 1722, and by the late eighteenth century Yaroslavl had become an important industrial centre, which it remains to this day.

There are many fine churches in Yaroslavl, including the Transfiguration Cathedral (1505–16) of the Saviour Monastery. The churches of Elijah the Prophet, Nikola Nadein, and St John the Baptist all date from the seventeenth century. The historical centre of Yaroslavl was awarded World Heritage Site status by UNESCO in 2005.

Perm

Perm's position on the navigable Kama River, leading to the Volga, and on the Great Siberian Highway (established in 1783) across the Ural Mountains helped it become an important trade and manufacturing centre; copper-smelting was once carried out there. Perm grew considerably as industrialization proceeded in the Urals during the Soviet period.

Modern Perm, with a population of just over 1 million, is the administrative centre of the Perm region in western Russia. The city, which extends for approximately 30 miles (50 km) along the high river-banks, is still a major railway hub and one of the chief industrial centres of the Urals region. Its diversified metallurgical and engineering industries produce equipment and machine tools for the petroleum and coal industries, as well as agricultural machinery. A major petroleum refinery uses oil transported by pipeline from the West Siberian oilfields, and the city's large chemical industry makes fertilizers and dyes.

Perm is a thriving cultural centre, with a university (the A. M. Gorky State University was established in 1916) and numerous theatres, including a puppet theatre. The P. I. Tchaikovsky Perm State Academic Opera and Ballet Theatre was founded in Russia's imperial past, and today the ballet company enjoys an international reputation and tours regularly. The Perm State Art Gallery, founded in 1922, has both local and international collections, exhibiting Perm wooden sculpture and work by classical and contemporary Russian artists, as well as pictures of the Italian, Dutch, and French schools of the fifteenth to the eighteenth centuries. The city offers many other opportunities for entertainment, from classical musical concerts (with the Philharmonic Orchestra), to folk concerts and folk dance, ice and circus shows, and many sporting events.

Yekaterinburg

Yekaterinburg lies along the Iset River, a tributary of the Tobol River, slightly east of the border between Europe and Asia, on the slopes of the Urals.

In 1723 a settlement on the site of an ironworks was named Yekaterinburg in honour of Catherine I, the wife of Peter I. The town grew as the administrative centre for all the ironworks of the Urals region, and its importance increased after 1783 when the Great Siberian Highway was built through it. After 1878 the Trans-Siberian Railway linked the city with Siberia. After the October Revolution of 1917, Yekaterinburg achieved notoriety as the scene of the execution of the last tsar, Nicholas II, and his family in July 1918. In 1924 it was renamed Sverdlovsk in honour of the Bolshevik leader Yakov M. Sverdlov, but the city reverted to its original name in 1991.

Modern Yekaterinburg is one of the major industrial centres of Russia. The city, laid out on a regular gridiron pattern, sprawls across the valley of the Iset – there dammed to form a series of small lakes – and the low surrounding hills. Boris Yeltsin, the first democratically elected president of Russia, was educated and spent much of his political career in the city.

Omsk

Omsk is another modern Russian city that owes its development primarily to the existence of the Trans-Siberian Railway and to its proximity to Siberia's mineral resources. Omsk is located in west-central Russia, on the Irtysh River at its junction with the Om. A settlement was founded in 1716 as a stronghold at the eastern end of the Ishim fortified line between the Tobol and the Irtysh: it developed as an agricultural centre and became a city in 1804. Its military function as headquarters of the Siberian Cossacks lasted until the late nineteenth century. In 1918–19 Omsk was the seat of the anti-Bolshevik government of Admiral Kolchak.

The building of the Trans-Siberian Railway in the 1890s and Omsk's position as a trans-shipment point on the Irtysh led to rapid commercial growth. Industrial growth was given great impetus during the Second World War, since when its population has more than trebled. Pipelines from the Volga–Urals and West Siberian oilfields supply the refinery and petrochemical industry, which makes synthetic rubber and tyres.

Engineering, especially the production of agricultural machinery, also dominates a wide range of industry. Other industries include the manufacture of cotton and woollen textiles, cord, footwear, and leather goods, and food processing. Timber working is also carried out. Among the cultural and educational facilities of Omsk are agricultural, engineering, medical, and veterinary institutes and other research and higher educational establishments. The city's population today reaches just over 1 million.

Novosibirsk

Novosibirsk is today the largest city in Siberia (with a population of nearly 1.5 million), and a major manufacturing and industrial centre as well as a communications hub. It is the chief city of western Siberia.

The city developed when the village of Krivoshchekovo on the left bank of the River Ob was chosen as the crossing point for the Trans-Siberian Railway in 1893. The settlement was then known variously as Gusevka or Aleksandrovsky, but in 1895 it was renamed Novonikolayevsk in honour of the accession of Nicholas II; in 1925 it was renamed again, this time as Novosibirsk, meaning "New Siberia". Its expansion was due partly to its strategic importance for communications and partly to its proximity to Siberia's vast natural resources, in particular the Kuznetsk coalfield to the east.

As the region's principal cultural and educational centre, Novosibirsk has an opera and ballet theatre, botanical gardens, an art gallery, and museums, as well as a symphony orchestra. There are also some two dozen institutions of higher learning, including the Novosibirsk State University, founded in 1959. With the large number of educational institutions, the proportion of students enrolled in higher education in the city is among the highest in Russia. The university and a number of these institutes are located in the satellite town of Akadem-gorodok, which since the 1960s has comprised Russia's largest cluster of basic science research institutes and personnel outside Moscow and St Petersburg. Most of these institutes belong to the Siberian Branch of the Russian Academy of Sciences. During the 1990s many scientists left the area and relocated outside Russia, though some of these researchers remained affiliated with their home institutions.

Irkutsk

The city of Irkutsk is the administrative centre of the Irkutsk region and an important cultural centre for eastern Siberia, in the Russian far east. Irkutsk lies along the Angara River at its confluence with the Irkut River. It was founded as a wintering camp in 1652, during the first Russian colonization of the area; a fort was built in 1661, and Irkutsk rapidly became the main centre of the region and of the Russian trade route to China and Mongolia. It acquired town status in 1686. Its importance grew after the coming of the Trans-Siberian Railway in 1898.

Modern Irkutsk, with a population of just over half a million, is one of the major industrial cities of Siberia and is especially noted for a wide range of engineering products. There are railway, aircraft, ship, and vehicle repair yards. Other industries include mica processing and consumer-goods manufacture. The Irkutsk hydroelectric station on the Angara River is within the city; its reservoir extends back to include Lake Baikal.

The city's attractions include its pleasing embankments along the river and many surviving wooden houses on its tree-lined streets, as well as its proximity to Lake Baikal, now a popular tourist destination. The Irkutsk State University (1918) and the Siberian branch of the Academy of Sciences are among the city's many teaching and research institutes.

Ulan-Ude

The capital of the Buryatiya republic, east-central Russia, Ulan-Ude lies in a deep valley between the Khamar-Daban and Tsagan-Daban mountain ranges. The wintering camp of Udinskoye, established there in 1666, became the town of Verkhne-Udinsk in 1783; it was renamed Ulan-Ude in 1934.

The city's development was greatly stimulated when the Trans-Siberian Railway reached it in 1900 and later by the construction of the branch line to Ulaanbaatar in Mongolia in 1949 – a branch extended to Beijing in 1956. Ulan-Ude's role as a major rail junction led to the establishment of large locomotive and carriage repair works.

Khabarovsk

The city of Khabarovsk is the administrative centre of the Khabarovsk territory, in far eastern Russia. It lies along the Amur River just below its confluence with the Ussuri. The town was named after the Russian explorer Yerofey Khabarov, who made several expeditions to the Amur River basin in the mid-seventeenth century. The modern city was founded in 1858 as a military outpost. Its nodal position at the point at which the Trans-Siberian Railway crosses the Amur made it an important focus of the Russian far east, and at one time it administered the entire area to the Bering Strait.

Modern Khabarovsk, with a population of about 600,000, spreads across a series of small valleys and ridges perpendicular to the Amur. The city has an attractive waterfront park and esplanade and a mixture of modern apartment blocks, factories, and old, one-storey wooden houses. It is a major industrial centre, with most enterprises located in the upstream district: they include a wide range of engineering and machine-building industries, oil refining, timber working, and furniture making, and many light industries. There are polytechnic, agricultural, medical, teacher-training, and railway-engineering institutes, and several scientific-research establishments. The city also boasts a number of theatres (including a puppet theatre), museums, picture galleries, and parks, and the Bolshekhekhtsirsky State Nature Reserve is nearby.

Vladivostok

Vladivostok is a seaport and the administrative centre of the Primorsky territory, in extreme south-eastern Russia. It is located around Zolotoy Rog ("Golden Horn Bay") on the western side of a peninsula that separates the Amur and Ussuri bays on the Sea of Japan. The town was founded in 1860 as a Russian military outpost and was named Vladivostok (variously interpreted as "Rule the East", "Lord of the East", or "Conqueror of the East"). Its forward position in the extreme south of the Russian far east inevitably led to a major role as a port and naval base. In 1872 the main Russian naval base on the Pacific was transferred there, and thereafter Vladivostok began to grow. In 1880 city status was conferred on it. The city also grew in importance after the construction of the Chinese Eastern Railway across Manchuria to Chita (completed in 1903), which gave Vladivostok a more direct rail connection to the rest of the Russian Empire. Today traces of this nineteenth-century heritage can still be found in the wooden architecture of that period, the old and the modern juxtaposed in many of the city's streets.

During the First World War, Vladivostok was the chief Pacific entry port for military supplies and railway equipment sent to Russia from the United States. After the outbreak of the Russian Revolution in 1917, the city was occupied in 1918 by foreign, mostly Japanese, troops, the last of whom were not withdrawn until 1922. The anti-revolutionary forces in Vladivostok promptly collapsed, and Soviet power was established in the region.

During the Soviet period Vladivostok remained the home of the Pacific Fleet, which was greatly enlarged in the decades after the Second World War. Vladivostok's military importance was such that it was closed to foreign shipping and other contacts from the late 1950s until the waning days of Soviet power in 1990. Its chief role as a commercial port subsequently re-emerged, both as a link to other Russian ports of the far east and as a port of entry for consumer goods from China, Japan, and other countries. The port is the eastern terminus of the Northern Sea Route along Russia's Arctic seaboard from Murmansk, and is the principal supply base for the Arctic ports east of Cape Chelyuskin.

The industrial base of Vladivostok was much diversified during the Soviet period. In addition to large ship-repair yards, there are railway workshops and a plant for the manufacture of mining equipment. Light industry includes instrument and radio factories, timber-working enterprises (notably those producing furniture and veneer), a chinaware works, and manufacturers of pharmaceutical products. Food industries are also important. In the 1990s, in the post-Soviet period, most industry declined, with the exception of food processing. Mechanical engineering continues to be important. A railroad town, Vladivostok is the eastern terminus of the Trans-Siberian Railway. The city also has an airport.

Vladivostok is the chief educational and cultural centre of the Russian far east. It is the site of the Far Eastern Branch of the Russian Academy of Sciences, the Far Eastern State University (founded 1920), and medical, art education, polytechnic, trade, and marine-engineering institutes – not surprisingly, students make up a significant proportion of the city's total population. The city's lively cultural life is also well served, with a symphony orchestra, theatres, galleries, and museums, including the V. K. Arsenyev Museum, devoted to regional lore, the Pacific Fleet History Museum, the Museum of Fishery and Oceanography, and an aquarium. Off the coast of Vladivostok is the Far East Marine Biosphere Reserve, an important area of marine biodiversity.

Sakhalin Island

Sakhalin Island lies off Russia's far-eastern coast, between the Tatar Strait and the Sea of Okhotsk, north of the Japanese island of Hokkaido. It may seem an unlikely place to visit, and indeed until the collapse of the Soviet Union foreigners were forbidden to do so. But today tourism is rapidly expanding, thanks largely to massive foreign investment in the island's offshore gas and oil resources.

The island was first settled by Japanese fishermen along its southern coasts; the first Russians arrived only in 1853. By an agreement of 1855 Russia and Japan shared control of the island, but in 1875 Russia acquired all Sakhalin in exchange for the Kuril Islands; it was then that the island soon gained notoriety as a Russian penal colony, where conditions were said to be among the harshest in the country. In 1945 the Soviet Union regained the southern half of the island, territory that Russia had lost in 1905 as a result of the Russo-Japanese War, and at the end of the Second World War Sakhalin's entire Japanese population was eventually repatriated.

Sakhalin is 589 miles (948 km) long from north to south and about 100 miles (160 km) wide, covering 29,500 square miles (76,400 square km). The landscape is wild and largely un-spoiled: the vegetation ranges from tundra and stunted forests of birch and willow in the north to dense deciduous forest in the south. Fishing is plentiful. Though there is a lowland plain in the north, most of the land is mountainous, reaching 5,279 feet (1,609 m) at Mount Lopatin, and snowboarding has become a tourist attraction. Other than the capital, Yuzhno-Sakhalinsk, there are no major towns; the town of Neftegorsk was largely destroyed in a major earthquake in 1995.

For devotees of the author and playwright Anton Chekhov the island has another fascination. In early 1890 Chekhov suddenly decided to escape the irritations of urban intellectual life by undertaking a one-man sociological expedition to the island. Chekhov's journey there was a long and hazardous ordeal by carriage and riverboat. After arriving unscathed, studying local conditions, and conducting a census of the islanders, he returned to publish his findings as a research thesis, which retains an honoured place in the annals of Russian penology: *The Island of Sakhalin* (1893–4).

INDEX

Note: Where more than one page reference is listed against a subject, page references in **bold** indicate significant treatment of the subject.